The Revolutionary and Anti-Imperialist Writings of James Connolly 1893–1916

Key Texts in Anti-Colonial Thought
Series Editor: David Johnson, The Open University

Available titles
The Revolutionary and Anti-Imperialist Writings of James Connolly 1893–1916
Edited by Conor McCarthy
African American Anti-Colonial Thought 1917–1936
Edited by Cathy Bergin

Forthcoming titles
Beyond 1968: Anti-Colonial Texts from Central American Student Movements 1929–1979
Edited by Heather Vrana

The Revolutionary and Anti-Imperialist Writings of James Connolly 1893–1916

Edited by Conor McCarthy

For Andrew Kincaid, Joe Cleary and Raymond Deane – friends and comrades

Edinburgh University Press is one of the leading university presses in the UK. We publish academic books and journals in our selected subject areas across the humanities and social sciences, combining cutting-edge scholarship with high editorial and production values to produce academic works of lasting importance. For more information visit our website: www.edinburghuniversitypress.com

© Conor McCarthy, 2016

Edinburgh University Press Ltd
The Tun – Holyrood Road
12(2f) Jackson's Entry
Edinburgh EH8 8PJ

Typeset in 10.5/13 Sabon by
Servis Filmsetting Ltd, Stockport, Cheshire

A CIP record for this book is available from the British Library

ISBN 978 1 4744 1066 3 (hardback)
ISBN 978 1 4744 1067 0 (webready PDF)
ISBN 978 1 4744 1068 7 (paperback)
ISBN 978 1 4744 1069 4 (epub)

The right of Conor McCarthy to be identified as the editor of this work has been asserted in accordance with the Copyright, Designs and Patents Act 1988, and the Copyright and Related Rights Regulations 2003 (SI No. 2498).

Contents

Series Editor's Preface	viii
Acknowledgements	ix
Introduction	1

1 **The Early Years and the Irish Socialist Republican Party** — 21
   Irish Socialist Republican Party (1896) — 21
   Socialism and Nationalism (1897) — 23
   Patriotism and Labour (1897) — 26
   Parnellism and Labour (1898) — 30
   The Sweating System (1899) — 31
   Physical Force in Irish Politics (1899) — 34
   Home Rulers and Labour: A Remonstrance Addressed to
      English Socialists (1901) — 37

2 **America and the International Workers of the World** — 42
   America and Ireland: Farmers' Demands (1899) — 42
   Our 'American Mission' (1902) — 45
   The American SDP: Its Origin, its Press and its Policies
      (1903) — 48
   A Political Party of the Workers (1908) — 53
   To Irish Wage Workers in America (1908) — 56
   Facets of American Liberty (1908) — 60

3 *Labour in Irish History* (1910) — 67
   Foreword — 67
   Chapter I: The Lessons of History — 74
   Chapter II: The Jacobites and the Irish People — 78
   Chapter III: Peasant Rebellions — 84

Chapter IV: Social Revolts and Political Kites and Crows	89
Chapter V: Grattan's Parliament	94
Chapter VI: Capitalist Betrayal of the Irish Volunteers	98
Chapter VII: The United Irishmen	110
Chapter VIII: United Irishmen as Democrats and Internationalists	115
Chapter IX: The Emmet Conspiracy	127
Chapter X: The First Irish Socialist: A Forerunner of Marx	131
Chapter XI: An Irish Utopia	140
Chapter XII: A Chapter of Horrors: Daniel O'Connell and the Working Class	152
Chapter XIII: Our Irish Girondins Sacrifice the Irish Peasantry upon the Altar of Private Property	160
Chapter XIV: Socialistic Teaching of the Young Irelanders: The Thinkers and the Workers	169
Chapter XV: Some More Irish Pioneers of the Socialist Movement	178
Chapter XVI: The Working Class: The Inheritors of the Irish Ideals of the Past – The Repository of the Hopes of the Future	181

4 **Empire and Revolution** 193
    The South African War I (1899) 193
    Imperialism and Socialism (1899) 195
    Resolution of Sympathy with the Boer Republics (1900) 199
    The Coming Revolt in India I: Its Political and Social Causes (1908) 200
    The Coming Revolt in India II: Its Political and Social Causes (1908) 206
    Our Duty in this Crisis (1914) 210
    A Continental Revolution (1914) 214
    In Praise of the Empire (1915) 217
    A War for Civilization (1915) 219

5 **The Lock-Out, the First World War and the Rising** 223
    Mr. John E. Redmond, MP: His Strength and Weakness (1911) 223
    The Dublin Lock-Out: On the Eve (1913) 228
    Glorious Dublin! (1913) 230
    Labour and the Proposed Partition of Ireland (1914) 233
    The Real Situation in Ireland (1914) 235

The Ballot or the Barricades (1914)	238
The Hope of Ireland (1914)	240
Ireland – Disaffected or Revolutionary? (1915)	243
What is a Free Nation? (1916)	246
We Will Rise Again (1916)	250
Labour and Ireland: Dublin Working Class, amid Great Emotion, Hoist and Salute the Flag of Ireland (1916)	252
Last Statement (1916)	254
Coda: Connolly's Afterlives	256
Index	259

Series Editor's Preface

Key Texts in Anti-Colonial Thought re-publishes selections of anti-colonial texts and locates them in their colonial/neo-colonial contexts. Leading scholars in Postcolonial Studies introduce a wide variety of hitherto hard-to-access anti-colonial writings. Each volume opens with a substantial introduction contextualising the selected texts, setting out the specific forms of colonial governance, economic exploitation and cultural imperialism they wrote against, as well as the communities of resistance, the solidarities and the distinctive political cultures that sustained them. In addition, the volumes provide extensive explanatory notes, annotated guides to further reading, and concluding discussions of the texts' relevance today. The series aims to counter the dependency of Postcolonial Studies on a narrow range of theorists and literary texts, and to provoke reflection on the connections between anti-colonial thought and contemporary resistance to global inequalities.

David Johnson

Acknowledgements

This book would not have happened without the invitation, encouragement and support of my old friend and comrade David Johnson. Any time my confidence in this project began to ebb, a conversation with David would loft my spirits and send me back to Connolly with renewed optimism and energy.

At Edinburgh University Press, Jackie Jones, Adela Rauchova, Rebecca Mackenzie, Geraldine Lyons and James Dale have been immensely helpful and patient. My warm thanks go to Janet Zimmerman for her work on the index.

I am indebted for advice and help regarding James Connolly to Lorcan Collins, Fintan Lane, Francis Devine, Frank Connolly, Terry Brotherstone, David Lloyd and P. J. Mathews. To Finbar Cullen and the Desmond Greaves School I owe thanks for their invitation in 2012 to talk about partition and class in Ireland.

The conversation and work of Declan Kiberd, Chris Lee, David Lloyd, Graham MacPhee, Barra O Seaghdha and Mark Quigley have been of inestimable importance to me over many years.

Emer Nolan, my Head of Department at Maynooth, has been a most supportive and helpful colleague and friend over the years, and even more during the time in which this book was in preparation. To her, and to former Head of Department Chris Morash, I owe the warmest thanks.

My colleagues in the Department of English at Maynooth have provided a warm and stimulating environment in which to work. I am grateful to the Maynooth University Publications Fund for financial assistance with the production of this book.

My comrades in the Ireland-Palestine Solidarity Campaign and Academics for Palestine have provided opportunities for rigorous discussion and political co-operation of the greatest importance to me.

Many friends and colleagues have given me the benefit of their support and kindness: Bashir Abu-Manneh, Michael Cronin, Sally Eberhardt, Dara Fox, Luke Gibbons, Nadia Hilliard, Sinead Kennedy, Marie-Violaine Louvet, Aideen Lynch, Peter McAuley, Natalya Pestova, Zohar Tirosh, and Kevin Whelan. I owe a long-standing debt to Norman Vance, as a mentor, exemplar and friend.

Conor McCarthy
March 2016

Introduction

James Connolly has a fair claim to being one of the most remarkable political figures in twentieth-century Irish history. He was a Marxist, a revolutionary, a union organiser, a writer and, finally, a guerrilla. Of all the notable Irish political leaders of the late nineteenth and early twentieth centuries, Connolly came from a uniquely poor working-class background. He was also an internationalist: his career took him from Scotland to Ireland to America and then back to Ireland. He was one of the leaders of the 1916 Rebellion in Dublin, and was court-martialled and executed as a consequence.

In 2010, the Irish national broadcaster Raidió Teilifís Éireann (RTE) conducted a poll – linked to a television documentary series – in which viewers chose the greatest person in Irish history. James Connolly ranked fourth. Yet in comparison to those placed ahead of him and below him – John Hume, Michael Collins, Mary Robinson and (more embarrassingly) Bono – Connolly's personal history and his ideas are nowadays relatively poorly known, in Ireland and internationally. This anthology aims to rectify that situation, and to locate in Connolly's work, ideas and writings an example of the political life lived honourably for our own times.

Connolly crammed into his nearly 48 years as much work and activism as might be achieved in several ordinary lives. He was constantly on the move – intellectually and politically, and at times geographically – and possessed a formidable will to resist, to critique, to act against, and to seek to overthrow the oppressive political and social conditions of his day, in the face of sometimes overwhelming odds. At the root of this tendency, however, was a relentless drive to improve the conditions of the very poorest in society – in Scotland, in America and in Ireland. His fighting will was expressed principally in the terms of the Marxism and socialism of his day, interwoven with ideas and organisations of militant

Irish republicanism and nationalism. Indeed much of his importance lies in his bringing the international discourses of revolutionary socialism and Marxism into an Irish context and idiom; but therein also lies his global interest, as he resolutely recast Ireland's struggles in an anti-imperialist framework.

Early Life

James Connolly was born in 1868 in the slum area of Cowgate, in Edinburgh, Scotland, of Irish parents. The Cowgate area is now one dedicated to urban nightlife, but in Connolly's time it was a very deprived part of the city, known as 'Little Ireland' because of the Irish immigrant community which was its primary population. The actual house in which the young James was born is gone, but a plaque stands on the building now on the site. This plaque reads as follows:

> TO THE MEMORY OF JAMES CONNOLLY
> BORN 5TH JUNE 1868 AT 107 COWGATE
> RENOWNED INTERNATIONAL TRADE UNION AND WORKING-CLASS LEADER
> FOUNDER OF IRISH SOCIALIST REPUBLICAN PARTY
> MEMBER OF PROVISIONAL GOVERNMENT OF IRISH REPUBLIC
> EXECUTED 12TH MAY 1916 AT KILMAINHAM JAIL DUBLIN

John Connolly was employed as a manure collector – a very humble line of work. Shortly after the birth of his third son, James, he was promoted to work as a gas lamp-lighter. His youngest son received his only formal education at St Patrick's School, a short distance from their home. In 1879, young James took up his first job, at the age of 11, as a printer's assistant. His elder brother John was working as a compositor at the *Edinburgh Evening News*. James's trade usefully equipped him over the many years of setting up and working on party and union newspapers – the chief conduit by which he would find and address an audience and a constituency.

Late Nineteenth-century Ireland

The last decades of the nineteenth century were marked by rising turbulence and excitement in Irish politics. Ireland was at this time a constituent nation of the United Kingdom, along with England, Scotland and Wales. Irish politicians sat in the Parliament of Westminster in London. The main Irish political party at this time was the Irish Parliamentary

Party (IPP), formed in 1882 by Charles Stewart Parnell, a Protestant landlord from Co. Wicklow, out of the remains of Isaac Butt's movement for Home Rule. At approximately the same time, the main popular political movement was that of the Irish National Land League, founded in 1879 by Michael Davitt and Parnell. The Land League was the latest in a long line of radical Irish agrarian organisations, going back to the eighteenth century, which sought to represent the grievances of poor tenants and farm labourers in rural Ireland. In the wake of the Great Irish Famine (1845–1852), economic and social conditions in the Irish countryside were dire, with rising rents, farm consolidation, and evictions of tenants unable to meet their landlords' charges. The Irish political context for the young Connolly was formed from the potent mixture of IPP and land-related political activity. But it must also be added that when Connolly arrived in Dublin as a socialist and labour organiser he found a fertile and active labour movement ahead of him. Forms of unionisation or 'combination' of rural labourers had been present in Ireland since the eighteenth century. Frequently illegal, their rise paralleled that of Whiteboy rural agitation. It should be noted, for example, that when Parnell formed the Irish National League out of the ruins of the Land League in 1882, the Irish Labour and Industrial Union, which represented rural workers primarily, dissolved itself into the new organisation: a crucial example of the subordination of Irish labour or class politics to Home Rule or nationalist politics. Equally, in the 1880s, Parnell and his IPP colleagues became masters in using the block of Irish MPs in Westminster as a powerful lever when the British Liberal or Conservative Parties could not attain working majorities. In consequence, one can say accurately that the politics of the Land League and Home Rule in Ireland produced powerful effects in Britain, and British political manoeuvres produced important effects in Ireland, even when not concerned directly with policy on Ireland.

Meanwhile, Ireland in the 1880s and 1890s was also undergoing an intellectual and cultural transformation of a very profound kind. Though Connolly was a political writer and activist, it is essential to note the wider Irish socio-cultural context and the ways in which he was both influenced by that context, and provided and embodied one of the most powerful critiques of that context in its own time. The nineteenth century had witnessed sweeping changes in Irish society – changes that could be characterised reasonably as the most radical since the plantations of the seventeenth century. Schematically, these changes might be put thus: 1) the emergence of a truly mass Anglophone politics, through the O'Connellite campaigns for Catholic Emancipation, and then for the repeal of the Act of Union; 2) the catastrophic effects of the Great Famine, which killed one million people by starvation and disease and which induced the emigration of another one million in those brief terrible years, and set in train a wider pattern of emigration which helped shape Irish society for the following century; 3) partly as a result of the Famine, and the politics of land and agriculture which came out of it – most notably the agitation of the Land League – the British government began in the 1870s a process of land reform which by the early twentieth century would have produced a new large and politically and culturally crucial class of small farmers. O'Connell succeeded in fostering an Anglophone politics of the masses, even before the Famine swept away the poorest of the rural population (and those most likely to speak Irish).

Exemplifying the structural paradoxes of nationalism, a political tendency which combines progressivist and democratising forward movement legitimated by a backward glance at a sometimes mythologised past, the very changes wrought by O'Connell and the Famine made possible, motivated and drove the cultural revival of the nineteenth century. Translations of ancient, mediaeval and more recent Irish writing were produced and circulated. In a society which was officially integrated into the United Kingdom, whose high politics was focused on London, whose economy traded mostly with Britain and America and where the machinery of the state – education, policing, welfare, the army – was overwhelmingly Anglophone, the rise of interest in and dissemination of songs, ballads, poetry and other kinds of writing translated from the Gaelic came with a powerful sense of discovery or re-discovery. By the late nineteenth century, this had issued in a battery of cultural, civic and political institutions. To the arrival of the Literary Revival – in the work of W. B. Yeats, Standish O'Grady, Lady Gregory, J. M. Synge, Lennox Robinson – in the sphere of high culture corresponded the creation of organisations such as the Gaelic League and the Gaelic Athletic Association in the sphere of mass culture. W. B. Yeats, Edward Martyn and Lady Augusta Gregory founded the Irish Literary Theatre in 1899, which became the Abbey Theatre in 1904. The Gaelic League was founded by Douglas Hyde in 1893, to promote the Irish language – even before the Famine, the language was in decline. And in 1884, Michael Cusack founded the Gaelic Athletic Association, which aimed to promote Irish field games and other aspects of Irish culture. The point is not that Connolly was a 'Revivalist' in any simple sense. He consistently argued the importance of the 'historical materialist' vision of history promulgated by Marx and Engels in the *Communist Manifesto* and the *German Ideology*, and as such was often sceptical of what would now be called 'culturalism'. Yet his radical activist and intellectual energy partakes of the general ferment in Irish society at this time, and his interest and effort in political propaganda, and his capacity to deploy various rhetorics or registers – speaking, writing – was frequently augmented by his love of poetry and literature. We see this in his frequent quotation of both poetry (James Clarence Mangan, Alfred Lord Tennyson) and popular song, buttressed by his sense of street theatre and the value of political balladry.

The upshot of such developments was the creation of a powerful, popularly-based and variegated culture of nationalism in Ireland. The point is not that national consciousness was simply new, but rather that in breadth and depth the movements of the late nineteenth century achieved a hegemony in Irish society unattained by either prior movements for constitutional change – the 'patriot politics' of Henry Grattan and Henry Flood in the 1780s, the 'Repeal' campaign of Daniel O'Connell of the 1840s, or Isaac Butt's Home Rule campaigning after the Famine – or prior revolutionary movements for change by force – the United Irishmen's rebellion of 1798, the Young Ireland rebellion of 1848, the Fenian rebellion of 1867.

Ireland at the end of the nineteenth century was primarily an agrarian society. Dublin, the capital, was the centre of the administration, and along with Belfast and Cork was the country's main port. But it was not a hub of manufacturing. That distinction fell to Belfast and its environs in the north-east, where, through the eighteenth and nineteenth centuries, industries such as rope-making, tobacco, heavy engineering, and pre-eminently linen and ship-building, made the city a major element in the Industrial Revolution in the United Kingdom, and integrated the city in the trading networks of the Empire. This development, combined with the much older sectarian divisions which developed after the colonisation of Ulster in the seventeenth century, contributed to the contention over Home Rule and independence which would be the crucial political frameworks for Connolly's political career in Ireland.

Connolly in Ireland 1882–1903

The young James Connolly, in a manner both symptomatic of Ireland's condition at this time and paradoxical in the light of his later career, first arrived in Ireland as a soldier in the British Army. At the age of 14, concluding that a decent career was impossible for him in Edinburgh, he enlisted in 1882. He was underage, of course, and his desertion in 1891 meant that he lived the rest of his life under the shadow of being caught and punished. He served several tours of duty in Ireland, but it was also at this time that he met his wife, Lillie Reynolds, in Edinburgh, and that he immersed himself, in the manner of a keen autodidact, in reading history and leftist political thought, including the work of Marx and Engels.

In the early 1890s, Connolly became involved in the socialist movement in Scotland. He became secretary of the Scottish Socialist Federation (SSF) in 1892, working with John Leslie. With the SSF, he learned the stress on education and 'propaganda' that he would develop later in Ireland. But he also noted the rise of what in the early 1890s was called the 'new unionism' in Britain: an outbreak of strikes and protests mostly by previously non-unionised workers. Connolly's work in America and Ireland would oscillate between promoting Marxist and socialist ideas via a party, and organising the workers into union movements. When the 'new unionism' was defeated, Connolly moved towards the Independent Labour Party (ILP), a moderate non-Marxist organisation, which aspired to electoral alliance with the Liberals: Connolly's political affiliations should not be presumed always to have been revolutionary, and indeed he quickly realised that the ILP, in its moderation and leanings towards the Liberals, was quite close to the offshoots of the Home Rule movement amongst the Irish immigrant community in Scotland.

While still in Scotland, Connolly moved further left in his positions, both in regard to Scottish politics – realising when the Liberals came to power the weakness of the ILP – and in regard to Ireland. In fact his early Scottish politics was suffused with Irish problematics. John Leslie's pamphlet, *The Irish Question*, influenced this move. Leslie mounted a direct attack on any linkage between the left and mainstream Irish nationalism. He argued for Irish independence, but suggested that the Irish nationalist elite, with its outriders amongst the migrant community in Scotland, was thoroughly in hock to capitalism and to Britain's economic domination of the smaller island. Irish nationalism was a middle-class formation, and the Irish working class needed to recognise and affiliate with its class allies beyond Ireland's shores: 'The emancipation of their class from economic bondage meant emancipation from all bondage ... if they refuse to be any longer the mere pawns in the great chess-game of the lay and clerical state gamblers for power and place, then they will clasp hands with the workingmen's parties of all other countries' (Leslie 1894: 12–13). This was a position that dominated most of Connolly's subsequent Irish political activity. For his pains, Connolly was then lambasted by the Irish National League, Parnell's party.

In 1895, Connolly ran in the St Giles ward in the Edinburgh local elections, as a 'socialist' candidate with the support of the SSF, but failed to win a seat. At around this time, he was invited by the Dublin Socialist Club to become its organiser, for the sum of £1 per week. He agreed to take up the position, and his full-scale immersion in Irish politics began.

Connolly quickly reorganised the Socialist Club and renamed it the Irish Socialist Republican Party (ISRP). Though this party remained tiny for its lifetime – it is estimated never to have had more than 80 members – it was a crucial formation in the history of the Irish left. In its very title, the party embodied the problematic around which a great deal of Irish left politics and thought has revolved in the century and more since Connolly set up the ISRP. This tension would lead to the party's dissolution in 1904, but the experience remained an essential one in his career. The ISRP ran candidates in local elections, and published a newspaper – much of it written by Connolly himself – *The Workers' Republic*: Ireland's first Marxist newspaper.

Connolly's was a Marxism of the Second International. What did this entail? The International was formed in 1889, the same year that Connolly joined the socialist movement in Scotland, and with its grim ending in 1916 his career can be seen to have paralleled this generation of Marxist thought and activity. Where the First International – the International Working Men's Association of Marx and Engels, founded in London in 1864 – was an affiliation of various socialist groups, the Second International was an umbrella organisation for the unions and socialist mass parties of Europe, dominated by the German Social Democrats, which could muster millions of voters and hundreds of parliamentary seats. Strikingly, the expansion of the socialist movement in Europe, while spurred by a major recession in European economies between the 1870s and the 1890s, ran concurrently with the economic boom of the turn of the century, the era of high imperialism and monopoly capitalism. That the International was both a source of opposition to that form of capitalism, and fundamentally imbricated with it, is illustrated by its benefiting from parliamentary reforms across Europe which opened the vote to working men in Britain and Ireland in 1884, in Germany in 1871, and in Spain in 1890. This parallel of the expansion of socialism and the expansion of empire and monopoly capital is in part to be expected – an expanding capitalism was producing an expanding proletariat – but it brought with it tensions which would be exposed to devastating effect with the coming of the First World War.

Despite their growth, the socialist parties of Europe were still largely marginal to the overall political systems in which they operated.

Consequently, they were mostly reformist in orientation: their rhetoric was usually far in advance of their actual policies. Parties spoke aggressively about capitalism, while the unions to which they were often affiliated sought modest adjustments in the workplace. Their Marxism was inherited from Engels and was often interpreted in a dogmatic and pseudo-scientific manner. So they saw the demise of capitalism and the rise of socialism as inevitable, and the task of socialist parties as being to help that trend on its way.

Connolly's thought is to be located in this context, though he also strains against it. If the collapse of capitalism was a foregone conclusion, then, as Karl Kautsky suggested, it was only a matter of time before this came about, and it would occur in accordance with 'laws' of historical development which operated no matter what human actors did (Kautsky 1910). This tendency to see history move through 'stages' was problematic for a thinker and activist from the periphery of Europe, such as Connolly. The briefest study of Irish history revealed various deviations from the patterns of development of the core countries of Europe. Not merely this, but the determinism of this strain of Marxism seemed to leave little room or need for human agency: if the process of the breakdown of capitalism and the rise of socialism is inevitable of itself, what need is there for activism, campaigning, strike or protest, legal measures, parliamentary manoeuvre? In fact, it was not until Lenin's break with the International that a less mechanical model of socialist development and action was put forward.

In the face of the self-propelling nature of the historical process, the task for parties and activists, according to the Second International, was consciousness-raising and the making of propaganda. Connolly subscribed to this, and he also accepted the International's enthusiasm for parliamentary politics. This issue had given rise to the expulsion of the anarchists from the International's Congress of 1893. At least until his departure for America in 1903, Connolly saw value in parliamentary activity and electoral politics. Though he gave the state rather little consideration in his writings – either with a view to its seizure or destruction, or its internal workings; he tended simply to see the state machinery as the managing apparatus of capitalism – he clearly believed in its malleability. Accordingly, for most of his career, this put considerable distance between Connolly and the conspiratorial approach of Irish republican revolutionaries.

So Connolly differed from the International in the voluntarism of his politics, and in his sense of Irish history. Yet the 'stage' model of history as a general rule retained its attraction for him, and this produces torsions and paradoxes in his views on history as they pertain to other peripheral parts of Europe or the empires. For Connolly was also aware, and was keen to show, that the lineages of Irish history have at times run athwart metropolitan European patterns. At the root of this paradox is Ireland's status as an old English colony and zone of influence dating back to the high Middle Ages, which after 1800 and the Act of Union was constitutionally folded into the British metropolis. Yet this incorporation came, we might say, too late: it occurred only after a modern Enlightenment civic nationalism had found expression (in the late eighteenth century in the form of Grattan's Parliament and then the United Irishmen's rebellion), and this meant that though Ireland was formally a part of the United Kingdom in Connolly's time, it was also developing an ever-more pervasive secessionist nationalism which manifested itself in terms we would now call 'anti-imperialist' and 'anti-colonial'. This peculiarity is crucial to Connolly's interest in his own time and in ours.

Developing Socialist Republicanism

The activities and positions of the ISRP, then, reflected this unusual intellectual and political location. On the one hand, Ireland was a country of very great class divisions, cross-cut with sectarian and regional differences – between Catholicism and forms of Protestantism, between the industrialised north-east and the agrarian south and west, between a residual 'Ascendancy' landed gentry class and the mass of small farmers or tenants. Connolly found himself prosecuting the class struggle in a political context where various rival 'oppositional' politics jostled him and his comrades for space, electorally and ideologically. Constitutional nationalists – the Home Rule politics of Parnell's United Irish League and the various groupings into which it split after Parnell's fall in 1891 – and revolutionary republicans (the Irish Republican Brotherhood (IRB) and its variants), parliamentarians and revolutionaries all competed for the attention of the public, where the electoral franchise had been expanded in 1884, and where local government became an arena for working-class politics with the Local Government Act in 1898. The ISRP's programme was largely at one with the tendencies of the other parties in the Second International, but it also sought to secularise education, and to argue – long before Sinn Féin – for an independent Irish republic. But asserting this position compelled Connolly constantly to work out his location and that of his party on the plane of ideas and policies. He argued that the Irish nationalist movement had been taken over by – if it had not always been in the control of – middle-class or bourgeois forces, and equally that revolutionary republicanism was largely lacking in a class analysis of the Irish situation. Connolly's overall point – and this remained consistent for the rest of his career – was that nationalism – parliamentary or militant – was likely to reproduce the existing distribution of wealth and privilege in any autonomous or independent Ireland that might emerge under its aegis.

Connolly's felt need to articulate simultaneous critiques of bourgeois constitutional nationalism and revolutionary republicanism is related to his anti-imperialism. We should note here that at this time, the term 'imperialism' referred specifically to the imperial polities of Europe – the British Empire, the Austro-Hungarian Empire, the Russian Empire – and their rivalries and alliances, and not so much to the projection of power overseas, and the relationship of metropolises with peripheries that the term has come to mean in more recent times. This usage prevailed even with the Marxist thinkers of this generation (with the possible exception of Rosa Luxemburg). This usage must be borne in mind when considering Connolly as an anti-imperialist thinker.

Irish History and the Colonial Present

Two events in the 1890s serve to highlight Connolly's complex location: firstly, the involvement of the ISRP in the 1798 centenary celebrations, and secondly, the South African War (1899–1902). Committees sprang up around the country in 1897 called '98 Committees, and the ISRP set up its own 'Rank and File '98 Club'. The purpose of this was to strip away the nationalist sentiment that had clouded memory of the rebellion and had obscured understanding of Wolfe Tone's ideas. Connolly sought to reveal that the 'unity' for which the United Irishmen stood in 1798 was a unity of creeds, not a unity of classes. Tone's ideas were revolutionary, for Connolly, insofar as they touched on matters of class, but it was crucial to realise that the rebellion was betrayed as much by Irish constitutional nationalists as by failures of French assistance. Connolly also deployed the Rank and File '98 Club in a protest against the celebration of the Diamond Jubilee of Queen Victoria. In June 1898, he organised a demonstration, attended by Maud Gonne (famous as the beloved of W. B. Yeats but a substantial republican political campaigner in her own right), in which the protestors carried a symbolic coffin. At O'Connell Bridge, in the heart of Dublin, stopped by a cordon of police, the crowd tipped the coffin into the River Liffey, to cries of 'To Hell with the British Empire!'

In 1899, the Second Boer War began, between Britain and the

Transvaal Republic and Orange Free State. Britain had long sought control of valuable natural resources in the region, and had fought an earlier war in the effort to annex the Boer Republics. Now war broke out again, and the cause of the Boers attracted intense Irish attention and interest. The 1890s had witnessed a movement of some Irish to Johannesburg and other areas in the Transvaal, including Arthur Griffith and John MacBride. The latter was invited to lead an Irish brigade to fight with the Boer republics; though he turned the command down, he went on to take part in the fighting. Three hundred Irishmen joined the 'commando'. Pro-Boer sentiment gripped Dublin, with street protests and the flying of the Transvaal flag. Advanced nationalists openly supported the Dutch settlers. And so also did Connolly and the ISRP. Connolly argued that the war showed that Britain felt comfortable stripping its garrison in Ireland to provide troops for its war in southern Africa because it now regarded Ireland as entirely passive and pacified. He welcomed any struggle in which the British Army might be defeated or damaged. As with the '98 Committees and the Jubilee protests, nationalist and republican sentiment was intensely aroused by the Boer cause, but to Connolly's disgust, when a 'Transvaal committee' was formed, republicans invited Home Rule constitutional nationalists to join it. Again, Connolly found parliamentary and 'physical force' nationalists prepared to ally with each other, and the willingness of the republicans to abandon the class dimension of Irish protest and agitation, turning their backs on his organisation and on the working class. But it was not only the local Irish politics of the Boer War that were complicated for Connolly. We also note his failure to recognise that while the Boers were bravely resisting incorporation by the British Empire, their resistance was predicated on a colonial-racist occlusion of the native peoples of southern Africa. Black Africans were simply invisible, either as displaced or oppressed victims or as historical and political agents. Yet just 13 years later, the South African Native National Congress, the forerunner to the African National Congress, was formed in Bloemfontein by, amongst others, John Dube and Sol Plaatje. This historical development was unforeseen by Connolly, and renders our understanding of him as an anti-imperialist thinker rather more complicated.

A Vision of Irish History

In 1897, Connolly had published his first pamphlet, *Erin's Hope*. This essay is a precursor to *Labour in Irish History* (1910). It shows the influence of James Fintan Lalor, a figure on the left of the Young

Ireland movement of the 1840s who advocated the mobilisation of the Irish peasantry and argued the importance of the land question in rural Ireland. Connolly argued, in a manner that went beyond Marxist thinkers to include nationalist historians such as Alice Stopford Green, that feudalism and eventually capitalism in Ireland were accretions of Norman and English colonisation. Gaelic Ireland was characterised by a form of 'primitive communism', as described by Marx and Engels. Under the Irish Brehon legal code, land was held in common, and this system had persisted longer in Ireland than elsewhere. Not merely this, but this arrangement offered a model for socialism in the future in what was still primarily an agrarian society. Irish capitalism, meanwhile, had developed too recently, and too much under English control, for it to grow in the future. A shift to socialism could actually bypass industrialisation.

Connolly's approach, in other words, here, and later in *Labour in Irish History*, is highly unorthodox. It is also problematic, on several counts. Marx and Engels had not shared Connolly's positive evaluation of primitive communism, and had seen its replacement by capitalist accumulation and private property as inevitable and progressive, as only by these means could the productive forces be expanded. Furthermore, Connolly's vision was coloured, we might say, by Irish Revivalism – his view of the Gaelic past was much more positive than the historical evidence warrants. Having asserted powerfully the need for a socialist solution to the national question, Connolly was entering into paradoxes which would persist through his career. His assumption that class society and capitalism were essentially foreign to Ireland would lead him at times to a more optimistic view of nationalism than was warranted by his own analyses and instincts. Not merely this but Connolly's tendency to see a contradiction between republicanism and capitalism would lead him occasionally to misunderstandings of Irish capitalism and of republicanism's revolutionary potential, exemplified in his attempts to forge links with Arthur Griffith and Sinn Féin. Griffith, with whom Connolly co-operated in the Boer War protests, was a member of the IRB and was anti-imperialist. But his opposition to the British war against the Boers was based on openly racist and supremacist views, and he anticipated eagerly the expansion of capitalism in any independent Irish state which might eventually be won.

Connolly in America 1903–1910

By the early 1900s, while trying to build up the ISRP, Connolly had become aware of the Socialist Labor Party (SLP) in America, and its dynamic new leader, Daniel De Leon. De Leon had led a left-leaning faction from which the mainstream eventually broke away to form the Social Democratic Party (SDP). De Leon's SLP was an aggressively revolutionary party; the SDP was reformist. Connolly became aware of these debates specifically in the context of a quarrel within the Second International regarding coalition with bourgeois parties, and was impressed by De Leon's clear-cut opposition which was matched by that of the ISRP. Connolly then used the example of the SLP as a lever to try to force a leftward shift in British socialism, with its ongoing tendency to support Home Rule parties in Ireland. He went briefly to Scotland in 1903, to set up a new party, the Scottish Labour Party, and arranged the distribution of the American SLP's newspaper in Scotland. But the party remained tiny, and refused to support him as organiser. With the ISRP in comparably dire straits in Ireland, Connolly emigrated to America.

His American years brought Connolly to new debates, and some new positions, which we will sketch briefly here. Firstly, he quite quickly found De Leon dogmatic, authoritarian and aggressive in debate on socialist and Marxist principles and ideas. This led rapidly to a falling-out between the two men. They quarrelled, in public, over analyses of wages – an important matter, as Connolly feared that De Leon's pessimism over the benefits of wages rises for workers had the potential to reduce the activity of unions allied to the SLP to passivity – and over the matters of marriage and religion. Since his Edinburgh days, Connolly had tended to see the personal or intimate sphere of life as beyond the purview of his politics, but now he took the position that advocacy of divorce was a bourgeois position. And in regard to religion, he found that Irish Catholic workers in America were often attacked for their religion. This led eventually to his founding of the Irish Socialist Federation, a small group set up to cater to the Irish-American proletariat.

As Connolly came into conflict with De Leon and aspects of SLP policy, so also he was becoming involved in a new organisation, the International Workers of the World (nicknamed 'the Wobblies'). The IWW was an explicitly syndicalist organisation, projecting 'one big union' – as against trade-specific craft unions – and appealed to the most impoverished workers. Emerging out of the struggles of American miners, it burst on the scene in 1905. It was positioned well to the left of the SDP, and was equally critical of the elitism and corruption of the American Federation of Labor (AFL), which had never made any effort to organise or campaign for the unskilled or immigrant workers, and which espoused racist and sexist attitudes to black and female workers. It was also a product of the galvanisation of the international labour movement by the Russian Revolution of 1905, which seemed to demonstrate the power of the general strike. Connolly gradually moved away from the SLP and towards the IWW in his activities.

Syndicalism helped to shape Connolly's attitudes and positions not only during his time in America, but also to events and politics in Ireland when he returned there. Its prioritising of the workers and its stress on direct action (as against negotiation or bargaining, and as against elections) would influence the formation of the Irish Transport and General Workers' Union in 1909. In a substantial pamphlet he wrote at this time, *Socialism Made Easy*, Connolly set out his ideas. The crux of the matter for him was the need for what he called 'industrial unionism'. Unionised workers could gradually wrest control of industries away from managers and capitalists. The socialist republic of the future could itself start to take form within the shell of industry, by the activity of the union. This was a powerfully motivating idea, though it was also one which was perhaps naïve about the potential resistance of the bosses, and which simply played down the power of the state either to channel or simply to resist and break such activity. In keeping with the quasi-anarchist ideas of the syndicalists, Connolly also saw little role for the state in the new society to come; unlike the Bolsheviks, say, he saw no need for the workers' state.

Connolly's later years in America were marked by some ideological confusion. The IWW took him away from the SLP. In 1907, the Wall Street financial markets crashed, and the ensuing recession severely damaged the IWW. In this context, he joined the Socialist Party of America, a party of which he had previously been critical and scornful. This move, while understandable at the time, brought with it uncomfortable compromises: the party's leadership was racist, and its leadership sat on the rightward end of the spectrum of socialism. But the wider matter was that his experience of syndicalism had led Connolly to doubt the value of the political party as a mechanism for organisation and ideological battle. Though he was himself an avid student of history and politics, he also evinced little sympathy for 'theory', seeing the practical action of a union as more valuable.

Labour in Irish History

This short book is the most sustained piece of writing Connolly produced. In 16 short chapters, he offers a critique of mainstream Irish history of a ruthlessness and power few modern 'revisionists' can equal. Again and again, the highlights of Irish nationalist political history are examined and found wanting in class terms. Readings of Jacobite heroes, of the 'patriot' politics of the late eighteenth century, of even the United Irishmen, and of O'Connell show the kind of class compromises that were repeatedly made. Connolly sees nationalism as the 'idealised expression of class interests', but he also holds out hope for a 'real' or authentic nationalism.

The contradictions that complicate Connolly's work are those we have already observed. On the one hand, he recognises that there is, and for long has been, greater identity of interest between the Irish bourgeoisie and the English bourgeoisie than between the Irish bourgeoisie and the Irish workers and peasants. On the other hand, he wishes, partly for tactical political reasons, to find resources for action in the Irish revolutionary tradition, which is dominated by republicanism. So part of his purpose is to scour the republican tradition for elements of class progressivism. We need to read this endeavour with a combination of sympathy and scepticism.

At the root of the complexity of Connolly's text is the argument that Irish nationalism had led to a different idea of property rights from those held in England. Following on from this, there is the suggestion that feudalism and eventually capitalism itself are imports or impositions that arrived from England. This vision of history had already been advanced in *Erin's Hope*, as we saw earlier. Here, in this later and more substantial work, the stakes, both politically and intellectually, are higher.

The complicating matters turn on Irish nationalism. Connolly himself wrote that *Labour in Irish History* was a text of the Irish Revival, and this is not just a matter of its historical moment of production but runs into its intellectual substructure. In a manner similar to the discovery or rediscovery of an ancient Irish Gaelic culture, and hence nation, which we see in cultural nationalists of Connolly's time such as Standish O'Grady or W. B. Yeats, Connolly retrojects an idea of Irish national character, an idea of national consciousness, deeper into Irish history than many mainstream Irish historians would accept was warranted, and he ascribes to it attributes of resistance and coherence which are difficult to verify in positivist terms. Most obviously, his chapters on agrarian radicalism of the eighteenth and nineteenth centuries are both provocative and problematic. In the movements of Whiteboys in the south, and Steelboys and Hearts of Oak in the north, Connolly risks seeing a coherent national (as against local) programme of resistance. Though he places a great emphasis in his book on the period of the late eighteenth and early nineteenth centuries, in his move (rightly) to criticise 'patriot' politics as bourgeois, he does not see the importance of the rising Protestant and Catholic middle classes to what would issue as nationalism after the failed rebellion of 1798. Connolly is reluctant to see a kind of radicalism in middle-class movements for separatism, or to recognise an 'authentic' middle-class nationalism, and this to a degree blinds him. Further, he reads into the agrarian movements a wish for a return to the putative ancient Gaelic modes of common landholding. The implication is that Irish primitive communism is lying dormant in the people, waiting to be revived.

These tendencies feed into Connolly's positive assessments of the United Irishmen, and, amongst the Young Ireland generation of the mid-nineteenth century, of James Fintan Lalor. He is persuaded by Wolfe Tone's fierce Jacobinism and is reluctant to acknowledge fully the bourgeois character of the United Irishmen (whose *Northern Star* newspaper resolutely defended property rights). As we have already seen in regard to *Erin's Hope*, he is impressed by Lalor's emphasis on the potential of a radicalised or nationalised peasantry, and he overlooks John Mitchel's late-career endorsement of slavery in the southern United States. Nevertheless, *Labour in Irish History* is a remarkable work. It has been read and argued over ever since its appearance. As Connolly's masterpiece, it has been the focus for debates on the Irish left in every generation.

Connolly and Revolutionary Ireland 1910–1916

The Ireland to which Connolly returned from the United States in 1910 was one which was ever-more agitated by various struggles. The chief of these were the Home Rule and Ulster Crisis of 1912–1914, the Dublin Lock-Out of 1913, and the outbreak of the First World War in 1914. These tumultuous events demanded an exceptional agility of Connolly, organisationally and ideologically. All the time, he was also reflecting on revolutionary movements elsewhere: in other parts of the British Empire such as Egypt and India, and also in Russia, and in other parts of Europe. The Ulster Crisis was problematic for him, in that it demonstrated that the most industrialised part of Ireland also harboured the most powerful anti-revolutionary forces on the island. The Lock-Out was a tremendous battle with the Dublin property-owning classes, and is often seen as a formative struggle, and ultimately defeat, in the history of the Irish left. The First World War blew open the ideological and political context for Connolly's Irish efforts, and helped to channel him towards his eventual participation in the Easter Rising of 1916.

Events in Ulster, such as the signing of the Ulster Covenant, the formation and arming of the Ulster Volunteers, and the alliance between the Conservative Party in Britain and Ulster Unionism, operated to display in the most formidable manner the efforts of landowners and capitalists to maintain their linkage to the British and imperial economy, by deploying an ideology of sectarian priority and privilege. In Connolly's eyes, and despite his efforts, the Ulster working class, predominantly Protestant, faced a choice between class solidarity with the poor elsewhere in Ireland or ethno-religious community. It chose the latter, for the most part. This was a forerunner of the problems of class and nationalism just a few years later. The Lock-Out was a product of an improvement in the British and Irish economies without a parallel rise in wages. The workers of Dublin, increasingly unionised due to the efforts most famously of James Larkin, were in militant mood. Dublin business-owners, looking forward to Home Rule after 1912, faced a rebellious workforce. The most aggressive of the Dublin capitalists, William Martin Murphy, advocated breaking the workers' movement, to help produce quiescent unions when Home Rule arrived. Larkin and Connolly fought the Lock-Out by the tactic of the sympathetic strike. They stretched their campaign to Britain itself, appealing to workers and unions there for support. Their efforts in Ireland were damaged by Church intervention. For a brief time, the labour movements of Britain and Ireland collaborated effectively, but eventually the workers were defeated. Nevertheless, Connolly could find that the Lock-Out had shown the finest points of the British labour movement.

With the coming of the First World War, Irish struggles of this kind came into a new context. Most grievous for Connolly was the collapse of the Second International. On or shortly after 4 August 1914, socialist politicians all over Europe declared their patriotic support for their governments: only the Russians and the Serbians took a principled stand. In Ireland, Orange forces declared support for the Empire. Home Rule politicians supported war, and the Irish Volunteers, a nationalist militia, eventually split after encouragement from John Redmond, the Home Rule leader to take part in the war. On the Irish left, too, opinion was severely divided. Even Irish syndicalists showed support for Britain's war effort. Connolly was one of a handful of figures, including Lenin and Luxemburg, who adhered to the best principles of the Second International, and rejected the 'humanitarian' pacifist arguments of figures such as Kautsky, rather seeing the war as an opportunity for revolutionary action. Connolly had never rejected violent practice; his point was that revolutionary action by the workers would at some point be necessary. That moment was now at hand.

The failure of the Second International was a significant factor in pushing Connolly towards armed insurrection. His first response was to call for continent-wide general strike. He was convinced that immediate general action by the working classes of the great powers could bring the war to a halt. But the call fell on deaf ears, including in Ireland. By 1916, Connolly was dismayed by the failures of both Irish nationalists and the Irish working class to show resistance to the war. Nationalists had responded in large numbers to Redmond's appeal to show 'loyalty' by joining up, in the hope of winning political favours at the war's end (when the suspended Home Rule process would be set in motion). Edward Carson had argued that unionists should act in the same way on the same premise but with the opposite goal in mind: unionist support for the war effort would help stop Home Rule. But the workers had not responded to Connolly's call in any significant numbers. The bases on which Connolly asserted Irish anti-imperialism and anti-capitalism were eroded before his eyes.

Connolly was now forced to conclude that the methods hitherto espoused by the Second International were ineffective and inappropriate in wartime. By 1915, he was arguing that 'we believe in constitutional action in normal times; we believe in revolutionary action in exceptional times. These are exceptional times.' And so his scepticism regarding the republican movement underwent a change, and this ultimately allowed him to ally himself with republicans in planning rebellion. The change was that the republican movement, and its militia the Volunteers, which had been gradually taken over by mainstream Home Rule ideas – Redmond saw the Volunteers as acting purely to defend Ireland in wartime – was now split. The Volunteers in late 1914 divided. The great majority responded to Redmond's call and changed their name to the National Volunteers. A rump of 10,000 was left, but now radicalised and open to IRB plans for armed rebellion. This gave Connolly his opportunity. He quickly moved closer to the IRB (which included figures such as Patrick Pearse and Thomas Clarke), and became party to their plans for insurrection.

Connolly and the Meaning of the Rising

The story of the Easter Rising itself is well known. Connolly's leadership is recorded as having been important and inspiring. His court-martial and execution, as with those of the other 1916 leaders, was swift, ruthless and quickly revealed to be politically misguided. But it is worth noting that Connolly's military experience was important in his participation in the rebellion, and that the Irish Citizen Army, the tiny militia Connolly had set up in the wake of the Lock-Out, to defend workers' protests, brought out almost its entire strength to take part in the Rising.

The Easter Rising, though it failed in its overt intent, was a hinge event in Ireland's struggle for independence. Most obviously, it was a hammer-blow directed at the parliamentary and constitutional Home Rule movement as much as at Britain. In class terms, it represented a shift away from the bourgeois elite politics of even Parnell, and a move towards lower-middle-class leadership of the independence movements, both political and militant. The Rising's import, and Connolly's participation in it, has been argued over ever since.

At the time, the European left responded to the rebellion in various ways. Elements of the British left saw it as militarist and as a betrayal of the British people. But internationally, the response was more positive. Just at the moment of the Rising itself, the Austrian Karl Radek had argued that peripheral nationalist movements were ineffective in opposing imperialism. On 9 May 1916, writing in *Berner Tagewacht* three days before Connolly's execution, Radek saw the Rising as a petty-bourgeois *putsch*, devoid of progressive class content due to the process of land reform which had been underway in the Irish countryside since the 1870s (O'Connor Lysaght 1993: 57). Trotsky had a more nuanced sense of Irish class politics, but nevertheless gloomily opined that the 'basis for a national revolution has disappeared, even in backward Ireland' (O'Connor Lysaght 1993: 59). It fell to Lenin to draw the positive and more properly dialectical lessons from the Rising. Writing about the insurrection the following autumn, and anticipating the coming European revolutions, Lenin declared that the Irish rebellion was premature, but that to dismiss it merely as a brief flaring of possibly reactionary petty-bourgeois sentiment and militancy was historically mistaken: 'The dialectics of history are such that small nations, powerless as an *independent* factor in the struggle against imperialism, play the part of one of the ferments ... which help the *real* anti-imperialist force, the socialist proletariat, to appear on the scene' (O'Connor Lysaght 1993: 64; italics in original). Coming at the end of a very long Irish revolutionary tradition, the Rising showed that the general crisis of capitalism and imperialism would be driven by revolutionary action both in the colonies *and* in the metropolitan cores.

Looking back at Connolly's career, then, we are left with a sense of an extraordinary life of labour activism, political militancy and radical thought, all of them shot through with both grace and steel. Connolly stands out amongst his Irish peers and contemporaries, and in the international labour movement of his time, for his combination of courage and principle, and for his ability to recognise all of the intersecting vectors determining radical action in a globalised world – transnational capital, solidarity across national borders, the agency of ordinary people. His agility and fertility of thought and action remain exemplary to this day.

Works Cited

Kautsky, Karl (1910), *The Class Struggle*, Chicago: CH Kerr.
Leslie, John (1894), *The Present Position of the Irish Question*, London: The Twentieth Century Press Ltd.
O'Connor Lysaght, D. R. (1993), *The Communists and the Irish Revolution: The Russian Revolutionaries on the Irish Question 1899–1924*, Dublin: LiterÉire Publishers.

Further Reading

Allen, Kieran (1990), *The Politics of James Connolly*, London: Pluto Press. Trenchant and thoughtful study by a contemporary Trotskyist scholar.
Anderson, W. K. (1994), *James Connolly and the Irish Left*, Dublin: Irish Academic Press. Valuable study of Connolly's ideas and their legacies.
Collins, Lorcan (2012), *James Connolly*, Dublin: O'Brien Press. Lively and compelling popular biography, in a fine series (*16 Lives*) on the 1916 leaders.
Greaves, C. Desmond (1961), *The Life and Times of James Connolly*, London: Lawrence and Wishart. The earliest scholarly biography.
Kostick, Conor (2009), *Revolution in Ireland: Popular Militancy 1917–1923*, Cork: Cork University Press. Eye-opening portrayal of the wide range of forms and ideologies of protest and revolt released under revolutionary conditions.
Lane, Fintan (1997), *The Origins of Modern Irish Socialism 1881–1896*, Cork: Cork University Press. Useful and valuable background.
Lynch, David (2005), *Radical Politics in Ireland: The Irish Socialist Republican Party 1896–1904*, Dublin: Irish Academic Press. Detailed study of the short life of the ISRP.
McCracken, Donal (2003), *Forgotten Protest: Ireland and the Anglo-Boer War*, Belfast: Ulster Historical Foundation. Useful contextualisation of Connolly's positions on the South African War.
Nevin, Donal (2005), *James Connolly: 'A Full Life'*, Dublin: Gill and Macmillan. The major recent life of Connolly.
O'Connor, Emmet (2011), *A Labour History of Ireland 1824–2000*, Dublin: University College Dublin Press. An excellent interpretative survey.

Chapter 1
The Early Years and the Irish Socialist Republican Party

Irish Socialist Republican Party

(1896)

This document is the founding manifesto of the ISRP, and so is of interest as one of the earlier codified and institutionalised statements of Connolly's position. Most notably, it breaks with the position of the Second International regarding the working classes of Europe's colonies. Where conservatives within the International saw colonisation as a civilising process, and centrists saw no necessary link between the struggles of colonised peoples and those of the metropolitan working class, Connolly asserts powerfully the revolutionary potential of the downtrodden colonised, the futility of waiting on the benevolence of the metropolis, and the necessity of national self-determination to the defeat of capitalism in Ireland.

'The great appear great to us only because we are on our knees;
LET US RISE'[1]

OBJECT

Establishment of AN IRISH SOCIALIST REPUBLIC based upon the public ownership by the Irish people of the land, and instruments of production, distribution and exchange. Agriculture to be administered as a public function, under boards of management elected by the agricultural population and responsible to them and to the nation at large. All other forms of labour necessary to the well-being of the community to be conducted on the same principles.

---

[1] This famous maxim is attributed to James Larkin (1876–1947), Irish trade unionist, leader with Connolly of the Dublin workers during the 1913 Lock-Out, and founder of the Irish Transport and General Workers' Union.

PROGRAMME

As a means of organising the forces of the Democracy in preparation for any struggle which may precede the realisation of our ideal, of paving the way for its realisation, of restricting the tide of emigration by providing employment at home, and finally of palliating the evils of our present social system, we work by political means to secure the following measures:
1. Nationalisation of railways and canals.
2. Abolition of private banks and money-lending institutions and establishments of state banks, under popularly elected boards of directors, issuing loans at cost.
3. Establishment at public expense of rural depots for the most improved agricultural machinery, to be lent out to the agricultural population at a rent covering cost and management alone.
4. Graduated income tax on all incomes over £400 per annum in order to provide funds for pensions to the aged, infirm and widows and orphans.
5. Legislative restriction of hours of labour to 48 per week and establishment of a minimum wage.
6. Free maintenance for all children.
7. Gradual extension of the principle of public ownership and supply to all the necessaries of life.
8. Public control and management of National schools by boards elected by popular ballot for that purpose alone.
9. Free education up to the highest university grades.
10. Universal suffrage.

THE IRISH SOCIALIST REPUBLICAN PARTY

That the agricultural and industrial system of a free people, like their political system, ought to be an accurate reflex of the democratic principle by the people for the people, solely in the interests of the people.

That the private ownership, by a class, of the land and instruments of production, distribution and exchange, is opposed to this vital principle of justice, and is the fundamental basis of all oppression, national, political and social.

That the subjection of one nation to another, as of Ireland to the authority of the British Crown, is a barrier to the free political and economic development of the subjected nation, and can only serve the interests of the exploiting classes of both nations.

That, therefore, the national and economic freedom of the Irish people must be sought in the same direction, viz., the establishment of an Irish Socialist Republic, and the consequent conversion of the means of production, distribution and exchange into the common property of society, to be held and controlled by a democratic state in the interests of the entire community.

That the conquest by the Social Democracy of political power in Parliament, and on all public bodies in Ireland, is the readiest and most effective means whereby the revolutionary forces may be organised and disciplined to attain that end.

BRANCHES WANTED EVERYWHERE. ENQUIRIES INVITED. ENTRANCE FEE, 6d. MINIMUM. WEEKLY SUBSCRIPTION 1d. Offices: 67 MIDDLE ABBEY STREET, DUBLIN.

Socialism and Nationalism

Shan Van Vocht (January 1897)

Shan Van Vocht was a nationalist magazine published in Belfast between 1896 and 1899 by Alice Milligan and Anna Johnston. The name is derived from the Irish Gaelic term *An tSean Bhean Bhocht*, which means 'the poor old woman', a traditional personification of Ireland. We should note in this article Connolly's critique of bourgeois republicanism, and his argument for alliance between the urban and rural poor.

In Ireland at the present time there are at work a variety of agencies seeking to preserve the national sentiment in the hearts of the people.

These agencies, whether Irish Language movements, Literary Societies or Commemoration Committees, are undoubtedly doing a work of lasting benefit to this country in helping to save from extinction the precious racial and national history, language and characteristics of our people.

Nevertheless, there is a danger that by too strict an adherence to their present methods of propaganda, and consequent neglect of vital living issues, they may only succeed in stereotyping our historical studies into a worship of the past, or crystallising nationalism into a tradition – glorious and heroic indeed, but still only a tradition.

Now traditions may, and frequently do, provide materials for a glorious martyrdom, but can never be strong enough to ride the storm of a successful revolution.

If the national movement of our day is not merely to re-enact the old sad tragedies of our past history, it must show itself capable of rising to the exigencies of the moment.

It must demonstrate to the people of Ireland that our nationalism is not merely a morbid idealising of the past, but is also capable of formulating a distinct and definite answer to the problems of the present and a political and economic creed capable of adjustment to the wants of the future.

This concrete political and social ideal will best be supplied, I believe, by the frank acceptance on the part of all earnest nationalists of the Republic as their goal.

Not a Republic, as in France, where a capitalist monarchy with an elective head parodies the constitutional abortions of England, and in open alliance with the Muscovite despotism brazenly flaunts its apostasy to the traditions of the Revolution.

Not a Republic as in the United States, where the power of the purse has established a new tyranny under the forms of freedom; where, one hundred years after the feet of the last British red-coat polluted the streets of Boston, British landlords and financiers impose upon American citizens a servitude compared with which the tax of pre-Revolution days was a mere trifle.

No! the Republic I would wish our fellow-countrymen to set before them as their ideal should be of such a character that the mere mention of its name would at all times serve as a beacon-light to the oppressed of every land, at all times holding forth promise of freedom and plenteousness as the reward of their efforts on its behalf.

To the tenant farmer, ground between landlordism on the one hand and American competition on the other, as between the upper and the nether millstone; to the wage-workers in the towns, suffering from the exactions of the slave-driving capitalist to the agricultural labourer, toiling away his life for a wage barely sufficient to keep body and soul together; in fact to every one of the toiling millions upon whose misery the outwardly-splendid fabric of our modern civilisation is reared, the Irish Republic might be made a word to conjure with – a rallying point for the disaffected, a haven for the oppressed, a point of departure for the Socialist, enthusiastic in the cause of human freedom.

This linking together of our national aspirations with the hopes of the men and women who have raised the standard of revolt against that system of capitalism and landlordism, of which the British Empire is the most aggressive type and resolute defender, should not, in any sense, import an element of discord into the ranks of earnest nationalists, and would serve to place us in touch with fresh reservoirs of moral and physical strength sufficient to lift the cause of Ireland to a more commanding position than it has occupied since the day of Benburb.

It may be pleaded that the ideal of a Socialist Republic, implying, as it does, a complete political and economic revolution would be sure to alienate all our middle-class and aristocratic supporters, who would dread the loss of their property and privileges.

What does this objection mean? That we must conciliate the privileged classes in Ireland!

But you can only disarm their hostility by assuring them that in a *free* Ireland their 'privileges' will not be interfered with. That is to say, you must guarantee that when Ireland is free of foreign domination, the green-coated Irish soldiers will guard the fraudulent gains of capitalist and landlord from 'the thin hands of the poor' just as remorselessly and just as effectually as the scarlet-coated emissaries of England do today.

On no other basis will the classes unite with you. Do you expect the masses to fight for this ideal?

When you talk of freeing Ireland, do you only mean the chemical elements which compose the soil of Ireland? Or is it the Irish people you mean? If the latter, from what do you propose to free them? From the rule of England?

But all systems of political administration or governmental machinery are but the reflex of the economic forms which underlie them.

English rule in England is but the symbol of the fact that English conquerors in the past forced upon this country a property system founded upon spoliation, fraud and murder: that, as the present-day exercise of the 'rights of property' so originated involves the continual practice of legalised spoliation and fraud, English rule is found to be the most suitable form of government by which the spoliation can be protected, and an English army the most pliant tool with which to execute judicial murder when the fears of the propertied classes demand it.

The Socialist who would destroy, root and branch, the whole brutally materialistic system of civilisation, which like the English language we have adopted as our own, is, I hold, a far more deadly foe to English rule and tutelage, than the superficial thinker who imagines it possible to reconcile Irish freedom with those insidious but disastrous forms of economic subjection – landlord tyranny, capitalist fraud and unclean usury; baneful fruits of the Norman Conquest, the unholy trinity, of which Strongbow and Diarmuid MacMurchadha – Norman thief and Irish traitor – were the fitting precursors and apostles.[2]

---

[2] Diarmaid MacMurchadha (*c.*1110–*c.*1170), Irish warrior and king, King of Leinster, displaced from his throne by the High King of Ireland, he sought the help of Richard de Clare, 2nd Earl of Pembroke, nicknamed Strongbow, to attain his reinstatement, thereby facilitating the Norman invasion of Ireland.

If you remove the English army to-morrow and hoist the green flag over Dublin Castle, unless you set about the organisation of the Socialist Republic your efforts would be in vain.

England would still rule you. She would rule you through her capitalists, through her landlords, through her financiers, through the whole array of commercial and individualist institutions she has planted in this country and watered with the tears of our mothers and the blood of our martyrs.

England would still rule you to your ruin, even while your lips offered hypocritical homage at the shrine of that Freedom whose cause you had betrayed.

Nationalism without Socialism – without a reorganisation of society on the basis of a broader and more developed form of that common property which underlay the social structure of Ancient Erin – is only national recreancy.

It would be tantamount to a public declaration that our oppressors had so far succeeded in inoculating us with their perverted conceptions of justice and morality that we had finally decided to accept those conceptions as our own, and no longer needed an alien army to force them upon us.

As a Socialist I am prepared to do all one man can do to achieve for our motherland her rightful heritage – independence; but if you ask me to abate one jot or tittle of the claims of social justice, in order to conciliate the privileged classes, then I must decline.

Such action would be neither honourable nor feasible. Let us never forget that he never reaches Heaven who marches thither in the company of the Devil. Let us openly proclaim our faith: the logic of events is with us.

Patriotism and Labour

Shan Van Vocht (August 1897)

Connolly uses the term 'patriot' here both in its general sense, referring to love of country, and in its eighteenth-century Irish sense, referring to the 'patriot' politics of figures such as Henry Grattan, who combined an Irish identity with an alliance with Liberals or Whigs in Britain, and who sought Irish political autonomy within the British Empire.

What is Patriotism? Love of country, someone answers. But what is meant by 'love of country'? 'The rich man', says a French writer, 'loves his country because he conceives it owes him a duty, whereas the poor man loves his country as he believes he owes it a duty'. The recognition of the duty we owe our country is, I take it, the real mainspring of patriotic action; and our 'country', properly understood, means not merely the particular spot on the earth's surface from which we derive our parentage, but also comprises all the men, women and children of our race whose collective life constitutes our country's political existence. True patriotism seeks the welfare of each in the happiness of all, and is inconsistent with the selfish desire for worldly wealth which can only be gained by the spoliation of less favoured fellow-mortals.

Viewed in the light of such a definition, what are the claims to patriotism possessed by the moneyed class of Ireland? The percentage of weekly wages of £1 per week and under received by the workers of the three kingdoms is stated by the Board of Trade report to be as follows: England, 40; Scotland, 50; and Ireland, 78 per cent. In other words, three out of every four wage-earners in Ireland receive less than £1 per week. Who is to blame? What determines the rate of wages? The competition among workers for employment. There is always a large surplus of unemployed labour in Ireland, and owing to this fact the Irish employer is able to take advantage of the helplessness of his poorer fellow-countrymen and compel them to work for less than their fellows in England receive for the same class of work.

The employees of our municipal Corporations and other public bodies in Ireland are compelled by our middle-class town-councillors – their compatriots – to accept wages of from 4s. to 8s. per week less than English Corporations pay in similar branches of public service. Irish railway servants receive from 5s. to 10s. per week less than English railway servants in the same departments, although shareholders in Irish railways draw higher dividends than are paid on the most prosperous English. In all private employment in Ireland the same state of matters prevails. Let us be clear upon this point. There is no law upon the statute book, no power possessed by the Privy Council, no civil or military function under the control of Prime Minister, Lord Lieutenant, or Chief Secretary which can, does or strives to compel the employing class in Ireland to take advantage of the crowded state of the labour market and use it to depress the wages of their workers to the present starvation level.

To the greed of our moneyed class, operating upon the social conditions created by landlordism and capitalism and maintained upon foreign bayonets, such a result is alone attributable, and no amount of protestations should convince intelligent workers that the class which grinds them down to industrial slavery can, at the same moment, be leading them forward to national liberty. True patriotism seeks the welfare of each in the happiness of all, and is inconsistent with the selfish desire for worldly wealth which can only be gained by the spoliation of less favoured fellow-mortals. It is the mission of the working class to give to patriotism this higher, nobler, significance. This can only be done by our working class, as the only universal, all-embracing class, organizing as a distinct political party, recognizing in Labour the cornerstone of our economic edifice and the animating principle of our political action.

Hence the rise of the Irish Socialist Republican Party. We are resolved upon national independence as the indispensable groundwork of industrial emancipation, but we are equally resolved to have done with the leadership of a class whose social charter is derived from oppression. Our policy is the outcome of long reflection upon the history and peculiar circumstances of our country. In an independent country the election of a majority of Socialist representatives to the Legislature means the conquest of political power by the revolutionary party, and consequently the mastery of the military and police forces of the State, which would then become the ally of revolution instead of its enemy.

In the work of social reconstruction which would then ensue, the State power – created by the propertied classes for their own class purposes – would serve the new social order as a weapon in its fight against such adherents of the privileged orders as strove to resist the gradual extinction of their rule.

Ireland not being an independent country, the election of a majority of Socialist Republicans would not, unfortunately, place the fruits of our toil so readily within our grasp. But it would have another, perhaps no less important, effect. It would mean that for the first time in Irish history a clear majority of the responsible electorate of the Irish nation – men capable of bearing arms – had registered at the ballot-boxes their desire for separation from the British Empire. Such a verdict, arrived at not in the tumultuous and, too often, fickle enthusiasm of monster meetings, but in the sober atmosphere and judicial calmness of the polling-booth, would ring like a trumpet-call in the ears alike of our rulers and of every enemy of the British imperial system. That would not long survive such a consummation. Its enemies would read in the verdict thus delivered at the ballot-box a passionate appeal for help against the oppressor, the moral insurrection of the Irish people, which a small expeditionary force and war material might convert into such a military insurrection as would exhaust the power of the empire at home and render its possessions an easy prey abroad. How long would such an appeal be disregarded?

Meanwhile, there is no temporary palliative of our misery, no material benefit which Parliament can confer that could not be extorted by the fear of a revolutionary party seeking to create such a situation as I have described, sooner than by any action of even the most determined Home Rule or other constitutional party. Thus, alike for present benefits and for future freedom, the revolutionary policy is the best. A party aiming at a merely political Republic and proceeding upon such lines, would always be menaced by the danger that some astute English Statesman might, by enacting a sham measure of Home Rule, disorganize the Republican forces by an appearance of concessions, until the critical moment had passed. But the Irish Socialist Republican Party, by calling attention to evils inherent in that social system of which the British Empire is but the highest political expression sign, founds its propaganda upon discontent with social iniquities which will only pass away when the Empire is no more, and thus implants in all its followers an undying, ineradicable hatred of the enemy, which will remain undisturbed and unmollified by any conceivable system of political quackery whatever.

An Irish Socialist Republic ought, therefore, to be the rallying cry of all our countrymen who desire to see the union and triumph of Patriotism and Labour.

Editorial Note
Whilst in full sympathy with Mr Connolly's views on the labour and social questions, we are absolutely opposed to the scheme he puts forward for the formation of an Irish Republican party in the British Parliament. Any conscientious Republican would stick at the oath of allegiance and no reliance could be placed on what John O'Leary calls 'double-oathed' men. John Mitchel allowed himself to be returned as a representative, but absolutely refused to entertain the idea of claiming his seat. He looked upon his election merely as a declaration in favour of his unalterable rebel principles. We would like to have this question debated.

Parnellism and Labour

Workers' Republic (8 October 1898)

The Workers' Republic was the newspaper of the ISRP, and the first Marxist newspaper in Ireland. Connolly's training as a print-worker was useful in its production, though it was always a modest journal. It was sold at meetings and rallies. Its articles frequently reflected or reproduced the topics addressed by Connolly at public meetings. Over its short life, it also reflected the interests of the international socialist movement, carrying articles by figures such as Karl Marx, Friedrich Engels, Paul Lafargue and Ferdinand Lassalle. It also carried short news items about the progress and reversals of socialist movements across the world. By 'Parnellism', Connolly refers to mainstream nationalist constitutionalist/parliamentary politics and its drive towards Home Rule.

So long as they seek for Home Rule – for mere changes within the Constitution – our Irish parties at Westminster are, and must ever be, in the position of political hucksters seeking a good price for the votes they offer as wares. Their 'independence' is only the fraudulent cloak with which they strive to cover their venality and lack of spirit.

We must not omit to specify one other cause of the decay of the official Parnellite party, viz., their unsatisfactory attitude towards labour. When Charles Stewart Parnell was basely deserted in Committee Room 15 by the crowd of adventurers and hack journalists out of whom he had constructed a formidable political party; when he was attacked in Ireland by the tenant farmers who owed much of whatever security they possessed to his skilful leadership; when the priesthood, whom he had elevated to power in the branches of the National League, turned to rend the man under whose firm guidance their influence might have become a power for freedom; when he was, in fact, deserted by the men who had ever been most loud-mouthed in their adulation of his person, it was the real and true-hearted workingmen of Ireland who sprang to his side and fought his battles.[3] They had never gained, but ever lost by his agitation, but in the supreme crisis of his destinies they rose superior to all other

---

[3] Charles Stewart Parnell (1846–1891), Irish politician, land reform leader and founder of the IPP. The crucial vote over the leadership by Parnell of the Irish National League (the main party of the IPP in Westminster), in the wake of the revelation of his relationship with Katherine O'Shea, took place at Committee Room 15 in the Palace of Westminster on 29 November 1890. The result was the splitting of the Party and the end of Parnell's career.

considerations and fought for the man battling against an insulting form of foreign dictation. They asked no reward – and got none. During the early days of the split Mr. Parnell did, indeed, adopt a programme laid before him by Dublin workingmen – a programme embodying nearly every measure advocated as palliative measures by the Socialist parties, but with his untimely death disappeared every hope of seeing that programme adhered to by any Home Rule party. Every succeeding year has seen the Parnellite party become more and more conservative and reactionary. Today, in direct opposition to the policy of their great leader, we find the Parnellite chiefs seeking every opportunity to hob-nob with the representatives of Irish landlordism; hailing their feeblest utterances upon a financial question as the brightest scintillations of wisdom; and not scrupling to tell at Cambridge an audience, composed of the young fledglings of English aristocracy, that the realisation of Ireland's independence was neither possible nor desirable.

Followers of Parnell they are indeed, but they follow at such a respectable distance they have lost sight not only of the leader but of his principles.

Meanwhile, the manhood of Ireland, no longer dazzled by the glare of a great personality, have had time to more closely examine their position, social and political. As a result they turn alike from the men who sold their leader at the bidding of an unscrupulous politician; from the incapable gang whose only hope of existence is to live like political cannibals upon the reputation of the dead; and from the pitiful compromise of the National Demand which scarce even the genius of Parnell could make appear respectable.

The working class of Ireland trusts no more the charming of the middle-class politician, charm he never so plausibly; strong in its own power it marches irresistibly forward to its destiny, the Socialist Republic.

The Sweating System

Workers' Republic (3 June 1899)

This essay shows Connolly's capacity to focus on a very specific labourers' issue, and to analyse the minutiae of oppression in the workplace. Note the appeal to socialism, and to class consciousness, pointing towards the remedy to such practices.

We are unfeignedly glad to see the members of the tailoring trade in Dublin bestirring themselves to put an end to the sweating system in connection with that industry. Unfortunately in a great many of our most important trades any discontent which exists is too often attributed to merely imaginary causes, and the money and energy of the workers frittered away in a foolish effort to win the co-operation of the employers in an attempt to better the condition of Labour.

In this move of the tailoring craft, however, there are to be found the tokens of a recognition on the part of the men that, from whatever quarter assistance may voluntarily come, from the side of the masters nothing can be hoped for, – except by pressure of the Union on the one hand or the threat of withdrawal of custom on the other. This fact helps to clear the air and will, no doubt, be highly beneficial to the men in so far as it will serve to solidify their ranks and compel them to realise that it is only by the financial and moral strength of their organisation they can hope to achieve success, and not at all by any reliance upon the goodwill of employers.

For the benefit of the general public we may here set down some of the principal factors in the dispute alluded to. The central grievance upon which attention is directed, if not the only one at present, lies in the employment of what are known as 'outworkers'. Such outworkers are men or women for whom the employer provides no workshop or other facilities, but who execute at home whatever work they receive. This system has a double disadvantage for those workers who work only in the shop, or as it is technically termed, on 'the board'. In the first place, it makes impossible any effective supervision of the conditions under which the work is performed – and thus opens the way for all manner of inroads on the 'log', or price list, and provides the employing class with a reserve of unorganised labour continually competing with the organised workers, and continually offering facilities to the employer in his struggles with his workmen. In the second place, whereas the regular union worker can only work for one employer at a time, and must take all chances incidental to the fluctuations of that employer's business, the outworkers can serve two or three firms at once and thus assure themselves of work, if not from one, then from the other. The result being that the union worker, having insecurity of employment to reckon with, must necessarily seek for such a rate of wages as will counterbalance such insecurity, but the outworkers having greater facilities for procuring work can, and do, accept lower wages. Add to this the fact that even if both sections of workers got the same wages IN CASH yet, owing to their peculiar circumstances, the outworkers would be the less costly to the employer as they would be providing their own workshop, fires, etc. Under such conditions it is no wonder that the regularly organised members of the tailoring craft regard the existence of the outworking, or sweating, system as a danger to their best interests. Indeed it were a wonder were it otherwise, for the facts herein set forth give but the faintest outline of the evils contained in the system of outworking. For instance the fact of such work being performed within the small compass of a working-class 'home' is fatal to the health of those employed upon it, and engenders fever and other contagious diseases which, through the medium of the garments, are spread throughout the entire community. Then, like all other 'home' work, it invariably leads to female and child labour – all the members of the family being pressed into the service. Thus a crop of evils of the most serious nature are fostered by this system of sweating against which our friends of the tailoring craft are now arrayed.

But what of the remedy? We might, were we so minded, placidly – and quite correctly – point out to our tailoring friends that the only remedy is Socialism, that nothing short of the public ownership and democratic control of the means of life will finally rid them of their industrial troubles; that sweating is but the natural child of Capitalism, and that to get rid of the one you must abolish the other. But this is not our attitude, nor is it the attitude of the scientific Socialist wherever he is found. Socialism is indeed the only permanent remedy, but Socialists seek for a mitigation of present evils even whilst pressing for the abolition of the source from whence they sprung. Indeed, Socialists are the most imperative of all in agitating for immediate reforms because we know that no measure of relief to the cause of Labour is to-day possible, which does not carry within it the germ of Socialist principles – is not in a greater or less degree an application to industrial life of the Socialist idea. Thus the only radical and effective remedy for the evils of sweating, viz. the entire suppression of outworking, is perhaps too herculean a task for mere trade-union effort to accomplish, but lies well within the range of what the workers might accomplish by political action *as a class*. And as the regulation of industrial activity by the workers themselves, instead of by a dominant class, is the very essence of the Socialist conception so even that partial application of the principle which would be shown in the spectacle of working-class representatives in the House of Commons forcing this upon the employers, lies along those lines of progress we desire to travel. We would advise our friends to study that fact well, and then ask themselves why it is that our Home Rule representatives, so ready to serve the class interests of the tenant farmers, are so utterly indifferent to the class interests of the town workers.

Meanwhile in every effort their union may make towards abolishing the evils of sweating, the tailoring trade can count upon our heartiest co-operation.

Physical Force in Irish Politics

Workers' Republic (22 July 1899)

'Physical force' militancy in Irish politics, in Connolly's time and since, traces its lineage to the United Irishmen and their rebellion of 1798. In the 1890s, the grouping that represented this tradition was the IRB.

Ireland occupies a position among the nations of the earth unique in a great variety of its aspects, but in no one particular is this singularity more marked than in the possession of what is known as a 'physical force party' – a party, that is to say, whose members are united upon no one point, and agree upon no single principle, except upon the use of physical force as the sole means of settling the dispute between the people of this country and the governing power of Great Britain.

Other countries and other peoples have, from time to time, appealed to what the first French Revolutionists picturesquely described as the 'sacred right of insurrection', but in so appealing they acted under the inspiration of, and combated for, some great governing principle of political or social life upon which they, to a man, were in absolute agreement. The latter-day high falutin 'hillside' man, on the other hand, exalts into a principle that which the revolutionists of other countries have looked upon as a weapon, and in his gatherings prohibits all discussion of those principles which formed the main strength of his prototypes elsewhere and made the successful use of that weapon possible. Our people have glided at different periods of the past century from moral force agitation, so-called, into physical force rebellion, from constitutionalism into insurrectionism, meeting in each the same failure and the same disaster and yet seem as far as ever from learning the great truth that neither method is ever likely to be successful until they first insist that a perfect agreement upon the end to be attained should be arrived at as a starting-point of all our efforts.

To the reader unfamiliar with Irish political history such a remark seems to savour almost of foolishness, its truth is so apparent; but to the reader acquainted with the inner workings of the political movements of this country the remark is pregnant with the deepest meaning. Every revolutionary effort in Ireland has drawn the bulk of its adherents from the ranks of the disappointed followers of defeated constitutional movements. After having exhausted their constitutional efforts in striving to secure such a modicum of political power as would justify them to their own consciences in taking a place as loyal subjects of the British Empire, they, in despair, turned to thoughts of physical force as a means of attaining their ends. Their conception of what constitutes freedom was in no sense changed or revolutionised; they still believed in the political form of freedom which had been their ideal in their constitutional days; but no longer hoping for it from the acts of the British Parliament, they swung over into the ranks of the 'physical force' men as the only means of attaining it.

The so-called physical force movement of today in like manner bases its hopes upon the disgust of the people over the failure of the Home Rule movement; it seeks to enlist the people under its banners, not so much by pointing out the base ideals of the constitutionalists or the total inadequacy of their pet measures to remedy the evils under which the people suffer, as by emphasising the greater efficacy of physical force as a national weapon. Thus, the one test of an advanced Nationalist is, in their opinion, one who believes in physical force. It may be the persons so professing to believe are Republicans; it may be they are believers in monarchy; it may be that Home Rule would satisfy them; it may be that they despise Home Rule. No matter what their political faith may be, if only they are prepared to express belief in the saving grace of physical force, they are acclaimed as advanced Nationalists – worthy descendants of 'the men of '98.' The '98 Executive, organised in the commencement by professed believers in the physical force doctrine, started by proclaiming its adherence to the principle of national independence 'as understood by Wolfe Tone and the United Irishmen', and in less than twelve months from doing so, deliberately rejected a similar resolution and elected on its governing body men notorious for their Royalist proclivities. As the '98 Executive represents the advanced Nationalists of Ireland, this repudiation of the Republican faith of the United Irishmen is an interesting corroboration of the truth of our statement that the advanced Nationalists of our day are utterly regardless of principle and only attach importance to methods – an instance of putting the cart before the horse, absolutely unique in its imbecility and unparalleled in the history of the world.

It may be interesting, then, to place before our readers the Socialist Republican conception of the functions and uses of physical force in a popular movement. We neither exalt it into a principle nor repudiate it as something not to be thought of. Our position towards it is that the use or non-use of force for the realisation of the ideas of progress always has been and always will be determined by the attitude, not of the party of progress, but of the governing class opposed to that party. If the time should arrive when the party of progress finds its way to freedom barred by the stubborn greed of a possessing class entrenched behind the barriers of law and order; if the party of progress has indoctrinated the people at large with the new revolutionary conception of society and is therefore representative of the will of a majority of the nation, if it has exhausted all the peaceful means at its disposal for the purpose of demonstrating to the people and their enemies that the new revolutionary ideas do possess the suffrage of the majority; then, but not till then, the party which represents the revolutionary idea is justified in taking steps to assume the powers of government, and in using the weapons of force to dislodge the usurping class or government in possession, and treating its members and supporters as usurpers and rebels against the constituted authorities always have been treated. In other words, Socialists believe that the question of force is of very minor importance; the really important question is of the principles upon which is based the movement that may or may not need the use of force to realise its object.

Here, then, is the immense difference between the Socialist Republicans and our friends the physical force men. The latter, by stifling all discussions of principles, earn the passive and fleeting commendation of the unthinking multitude; the former, by insisting upon a thorough understanding of their basic principles, do not so readily attract the multitude, but do attract and hold the more thoughtful amongst them. It is the difference betwixt a mob in revolt and an army in preparation. The mob who cheer a speaker referring to the hopes of a physical force movement would, in the very hour of apparent success, be utterly disorganised and divided by the passage through the British Legislature of any trumpery Home Rule Bill. The army of class-conscious workers organising under the banner of the Socialist Republican Party, strong in their knowledge of economic truth and firmly grounded in their revolutionary principles, would remain entirely unaffected by any such manoeuvre and, knowing it would not change their position as a subject class, would still press forward, resolute and undivided, with their faces set towards their only hope of emancipation – the complete control by the working-class democracy of all the powers of National Government.

Thus the policy of the Socialist Republicans is seen to be the only wise one. 'Educate that you may be free'; principles first, methods afterwards. If the advocacy of physical force failed to achieve success or even to effect an uprising when the majority were unenfranchised and the secret ballot unknown, how can it be expected to succeed now that the majority are in possession of voting power and the secret ballot safeguards the voter?

The ballot-box was given us by our masters for their purpose; let us use it for our own. Let us demonstrate at that ballot-box the strength and intelligence of the revolutionary idea; let us make the hustings a rostrum from which to promulgate our principles; let us grasp the public powers in the interest of the disinherited class; let us emulate our fathers and, like the 'true men of '98,' place ourselves in line with the most advanced thought of our age and drawing inspiration and hope from the spectacle presented by the world-wide revolt of the workers, prepare for the coming of the day when the Socialist working-class of Ireland will, through its elected representatives, present its demand for freedom from the yoke of a governing master class or nation – the day on which the question of moral or physical force shall be finally decided.

Home Rulers and Labour: A Remonstrance Addressed to English Socialists

Workers' Republic (October 1901)

From his earliest involvement in socialist politics as a young man in the Irish community in Edinburgh, Connolly encountered and criticised the tendency of the British left to ally itself to Home Rule politics – i.e. bourgeois constitutional nationalism – in Ireland. This pattern cut against the principle of international working-class solidarity, and damaged the cause of labour in Ireland.

A few months ago we called attention in the columns of the *Workers' Republic* to the extraordinary utterances of certain English Socialists concerning the Home Rule party and its attitude towards Labour and Socialism. We pointed out that this Home Rule party was essentially a capitalist party, inspired solely by a consideration for capitalist interests, and that the few 'Labour men' in that party were of the type of the Woods, Burts and Pickards of the English Liberal party – were baits to lure the workers on to the official party hook.[4] We also expressed the opinion that the action of English Socialists in giving such commendatory

---

[4] Thomas Burt (1837–1922), English trade unionist, and one of the first working-class Members of Parliament. He stood with Liberal support. Benjamin Pickard (1842–1904), English miner, trade unionist and Member of Parliament. He stood with Liberal support. Henry Woods (1822–1882), English industrialist and Liberal Member of Parliament.

notices to the enemies of the Irish Socialists was nothing short of treason to the International Labour movement. This remonstrance of ours has been as entirely disregarded as if it had been but the fulmination of a Liberal conference. That section of the English Socialists to whom we refer are apparently as ready to sacrifice the interests of the Irish Socialists to suit their party convenience as their English masters have always been to sacrifice Ireland to suit their class interests. The phrase 'International Solidarity of Labour' which they mouth so glibly does not take in Ireland in its scope.

Have we no remedy? We have, and if the present remonstrance is as little heeded as the first we shall take that remedy into our own hands with results that we have no doubt will be somewhat disastrous to the election prospects of future ILP candidates in British constituencies where the Irish working class reside in any numbers. But first to explain the position. For some time past Mr Keir Hardie MP and his colleagues on the *Labour Leader* newspaper have been assiduously instilling into the minds of the British Socialists the belief that Mr John Redmond's Home Rule party are burning with enthusiasm for labour and are favourably inclined towards Socialism.[5] (We beg our readers in Ireland not to laugh at this; we are not exaggerating the case one whit.) Mr Keir Hardie has appeared on the platform with the Home Rule MPs at Irish gatherings, has given his most unqualified praise to them at gatherings of his own party – praise as staunch Labour men, please mark! – and in his paper, the aforesaid *Labour Leader*, he and another writer signing himself 'Marxian' have for the past few months left no stone unturned to imbue their readers with the belief that the Home Rule party are staunch democrats and socialistically inclined.

When Mr Keir Hardie was last in Parliament he on one occasion moved an amendment to an address to the throne – the amendment being in favour of finding work for the unemployed. The Home Rule members refused to support him. He moved an amendment to an address of congratulation on the birth of some royal baby, observing it should rather be a vote of condolence to the families of the Welsh miners who had just then been lost in a colliery disaster in Wales; the Home Rule members voted against him and in favour of royalty. The men who are leaders of the Home Rule party now, were the leaders of the party then also. This session they have voted in favour of several Labour

---

[5] James Keir Hardie (1856–1915), Scottish socialist; first Independent Labour Party Member of Parliament; a founder of the ILP and of the Labour Party. The *Labour Leader* was a newspaper founded by Hardie in 1888.

measures, and Mr Hardie and his friends seek to make great capital of this fact. But, paradoxical as it may seem to say so, their vote is not cast in favour of these measures, but against the Unionist government which opposed them. Had a Home Rule government been in power in England and opposed these Labour measures, the Home Rule Irish party would have supported the government against Labour as they did in the past.

The present leader of the Home Rule party, Mr John Redmond, is the gentleman who made himself notorious in Ireland by denouncing (at Rathfarnham) the agricultural labourers for forming a trade union. He is the gentleman who, when the Irish Working Class first got the Municipal franchise granted them in 1898, stumped this country asking the workers to vote for landlords to represent them – in order, he said, to show the English people that we would not make a revolutionary use of our power.

The Irish working class answered him by forming independent Labour Electoral organisations, and sending landlords and middle-class Home Rulers alike about their business. Mr Keir Hardie praised them in the *Labour Leader* for doing so; he now praises as the leader of the Irish democracy the very man whose insidious advice they rightfully scorned.

Mr Tim Harrington MP, and Lord Mayor of Dublin by the intrigues of the Home Rulers, is the gentleman who is notorious for having declared that sixteen shillings a week was enough wages for any working man.[6] He is also the gentleman who ousted from the Mayoral chair another Home Ruler, Lord Mayor Pile, whom he declared to be a traitor, and then became treasurer of a committee organised to present this 'traitor' with a valuable testimonial for his services to the city.[7]

One of the most highly placed men of the Executive of the United Irish League, the official Home Rule party, is Mr P. White, MP, who is well known to be the most detested employer of scab labour in the tailoring trade of the city of Dublin.

During the last municipal election in Dublin the Home Rule party ran as candidate for the North City Ward one Alderman McCabe who had earned the detestation of every trade unionist by voting in favour of giving painting contracts to non-union firms. Three Home Rule members of parliament, Messrs Tim Harrington, Pat O'Brien the Home Rule Whip, and Peter White were specially detailed to support

---

[6] Timothy Charles Harrington (1851–1910), Irish barrister, journalist, nationalist and Member of Parliament. Served three terms as Lord Mayor of Dublin.

[7] Thomas Devereux Pile (1856–1931), Irish Unionist politician and baronet. Welcomed Queen Victoria to Dublin in 1900.

this friend of blackleg labour against McLoughlin his Socialist opponent, although the latter had the unanimous endorsement of the Dublin Trades and Labour Council.[8]

But have not the Home Rulers declared in favour of Labour, has not Mr Redmond at Westport declared the fight against landlordism in Ireland to be a 'trade unionist fight'? The meaning of phrases can only be understood when you study the conditions out of which they arise. The Home Rule party in Ireland is today fighting for its very existence. The 'scenes' in Parliament are but the distant echo of the fight made by the Home Rulers to regain the support of the Irish Democracy. Despite all the puffing and booming of the press, despite the lavish expenditure of money on bands and faked up demonstrations, the United Irish League has not caught on in Ireland, and has not forty sound branches in all the country. The intelligent Irish Working Class despise the politicians. When after the first Local Government election in Ireland the professional politicians saw that the Irish workers had turned their backs upon them they took alarm, and in order to sidetrack the Labour movement in the next two elections they ran bogus labour candidates on their tickets in opposition to the independent candidates ran by genuine Labour organisations. This fact involved two sets of rallying cries. The Home Rule politician's election cry in such contests was, 'Nationality and Labour should go together'; that of the genuine Labour candidates was voiced by the then President of the Dublin Trades Council, Mr Leahy, when he said in reply that 'Labour should stand alone'.[9] We need not insist upon asking which side English Socialists should agree with. Imagine then our surprise and amusement when we found such utterances as that of Mr Redmond at Westport, and the Home Rule rallying cry we have quoted, both in their essence piteous appeals to the Irish workers to return to the Home Rule fold to be shorn, reproduced in the *Labour Leader* and ILP speeches, as 'magnificent utterances in favour of Labour'. When an English Liberal says 'we are fighting the cause of Labour', the ILP laughs him to scorn, and when an Irish Home Ruler says the same thing it is accepted as gospel truth. But not in Ireland, we know our men.

But we are told the Home Rulers are at least staunch democrats. So was Mr John Morley, yet Mr Keir Hardie made special efforts to defeat

---

[8] Patrick O'Brien (1847–1917), Irish Home Rule politician and Member of Parliament. William McLoughlin was a candidate for the ISRP in the 1901 Municipal Elections in Dublin.

[9] George Leahy, President of the National Association of Operative Plasterers.

him at Newcastle because he was not sound enough on the Labour question.[10] Staunch democrats! indeed, when they allowed an Irish National journal, the *United Irishman*, to be suppressed three times for its fight against the war, and refused to bring the matter up in the House of Commons, but made the world ring with denunciations when one of their own papers, the *Irish People*, was confiscated once.[11]

We ask Mr Keir Hardie to consider these facts; we challenge any of his Home Rule friends to dispute either the statements of the inference drawn therefrom. We do not agree with Hardie's general policy, would most decidedly not adopt it as our own, but we believe in his honesty of purpose. We ask nothing from the English democracy but we do not wish to cross one another's path. We believe the Irish working class are strong enough and intelligent enough to fight their own battles and we would be the last to advise them to trust to outside help in the struggle that lies before them. We do not propose to criticise Hardie's voting alliance with the Home Rulers, but a voting alliance need not be accompanied by indiscriminate praise of your temporary allies.

Finally if this is not heeded we shall have to take other methods of enforcing attention to our protest.

We shall ask the editors of the various Socialist papers of Great Britain to publish the above, and we shall take their attitude towards that request as an indication of the strength of that international Solidarity of which we hear so much and see so little.

Signed
Executive Committee
Irish Socialist Republican Party
138 Upper Abbey Street Dublin

---

[10] John Morley, 1st Viscount Morley of Blackburn (1838–1923), English writer and Liberal statesman; sometime Secretary of State for India, and biographer of William Gladstone; opponent of imperialism and the Boer War.

[11] The *United Irishman* was founded by Arthur Griffith in 1899, and was associated with Sinn Féin after the setting-up of that party in 1905. The *Irish People* was a nationalist and pro-Home Rule paper published by William O'Brien between 1899 and 1909.

Chapter 2
America and the International Workers of the World

America and Ireland: Farmers' Demands

Workers' Republic (21 October 1899)

This article demonstrates how Connolly was interested in America long before he moved to live and work there. His focus here on socialist parties in the United States shows his internationalism, but also prepares ideologically for his eventual alignment with the Socialist Labor Party (SLP) and his relationship with Daniel De Leon.

As a general rule we refrain from taking notice in our columns of the quarrels or discussions of the Socialist parties of the world. We regard ourselves as being, at present, primarily a missionary organ, founded for the purpose of presenting to the working class of Ireland a truer and more scientific understanding of the principles of Socialism than they could derive from a perusal of the scant and misleading references to that subject to be found in the ordinary capitalist press. This task also involves, as a matter of course, the criticism and exposure of all the quack remedies and political trickeries with which our masters, or their ignorant imitators in the ranks of the workers themselves, seek to impose upon the people as cure-alls for our social evils. We have all along acted upon the conviction that we must give the revolutionary principles of Socialism an Irish home and habitation before we venture to express our opinions on the minor matters dividing the party abroad. We can say now with some degree of confidence that we have succeeded in that task and that the Socialist Republican Party of Ireland is one of the factors which will play a big part in shaping the future history of this country, and being so confident we now propose to say a word upon a subject at present under discussion in the United States of America; and in which the name of our Party has been cited as following a course of action similar to that adopted by one of the disputants.

The matter is as follows:– There are in the States just now two distinct Socialist parties – The Socialist Labor Party, and the Social Democratic Party.[1] The first named is the longest established of the two and has repeatedly run candidates for the post of President of the United States, polling on the occasion of the last Presidential contest 36,664 votes. The last named has only come into existence since the last Presidential campaign, and is composed for the greater part of men and women who, while avowing themselves Socialists, disapproved of the policy and tactics pursued by the Socialist Labor Party. To the uninitiated in the economics and philosophy of Socialism it is hard to explain the exact point at issue, but it may be briefly summed up in the statement that the Socialist Labor Party adhere uncompromisingly to the policy of identifying themselves as a party with, and basing all their hopes upon, the struggle of the working class against every section of their exploiters, or employers. This involves opposition to every demand made in the interest of the master class, and an attitude of complacency, or even triumph, at the success of the great capitalist in crushing out his smaller competitor – this complacency arising from the, it seems to us, absolutely correct position that the crushing out of small capitalists by large ones will tend to increase the ranks of the working class, concentrate industry under centralised management, decrease the numbers of those interested in private property, and so make the ultimate attainment of Socialism easier.

In other words, theirs is the position known in Europe as the Marxist position, from its being first definitely formulated by the founder of Modern Socialism – Karl Marx.

The Social Democratic Party, on the other hand, look to the fact that the small middle class, and especially the farmers, still wield an enormous voting power, and, looking to the present rather than to the future, they have embodied in their programme certain 'Farmers' Demands' – proposals for legislation to enable the petty farmers to bear up against the competition of those mammoth farms for which the United States is so famous. The object being, of course, to win the votes of the farmers as a class.

Over those 'Farmers' Demands' a battle royal has been raging for

---

[1] The Social Democratic Party was a short-lived American socialist party, and a precursor to the Socialist Party of America. The SDP was formed in 1898, and dissolved in 1901.

some time between the two parties. The Socialist Labor Party denouncing them as reactionary and unscientific, the Social Democratic Party defending them as practical and useful. Lately some members of the latter party have themselves taken up the battle against those proposals being included in their programme, and demand their removal. In the course of this latter discussion in the columns of the *Social Democratic Herald* published at Chicago, Sept 25th, one writer, F.G.R. Gordon, in defending the proposals, cites our example as a party which, occupying an absolutely scientific position on Socialist doctrines, yet has its 'Farmers' Demands'. Here is the quotation:–

> The Irish Socialist Republican Party have their Farmers' Demands; and their party has been endorsed as the par excellent Scientific Socialist Party.[2]

No.3 of our programme is, we presume, the plank alluded to.

Now, we have no wish to be misunderstood by our comrades in America; we value our reputation as a straight Socialist Party too much to allow our name to be used as a cover for any kind of looseness in principles, tactics, or policy, even when it is used accompanied by flattery. Therefore, we would wish to point out to all whom it may concern that the cases of America and Ireland are not at all analogous. Agriculture in America has assumed already its company form, being in many cases administered purely on capitalist lines for the profit of non-resident owners; agriculture in Ireland is still in a semi-feudal form, the largest farm in Ireland would be classed as a petty farm in America, and the absorption of the working farmer by the capitalist managed estate of the non-resident farmer is practically unknown. Now observe this vital point of difference between the programme of the Socialist Republican Party of Ireland, and the programme of the Social Democratic Party of America. Both have demands for farmers, granted, but:–

1. The Farmers' Demands of the Social Democrats of America are demands which aim at the perpetuation of the system of petty farming by legislation to protect it from the effects of the competition of farms managed on those lines most nearly approximating to the Socialist form of industry, viz., the lines of centralised capital, and agricultural armies. American agriculture, *as such*, is not in any danger as a source of support for the agriculturist. His status may be endangered, not his existence.
2. The Farmers' Demands of the Socialist Republican Party of Ireland

---

[2] The *Social Democratic Herald* was the party newspaper of the SDP, published in Chicago from 1898 until 1913.

are demands which aim at preserving Agriculture in Ireland from being *annihilated as a native industry* by the competition of *foreign* agriculturists. Irish agriculturists are not threatened with absorption, but with extinction and enforced exile.

In other words the American Farmers' Demands are in the interest of one particular form of agricultural enterprise, as against another; the Irish Demands are directed towards rescuing agriculture itself, and teaching the agriculturist to look to national co-operation as the factor he should count upon for help in his struggle to remain in the country of his birth.

Things which look alike are not always alike. The apparent identity of the Irish and American proposals is seen to be non-existent when you take into account the different historical and industrial conditions of the two countries. Given American conditions in Ireland, the Irish Socialists would wipe their Farmers' Demands from off their programme, but in Ireland as it is with the rags of a medieval system of land tenure still choking our life and cramping our industry, with perennial famine destroying our people, with our population dwindling away by emigrations, we consider it right to point out, even if unheeded, that it is the duty of the State to undertake the functions of manufacture and custodian of all implements required for the one important industry of the country – agriculture. This is all we demand in that nature:–

Establishment at public expense of rural depots for the most improved agricultural machinery, to be lent out to the agricultural population at a rent covering cost and management alone.

It is not a sectional demand, but is the outcome of a national exigency.

'The practical application of the principles' (of Socialism), said Marx and Engels in their joint preface to the *Communist Manifesto*, 'everywhere, and at all times will depend on the historical conditions for the time being existing'.

Let our critics please remember that fact, and the Socialist Republicans of Ireland can confidently abide by the result.

Our 'American Mission'

Workers' Republic (August 1902)

This article prepares for Connolly's first lecture tour of America. Note how he distinguishes between prior (nationalist) political visitors to the United States who sought merely to elicit funds and political support for their campaigns, and his project, which is to assert the structural relationship of Irish and American workers under conditions of capitalism, and the need for their mutual solidarity.

We are pleased to be in a position to state that arrangements have been made between the Socialist Labour Party of America and the Socialist Republican Party of Ireland for Mr James Connolly, the editor of this paper, to proceed to the States on a lecturing tour on behalf of both organisations.[3] Our comrade leaves Liverpool on the fourth of September [1902], and will probably remain in America until the first week of December. Meetings are being organised already in many of the great industrial centres where Irishmen have made their home; the Cooper Union, the largest hall in New York, has been secured for his first meeting on the 15th September, and every effort will be made to enable our representative to place his message before the largest number possible of Irish-American workers.[4]

The fact that our comrade has spent so much of his own life (20 years) amongst the Irish exiles of Great Britain fits him in a peculiar manner for the task of understanding and speaking to those other exiles in America, while the thorough knowledge of Irish history and politics he has so well demonstrated in all his speeches and writings qualifies him for the position he now occupies as an exponent of that phenomenon in Irish politics – the revolt of the working class – seeking its independent political expression through the Socialist Republican Party.

We would direct our reader's attention to the great underlying significance of this visit to the States. All other Irish agitators have gone to America to beg funds for the support of agitations at home on the express or implied understanding that the desire of the agitation in Ireland was to erect in this country the political and economic institutions which prevail in America. Therefore every such agitator had praise of all things American on his tongue as part of his poor stock in trade. But this agitator knows that the misery of Ireland springs from an economic cause operating equally malignantly [in America] as it does in Ireland to the majority of the population; he knows that the comparative comfort of the more fortunate of the American workers is due primarily

---

[3] Note that Connolly here writes of himself in the third person.
[4] Established in Manhattan, New York City in 1859, the Cooper Union for the Advancement of Science and Art is a private higher education institution, whose admittance policy for most of its history has been predicated on offering every entrant a full scholarship.

to the state of the economic development of their country relatively to Ireland, and he knows also that the very nature of that economic development, its very power and insatiableness, will prevent all possibility of creating in Ireland industrial conditions at all similar to those in America. In other words, he knows well that to-day the very success of American enterprise in agriculture and industry strikes a death blow to the hopes of industry and agriculture on a grand scale *under capitalism* in Ireland, as the Americans are now our greatest competitors. He also knows and it will be his duty to preach that the terms 'American Success', 'American Domination', 'American Control' mean Success, Domination and Control by the American Capitalist Class, and that exercised not only against producers on this side of the Atlantic, but quite as relentlessly against the working class on the American side.

And whilst telling the workers of America of the new hope which has arisen in the breasts of the more intelligent of the working class of Ireland – the hope of a Socialist Republic in which our land will be purged of the contaminating presence of the foreign and native tyrants alike, a freedom for which the workers are learning to rely on themselves and on themselves alone – he will not fail to remind them that the progress of capitalism brings for the American worker a slavery as grinding and merciless as that we groan under to-day, even if many of the slaves be better fed and housed than are ours.

This campaign which our comrade Connolly is undertaking in America is, then, for the miscreants at home and abroad who have so long traded on our kindly sentiment to the undoing of the Irish workers, an ominous portent indeed. But to those who value truth, the facts which our comrade will lay before his audience upon the condition of that long neglected portion of the Irish nation, the working class, and the truths he will tell of the inwardness of the political position in Ireland, will make this visit a welcome relief from those of the attitudinising politicians who in the past have sold themselves to every American grinder-of-the-faces-of-the-poor who desired to parade an Irish leader on his platform as a catch for Irish votes.

A few words apropos of the party under whose auspices our representative will travel to the States will not be amiss. Shortly after the establishment of the Irish Socialist Republican Party in 1896 we opened up communications with the Socialist Labour Party of America.[5] An interchange of views took place between the two bodies, and we then

---

[5] The SLP was set up in 1876, initially under the name of the Workingmen's Party. It is the oldest socialist party in the United States and the second oldest in the world.

discovered that our ideas upon policy and tactics generally were practically identical, a discovery that immediately led to a friendship lasting to the present time. Since then both parties have gone through severe struggles, the SLP have been subjected to a revolt within and to a malevolent misrepresentation from without unequalled in the socialist movement for bitterness, and the ISRP has undergone a period of financial strain which has left its mark deep on the character and spirits of many of its members, but neither party has faltered, and both are as a result stronger than ever before.[6] Our confidence in our SLP friends is still unabated, and we can challenge the world to investigate our conduct, our policy, or our history. The SLP has the only Socialist daily newspaper in the English language, and we intend on the return of our editor from America to permanently re-establish the *Workers' Republic* on a weekly basis.

Verily, Labour Conquers All.

The American SDP: Its Origin, its Press and its Policies

The Socialist (July 1903)

The Socialist was a Scottish revolutionary socialist newspaper, published in Edinburgh, arising out of Connolly's encouragement of Scottish socialists to emulate the American Socialist Labor Party. Here, he contrasts the British Social Democratic Federation (whose journal was *Justice*) with the American SLP, deploying the American party as an exemplar.

In my article in the June issue of the *Socialist* I sought to place before our readers a correct picture of the position of the Socialist Labour Party of America, by contrasting it with the London SDF, and in doing so to expose the misrepresentations of Mr Hyndman and 'comrade *Justice*'. One point in the *Justice* American letter, however, I missed. It was the statement that the SLP had lost its place on the ballot in several states through corrupt practices. Of course no particulars were given, because none could be given as the statement was as destitute of any foundation in fact as the persons who made and retailed it were destitute of honour. Yet the persons who utter such slanders are they who whine about the 'outrageous language' of the writers in the *Socialist*. We would ask

---

[6] A group had just left the SLP and joined with the party's competitor the SDP to form the Socialist Party of America. The ISRP had gone through serious financial troubles, leading to some internal tensions.

those honest men who still remain in the SDF to require from the organ of the Twentieth Century Press the particulars, state, and date where the SLP lost its place through corrupt practices, and the name of the correspondent who makes the charge.

In this article I propose to give some details about the Social Democratic, or Socialist Party, the pet protege in American politics of the SDF. This party was established by Eugene V Debs, and at its foundation was not a political, but a colonising party.[7] That is to say, that it did not propose to realise Socialism through the conquest of the public powers of government by the working class marching to the ballot box in their respective localities. Oh, no! The bright brains of the leaders conceived a more brilliant plan than that. This plan was that all the Socialists in the United States should leave their then homes and move simultaneously into one State to be fixed upon by the party, and so secure a majority in that State. Then that they should elect the legislature of that State, appoint Socialists to administer the public powers, and so inaugurate the Socialist Republic. Then the theory ran that all the other States in the Union would be lost in admiration of the Socialist institutions in full working order, and would signify their admiration by rushing into Socialism. This plan was undoubtedly simple – so were the people who thought it practicable.

But the Socialist Labour Party men began attending the meetings of this SDP and asking irreverent questions. They wanted to know why, if Debs was a Socialist, he supported Bryan the Democrat in 1896. Considering there were already many unemployed in each State, how the Socialists, who gave up their situations in order to colonise, were going to find employment in the new State while waiting for the majority. Seeing that the United States Government was a capitalist government, and had already sent the Federal troops into Illinois in order to put down a strike, what would it do when the Socialist governors or legislature of Mr Debs' colony-state started in to socialise any capitalist property?

A few questions like these continually driven home and supplemented by vigorous criticism soon punctured the colony scheme, and eventually it was dropped by its promoters, thanks entirely to the light let in on the subject by the SLP men. But with the dropping of the colony scheme the SDP definitely entered politics as a Socialist party. In 1898 its ranks received an accession of numbers from those who had either

---

[7] Eugene Victor Debs (1855–1926), American union leader, a founder of the International Workers of the World, and four times a Socialist Party of America candidate for the American presidency.

been expelled from the SLP for treachery, or had incontinently fled its councils to escape expulsion. These formed what was styled the kangaroo party, and the circumstances attending its formation are worth recording.

The *People*, the organ of the Socialist Labour Party, was at that time published in the office of a private printing corporation, which was known as the Volkszeitung Corporation, from the fact that it had been established to print and publish a Socialist paper in the German language – the *Volkszeitung*.[8] This paper accepted capitalist advertisements, even the advertisements of capitalist politicians, and advocated all kinds of tax reform as Socialism. Eventually a motion was sent round the SLP sections, to be voted upon by the entire membership, in favour of placing the printing and publishing of the SLP organs and literature generally in the hands of the party itself. In passing, I may remark that in the SLP general votes are taken by individual membership and not by sections or branches. In the case of the vote under consideration, all those in favour of compromises, of conciliating the Debsites, and truckling for the support of pure and simple trade unionism, were in favour of leaving the paper in the control of the Volkszeitung Corporation. But as the vote came in gradually and was duly tabulated in the columns of the *People*, it was seen that the straight and uncompromising members were in the majority, and that the private ownership of the party press was doomed.

Affrighted at this, the unclean section of the party strove to avert disaster and keep the press in their hands by making a midnight raid on the premises of the National Executive, and by force to override the constitution of the party and set at naught its vote. They failed, but as a last measure formed another party and issued a rival paper, both party and paper usurping the titles of the original until compelled by law to abandon the fraudulent practice. Now they are called in New York the Social Democratic Party, and their organ is called the *Worker*, owned of course not by the party, but by the aforementioned private corporation.

In the presidential election of 1900, this element sent a deputation to the National Convention of the Debsite party and succeeded in getting their nominee, Job Harriman, nominated as candidate for Vice-President of the United States. This was to bring unity between the two sections of those opposed to the SLP, but it did not succeed, for as soon as the Convention was over Debs sent a letter to his press vehemently

---

[8] The *New Yorker Volkszeitung* was a German-language American radical newspaper published between 1878 and 1932.

denouncing what he termed the trickery and treacherous methods of the Harriman party. As a result, although the nomination held good for the election, the two candidates, who were supposed to be running in harness and harmony, never appeared on the same platform.

Some time ago a letter from that wonderful 'American Correspondent' appeared in *Justice* announcing the consummation of unity among the socialists of the United States, 'except the De Leonite faction', of course.[9] This unity was arrived at by means of a resolution at a convention in Indianapolis, if I remember aright, in which it was agreed that all sections should unite on the following basis:–

That each State should have full local autonomy in all matters, including policy and tactics.
That each State organisation should sail under whatever name it chose, or the laws of the State allowed.
That there should be no official organ of the party.

In other words, that everybody could join who chose, and could do what he blamed well pleased after joining. That each State should frame its own policy, even if that policy was in direct opposition to that of the party in the adjoining State, and that the party should have no official organ in case the members should get to know the muddled condition in which the party was. Thus was unity accomplished. What anarchist could desire more? The result of all this is made manifest in the present position of that united party. In some States it is named the 'Social Democratic', in some the 'Socialist', in some the 'Public Ownership', in some the 'Union Labour' party. Its policies are as varied as its names. In the Eastern States where the example and record of the SLP is to be reckoned with, it gives a lip adhesion to the principle of the class struggle, and appeals to the working class. In the Middle West, where capital is not so highly developed and the petty middle class is still a force, it trades mainly in schemes of municipalisation for the benefit of the taxpayer. In the Western Agricultural States it declares that the hope of the Social Revolution is in the farming class, and in California it withdrew its candidates in favour of those of a Union Labour Party formed by the trade union, and supported Mayor Schmidt of San Francisco, a Republican trade-unionist and enemy of socialism.

---

[9] Daniel De Leon (1852–1914), American socialist, journalist, union organiser and Marxist theorist; the leading figure in the SLP from 1890 until his death. Initially welcoming Connolly enthusiastically to America, De Leon would later clash with him vociferously over matters of both party organisation and Marxist theory.

Each faction of the party represented by those various policies has an organ in the press devoted to its interests, but always privately owned. The manner in which those various organs of the united party speak of their 'comrades' who belong to opposite factions makes the 'abusive language' of De Leon seem complimentary by comparison.

The following are the names and locations of the principal representatives in the press of the faction indicated:– the *Worker*, New York, the *Socialist*, Seattle, Washington, the *Chicago Socialist*, the *Social Democratic Herald*, Milwaukee, the *Los Angeles Socialist*, California. The body which acted as a National Executive of this hybrid organisation was situated at St Louis, Missouri, and its official designation was the 'Local Quorum'. Early in the present year its chief members made a furore by openly repudiating the principle that the wage worker and his interests should be the basis of the Socialist movement, and by insisting that the farmer was the real basis, and that our policy should be shaped accordingly. After a bitter and acrimonious discussion the members of Section St Louis met and suspended the chiefs of this local quorum for treason. Setting their suspension at defiance, the Local Quorum moved itself to Omaha, Nebraska, an agricultural State, and proceeded with their new propaganda. They were supported by the *Social Democratic Herald*, and denounced as traitors by the Seattle *Socialist*. The *Chicago Socialist* declared the seat of the Local Quorum as the party executive should neither be at St Louis nor at Omaha, but at Chicago, and the *Los Angeles Socialist* darkly hinted that both were wrong, that Salvation lay not in Socialist consolidation, but in Socialist support of trade union nominees.

This unity of purpose and principle is still further exemplified by the fact that in the Eastern States they support the American Federation of Labour, the head of which is Mr Samuel Gompers, and in the West they cater for the support of the Western Federation of Miners, whose official organ, the *Miner*, correctly stigmatises Mr Gompers as a 'traitor', a 'fraud', and a 'Judas'.[10] Quite recently this latter organisation enacted a rule to the effect that none of its members could be allowed to accept nomination for office by any capitalist party. This seems to show that it is marching towards the light, and I have no doubt that when it realises that the SDP is busy all through the States in accepting those capitalist nominations the Western Federation of Miners will not allow its members to accept, then it will not hesitate to throw that bundle of

---

[10] Samuel Gompers (1850–1924), American union leader and founder of the American Federation of Labor in 1886.

inconsistencies overboard and cleave to the Socialist Labour Party with its clean record and uncompromising policy.

This brief sketch of the SDP of America will explain why *Justice* has such an enthusiastic love for that organisation, viz., it seeks its affinity.

Inconsistency and sacrifice of principle for the sake of votes mark both organisations, and 'Be all things to all men' might be the watchword of either.

JAMES CONNOLLY.

A Political Party of the Workers

The Harp (January 1908)

The Harp was, as Connolly declares, the organ of the Socialist Federation, a group Connolly founded for Irish-American workers on the assumption that the various ethnic communities in the United States could and should be propagandised individually. This journal was published from January 1908 until June 1910. We should note here Connolly's affiliation of the Irish Socialist Federation (ISF) to the International Workers of the World (the 'Wobblies'), as contrasted to the reformism of the American Federation of Labor.

With the advent of an Irish Socialist paper in the labor movement of America will come of necessity a host of questions and questioners upon the attitude of the proprietors of that paper toward the political parties at present in the field for Socialism. Such questions are unavoidable, and it is therefore best that they be faced at once at the outset without delay or equivocation.

Let it be noted therefore that the *Harp* is the official organ of the Irish Socialist Federation in America, and that that body was founded with the intention, expressed and desired, of spreading the light of Socialism amongst the working class Irish in this country, and that, recognizing that the existence of two political parties of Socialism has had in the past and has now a confusing effect upon the minds of the American working class, the founders of the Federation recognized that it would be worse than folly to make allegiance to one or the other of these political divisions a test of membership in the newly founded camp of Irish Socialists in America.[11] The Federation is not founded for political action, it is

---

[11] The ISF was founded by Connolly in New York in 1907, expressly as a socialist organisation for the Irish-American working class.

founded for propaganda; it is not in existence to fashion a political machine, it is in existence to present Socialism as a historical development from capitalism and as the only remedy for the wage slavery of the workers. The task of presenting the Socialist side as against the side of the capitalists, with all their powerful allies and weapons, is a big enough job for us without also taking part in the campaigns of slander which form the stock in trade of the American Socialists when they condescend to refer to each other. In their mutual recriminations many wrong things have been said, many right things have been wrongly said, and we are convinced that if American Socialists in general had been more solicitous in finding and emphasizing the points they had in common, and less eager to stretch the importance of the points on which they differed, a great party – great in unity in essentials, great in numbers – might long ere this have been built up in America. And until that party does appear the ISF will confine its work to the making of Socialists; let its recruits when made choose their own political affiliations.

But, it may be said, since the Irish comrades deplore the existing division, have they no suggestion to offer whereby it may be ended? Is it not certain that as you make recruits to Socialism, and those recruits choose their own political affiliations, that in course of time their differing choices will result in bringing into the Federation the disputes which divide Socialists outside? That is true, and therefore it is to our interest as well as in conformity with our desires to find some common ground upon which in our opinion earnest revolutionary Socialists could meet to combine their forces in battle with the common enemy.

The common ground of action we favor is one for which a strong sentiment already exists in the rank and file of both existing parties. It has been adopted and endorsed by practically all the non-English using federations of Socialists in America, and has therefore strong organized forces already behind it, and it would, as a magnet, draw unto itself all the true proletarian Socialists and weld them into an irresistible force. A common ground of action to be effectual for its purpose cannot emanate from either SP or SLP; it cannot be furnished by unity conferences, no matter how earnest the conferees are; the ghost of all the hatreds and jealousies aroused by the past years of strife will perpetually rise between the most united unity conference and the realization of its hopes, and, finally, it cannot be realized by an amalgamation of the existing parties. There are too many leaders, save the mark! Too many 'saviors of the working class' whose reputations have been built upon disunion; too many petty personal ambitions which might be endangered did the rank and file have an opportunity to know and understand one another; and too much fear that a general reunion might mean a general housecleaning, and the consequent dumping upon the garbage heap of many great lights whose personal predominance is dearer to them than the power of the movement. Some men in the Socialist movement on both sides would rather have a party of ten men who unquestioningly accepted their dictum and called their blind faith 'democracy' than a party of half a million whose component elements dared to think and act for themselves. Unquestionably the realization of unity must have as its necessary concomitant the acceptance of the fact that the interests of the movement are greater than and superior to the prejudices or rivalries of its leaders.

What and where, then, is this common ground we have spoken of? As we have already stated, the ISF is pledged to no political party, but this neutrality on the political field is not extended to the economic. There, we believe, an assumption of neutrality would be a crime on our part. Between, on the one hand, the new economic organization, the Industrial Workers of the World, which prepares and organizes the administrative framework of society in the future, and at the same time furnishes the only effective method of resistance against present-day encroachments of the master class, and on the other hand the old-style pure and simple trade unionism of the AF of L with its system of dividing the working class and its professed belief in the identity of interests between Capital and Labor, between these two economic organizations our choice is as plain and unmistakable as between Socialism and Capitalism; indeed, it is the same proposition presented in different terms.[12] And as we believe that all working-class Socialists must realize that their place is in the only real economic organization truly worthy of the name of union, the IWW, so we believe that the same body has it in its power to solve the problem of Socialist unity. On the day that the IWW launches its own political party it will put an end to all excuse for two Socialist parties and open the way for a real and effective unification of the revolutionary forces. To it will flock all the real proletarians, all the loyal-hearted working class whom distrust and suspicion have so long kept divided: it will be the real Political Party of the Workers – the weapon by which the working class will register the decrees which its economic army must and shall enforce.

---

[12] The Industrial Workers of the World (IWW) was and is a radical, international union founded in 1905, influenced by various strands of left-wing activism and theory, including anarchism and syndicalism. The American Federation of Labour (AFL) was the first federation of unions in America, set up in 1886. In combination with the Congress of Industrial Organisations, which was originally a breakaway grouping, it remains the largest union group in the United States of America.

We do not say this will end forever all fear of the existence of two parties calling themselves Socialists, but it will end all possibility of two revolutionary Socialist parties claiming the allegiance of the working class at the same moment. Compromisers and schemers will still erect parties to serve their personal ends and satiate their lust for being worshipped; intellectual mannikins will still perch themselves upon the shoulders of the workers and imagining their high altitude is the result of transcendent ability on their part will call the world to witness how great they are; but they will be deprived of their power to delude the real revolutionist by the simple fact of the existence of a political party of Socialists dominated by and resting upon the economic movement of the working class.

This is our hope, our proposed solution of the problem of divided forces, and on the day that that hope is consummated if anyone looks around for the class-conscious Irish workers he will, we believe, find them alert and determined at the head of the fighters.

Ollamh Fódhla[13]

To Irish Wage Workers in America

The Harp (May 1908)

In this article, Connolly powerfully drives a wedge between Irish workers and the two great parties of American politics. If the Republican Party is that of large capital, the Democratic Party (often regarded as the 'natural' focus of Irish-American political aspiration) is actually a petty-bourgeois party, and both must be opposed by Irish-American workers as the local representatives of the forces that drove the impoverished Irish to migrate to the United States in the first place.

Fellow-Workers:
As all the political forces of the United States are busily engaged to-day in lining up for the great conflict of the Presidential election of 1908, as on every hand there is a measuring of strength, a scanning of 'issues', and a searching of souls we desire on our part to approach you for the purpose of obtaining your earnest consideration of our principles before determining where to cast your support in the campaign. Let us reason quietly together! We speak to you as fellow workers and as fellow countrymen, and we ask where do you stand in politics to-day? Hitherto the

---

[13] Ollamh Fódhla ('scholar of Fodhla') is a poetic name for Ireland.

Irish in the United States have almost entirely supported the Democratic Party, but the time has come when the majority of thoughtful Irishmen are beginning to realise that as the causes that originally led to that affiliation are no longer existent, the affiliation itself must be reconsidered. Political parties must thrive or fail according to the present development of the class in society they represent, and cannot be kept alive by a mere tradition of their attitude in past emergencies. The antagonism of the Democratic Party towards the Know Nothing movement in the past won for it the support of the Irish Workers, but Know Nothingism is not an issue to-day, and as the Democratic Party is going down to an unhonored grave because of its inability to grasp the problems of our own time shall we Irish Workers suffer ourselves to be dragged to social perdition with it?[14]

No; fellow countrymen, political parties are the expression of economic interests, and in the last analysis are carried to victory or defeat by the development or retardation of economic classes. Examine the history of America for the last decade in the light of this analysis of the springs of political action, and the truth of that contention will be at once apparent. The Republican Party is the political weapon of advanced capital, of great trusts and mammoth combination of wealth. Hence as during the last decade the whole trend of industry has been toward greater concentration of capital we find that the Republican Party has grown stronger and stronger and its hold upon the political institutions of the country has proportionately tightened. To-day the governmental machinery of the United States is completely in the hands of the servants of capital, and Senate and Congress are but instruments for registering the decrees of the trust magnates of the United States. On the other hand the Democratic Party is the party of the small business man, and of those narrow ideas upon economics and politics which correspond to the narrow business lines and restricted economic action of the middle class in general. Hence as the last decade has witnessed the continual absorption by the trusts of the business of its petty competitors so it has also witnessed the absorption by the Republican Party of the one time adherents of the Democracy; as it has witnessed the downfall of the middle class as a social factor so it is witnessing the downfall of the political party of the middle class and its elimination as a political factor. And just as the petty business man may hang on to a meagre existence

---

[14] The 'Know-Nothing' movement was an American political party of the 1850s, the Native American Party. Fiercely nationalist, anti-immigrant, anti-Catholic and anti-Irish, its mostly middle-class membership later split over the issue of slavery and emancipation.

in business whilst no longer seriously considering himself as a competitive factor in industry, so the political party of the Democracy may hang on to a sordid existence in local affairs by means of its control of graft whilst entirely eliminated as a serious aspirant to national power.

We Irish Workers are then not under the necessity of considering ourselves as bound by tradition to the Democratic Party; political parties are not formed by traditions, but by interests. Where then do our interests lie? Certainly not in the Republican Party – that is the party of our employers, and as our employers we know do not allow their actions to be governed by our interests we are certainly not under any moral obligation to shape our political activity to suit the interests of our employers. Where then? To answer that question properly we must ask ourselves why are we Irish here at all in this country, instead of in Ireland. Certainly we have no complaint to make against our native land, and we for the most part did not come here for pleasure. We came here because we found that Ireland was private property, that a small class had taken possession of its resources – its land, its lakes, its rivers, its mountains, its bogs, its towns and its cities, its railways, its factories, and its fisheries. In short, that a small class owned Ireland and that the remainder of the population were the bond slaves of these proprietors. We came here because we found that the government of the country was in the hands of those proprietors and their friends, and that army and navy and police were the agents of the government in executing the will of those proprietors, and for driving us back to our chains whenever we rose in revolt against oppression. And as we learned that since that government was backed and maintained by the might of a nation other than our own, and more numerous than us, we could not hope to overthrow that government and free our means of living from the grasp of those proprietors, we fled from that land of ours and came to the United States.

In the United States we find that every day the condition of matters for the working class drifts more and more in the direction of the conditions we left behind. Here the resources of the country are also in the hands of a small class – the land, the rivers, the lakes, the forests, the fisheries, the towns, the cities, the factories, the railroads, the entire means of life of eighty millions of people are in the hands of a class which every day grows smaller and whose rapacity and greed and lust for power grows as its numbers diminish. Here also we find that government is but the weapon of the master class, that the military and police forces of the nation are continually at the service of the proprietors in all disputes just as in Ireland, and that the 'rifle diet' is served out to workers in America oftener than to peasants in the old country. But here the analogy stops. In Ireland the government was a foreign government. It was outside our control and beyond our reach, and hence no political action of ours could completely master the situation or achieve our freedom from the oppression of the master class. That class sheltered behind the British Government, and our vote for freedom was answered by a foreign army shaking thirty thousand bayonets in our faces. But, in the United States, although the master class – the proprietors – rests upon the Government, and although that government rests upon armed forces to maintain and enforce its will, yet all alike, being native and not foreign, are within the reach of the political and economic action of the American workers, and can at any moment be mastered by them. Hence the hopelessness which at one time seized upon the popular mind in Ireland need never paralyze the action of the wage-slaves here. Freedom lies within the grasp of the American wage slave, he needs but the mind and knowledge to seize it.

What then is the lesson for the Irish Workers in America? We are not trust magnates, nor little business men, and the interests which bind us to those who work beside us and suffer with us are infinitely stronger than the traditions which draw us towards those of our race whose interests are those of our despoilers. Hence our duty is plain. We must fight against in America that which plundered and hunted us in Ireland. Here as there, and here greater than there, the enemy of our race is private property in the means of life. In Ireland it was fundamentally private property in land that was the original and abiding cause of all our woes; in America it is again private property in land and in machinery that recreates in the United States the division of classes into slavers and enslaved. In Ireland it was private property, immature but bloodthirsty, in America it is private property, grown mature from the sucking of human blood. In both it is the enemy of the human race. To quote the words of Ernest Jones, the Chartist leader of '48, friend of Ireland and fellow worker of John Mitchel in whose defense he spent one year in prison,

> 'The monopoly of land drives him (the worker) from the farm into the factory, and the monopoly of machinery drives him from the factory into the street, and thus crucified between the two thieves of land and capital, the Christ of Labor hangs in silent agony'.[15]

---

[15] Ernest Charles Jones (1819–1869), English poet and Chartist. A speech by Jones containing much (not all) of this formulation is reported by Marx in his article 'The Chartist Movement', *New York Tribune*, 25 August 1852.

We appeal to you then, fellow countrymen, to rally around the only banner that symbolizes hope for you in America as in Ireland – the banner of Socialism. Cast off all your old political affiliations, and organize and vote to reconquer society in the interests of its only useful class – the workers. Let your slogan be, the common ownership of the means of life, your weapons the Industrial and Political Organization of the Wage Slaves to conquer their own emancipation.

Facets of American Liberty

The Harp (December 1908)

Connolly here brilliantly skewers American 'liberty', which he shows to be more about freedom of capital than freedom of human beings.

'Where Liberty is, there is my country.'[16]

So said the enthusiastic 18th century revolutionist. But if he lived nowadays he would have a long search for his country – where Liberty is. The only liberty we know of now, outside the liberty to go hungry, stands in New York Bay, where it has been placed, I am told, in order that immigrants from Europe may get their first and last look at it before setting foot on American soil.

You see, it would be decidedly awkward for our Fourth of July orators to be orating to the newcomers about the blessings of American liberty and then to be asked by some ignorant European to tell where that liberty is to be found.

Some ignorant, discontented unit of the hordes of Europe, for instance, might feel tempted to go nosing around in this great country in search of liberty, and his search might take him into the most awkward places.

He might go down South and see little white American children of seven, eight and nine years of age working in our cotton mills enjoying their liberty to work for a boss at an age when other children are still compelled by tyrannical laws to stay on wrestling with the dreadful problems of reading, 'riting and 'rithmetic.

He might have visited Alabama and seen American citizens out on strike, driven out of their homes by the power of the capitalist mine-owner, and when they erected tents upon private land granted by a charitable farmer for that purpose, he might have seen a Democratic

---

[16] Attributed to Benjamin Franklin (1706–1790), American politician and scientist.

governor order in the state militia to cut down the tents and drive the American workers back to the mine at the point of the bayonet.

He might, being an ignorant European, visit Florida and see men lured from the big cities to the railroad construction camps and kept there on a hunger diet, compelled to endure blows and foulest insults, and when they attempted to escape he might see the power of the state detective force employed to arrest them as if they were criminals and take them back handcuffed to their slavery.

This ignorant representative of the scum of Europe might have visited Colorado in 1904 and seen armed militia invade newspaper offices and imprison printers and journalists alike without legal warrant or pretense at trial, trade union meetings suppressed, duly elected public officials compelled to resign under threat of lynching, respectable men taken out of their beds in the middle of the night and without [being] given a chance to even put their shoes on marched under armed guards across the state lines, hundreds of men thrown into cattle enclosures and kept there for months without trial, and Pinkerton detectives employed to manufacture outrages in order to hang innocent men.[17]

This pilgrim in search of liberty might have learned from the coal miners of Pennsylvania that their state is dotted over east and west with localities where union miners were shot down like dogs whilst peacefully parading the streets or roads in time of strikes, he might have learned that practically every industrial center in the country from Albany, N.Y., to San Francisco, California, from New Orleans to Minnesota, has the same tale to tell of the spilling of workmen's blood by the hirelings of the master class, and he might have attended the unemployed demonstration in Union Square, New York, and have seen the free American citizens rapped on the head for daring to ask for a job collectively, instead of begging for it individually.

Or this greenhorn might have strolled along West Street, New York, and interviewed some Irish longshoremen, who could tell him that when in Ireland they stayed at home and played cards and bothered the women of the house every time it rained (and in Ireland it rains oftener than it is fair), that they stopped work every time there was a fair day, or a Saint's Day, or a Feast Day, or a Home Rule, Nationalist, Gaelic

---

[17] The Pinkerton National Detective Agency, founded in 1850 by Allan Pinkerton, and once the largest private law enforcement organisation in the world, was used extensively by the forces of American business in struggles with the labour movement in the late nineteenth and early twentieth centuries.

League or Orange Demonstration, when they stayed up too long at a wake, or wished to go a few miles to attend a wedding.

But that since he became a participant in the freedom of America he has to turn out to his work rain or shine, winter and summer, and be ready to stand in line to be picked out of a gang as he used to pick out pigs at a fair at home, only that the pigs got fed, if they were or were not picked, whereas he and his family are likely to go hungry if he does not keep on the soft side of the boss and get picked. And if he does get picked for a job, he has to stand worse driving and foul abuse than an Irish ass ever received from its driver.

As for holidays – tell it not in Gath.[18] A holiday in Ireland meant rest and recreation for his body and mind; in America a holiday means a rest for his stomach and anxiety for his mind.

I think I can work in a joke here. There was once a hardworking Irish girl who married an enterprising Irish-American. On the day after the wedding she remarked, 'Well, thank God, now I can get a rest for my bones'.

''Deed, if you do, Mary', responded her loving spouse, 'it will be a rest for your jaw-bones'.

(This joke is going to be copyrighted.)

After making this pilgrimage through the state possibly our representative of the destitute alien might be impertinent enough to interrupt the Fourth of July orator with the demand to be shown where this American Liberty is.

Then the orator, thanks to Bartholdi, could arise in his dignity and crush the interrupter with the statement that Liberty is to be found outside in the Bay of New York.[19]

It is a waste of time to look inside for what is standing outside. Verb sap, or as we say in the Gaelic, 'An tuigeann tú?' In the classic language of the Bowery, 'Are you next?'

The Liberty we have in Bartholdi's statue is truly typical of liberty in this age and country.

It is placed upon a pedestal out of the reach of the multitudes; it can only be approached by those who have money enough to pay the expense; it has a lamp to enlighten the world, but the lamp is never lit, and it smiles upon us as we approach America, but when we are once in the country we never see anything but its back.

---

[18] Gath, often known as Gath of the Philistines, mentioned in the Old Testament, and the home city of Goliath.

[19] Frédéric Auguste Bartholdi (1834–1904), French sculptor and designer of New York's Statue of Liberty.

'Tis a great world we live in.

P.H.B., of Shaft, Pennsylvania, wrote to the *Harp* in September asking for enlightenment on several points connected with the practical workings of Socialism in the mining industry. The chief points he dealt with were the difficulty of having a system that would insure absolute justice to every individual, and who would do the dirty work, and who would be induced to waste his time in qualifying for a mining engineer when the ordinary miner would be as highly remunerated.

Our friend should remember that Socialists do not suppose that the substitution of common ownership for private ownership will of itself abolish all difficulties or solve all questions of administration. It will not. But it will make the solution of those questions on a just basis easier than it is to-day. In fact, to-day justice is simply not taken into account in such matters. Expediency and profit-making are all that are sought. Yet our friend, like many others, demands of Socialism perfect, absolute, flawless justice down to the minutest detail, and if he cannot be assured of it he will continue to support the capitalist system, although he knows it to be saturated with injustices of the most horrible description.

I presume that he would not ride on a railroad train until he had fully understood all the mechanism of a steam engine, all the principles and practice of steam propulsion, all the complicated appliances of signaling, points, switching and railroad telegraphing.

But that would not be his attitude in reality. No, he would say that he had no doubt there were difficulties in the way of railroading, but that the central principle being right he could trust the associated intelligence of those engaged in the industry to master those difficulties in line with the general principle. That, in fact, has been the general practical attitude of the human race toward all innovations, once the general principle of the new departure was accepted.

Under Socialism, mining, like every other industry, will be democratically administered by the workers in that occupation; foremen, managers, superintendents, etc., will all be elected from and by the rank and file of the workers, and those same workers will also elect the delegates who will represent them on the local and governing bodies of the land. All matters pertaining to the technical efficiency of the mines, and of labor, will be settled either by those experts whom the workers have elected as administrators, by discussion and vote of the men in the union of their industry, or by whatever method their common interest and sense of fairness can devise.

Such positions as mining engineers, or other professions, etc., can be filled by pupils chosen in a competitive examination. There will always be a sufficiency of candidates for any such post of honor, and as the cost of the education for such posts will be borne by the community, and not by the individual aspirant, they need not necessarily entail any disparity of salary.

As for the varying needs of individuals, each individual will require to 'cut his coat according to his cloth', to use a homely old saying. He whose tastes run to automobiles cannot expect to be strong on books, and he who desires the luxury of travel will have to forego the pleasures of a private garden and a secluded mansion. And so on *ad infinitum*.

Socialism will solve the problem of poverty by abolishing it, but it will not solve all problems, smooth all rough places, nor prevent all mistakes.

Under Socialism men will possibly often mistake their avocations in life, women will marry the wrong men, and men will marry the wrong women.

I know some Socialists say that there will be no marriage question under Socialism, but I do not see that that will necessarily be the case, and I am only concerned with what Socialism will necessarily do. I hold that under Socialism no woman will be compelled to marry a man for a livelihood or for riches, but I hold that it is quite possible that under Socialism a man and woman may imagine that they were destined for each other, love and marry, and after the lapse of years and closer intimacy find they had made a mistake and one came to hate the other.

And when that happens we will have a marriage and divorce question, or a sex question, if you will, and I do not see that the fact that each is economically independent of the other will alter that fact. If the woman desires to be rid of the man whilst the man still loves the woman, or vice versa, we will still have passion, and jealousy, and love, and hatred.

In fact, Socialism will not make us angels upon earth; it will only put a premium upon our better qualities instead of upon our baser, as is done by capitalism today. And that itself would be worth a revolution to realize, or a thousand revolutions.

Under any system of society there will be differences of opinion amongst men and women, and with some natures such differences will be intense and lead to much swinging of literary and verbal cudgels, and metaphorical belaboring with black thorns.

Talking of blackthorns reminds me of some fine verses I lately came across upon that inspiring subject. Here they are; you can read them while I mop my fevered brow:

LINES TO A BLACKTHORN

You're welcome to my hand, my fine blackthorn,
    That grew in beauty under Erin's skies;
Your blossom sweet, on many a bright May morn,
    Gave added fragrance to the summer's sighs.
Upon your branch the brown-robed linnet sang,
    The goldfinch chattered merrily his lay,
And at your feet the primrose joyous spring
    To welcome your sweet blossoms falling spray.
It moves the fount of memory to tears
    To think this fine 'Kippeen' had root upon
That Irish hillside, where my boyhood years
    In careless glee and innocence sped on,
I hear the lark with pulsing waves of song –
    Sweet herald of the dawn that knew no care –
Across the gulf of Time, again I long
    To feel the rapture of that matin prayer.
And when they cut you down, my fine blackthorn,
    They 'saysoned' you, like bacon in the smoke
Above the ample "hob", where night and morn
    The turf fire gave you heart and strength of oak.
And round the fire I hear the welcome cheer
    That burst in limpid music from the heart.
As neighbor entered with 'God save all here',
    And 'banact lat' as he would slow depart.
You are welcome to my hand, for like the rod
    At Moses' touch bloomed in the desert wild,
I see again dear Erin's verdant sod,
    And every flower that on her bosom smiled.
Sure you are nurtured by the same soft rain,
    Your veins were warmed by the same bright sun.
And so at your kind touch I live again
    The joyous hours with which life's morn begun.
    – William J. Dawson[20]

Another correspondent writes to ask me 'as a practical man' to tell what measures the Socialists would pass and what they would repeal in the city of St. Louis, in the state of Missouri, in the Senate or Congress if they got the victory. 'Tis a tall order.

In the first place I am not a practical man. To be practical under capitalism means that your ideas are consonant with the existence of

---

[20] William James Dawson (1854–1928), English clergyman and poet. 'Banact lat' is an Anglicization of the Irish Gaelic phrase 'Beannacht leat', which means 'Bless you'.

capitalism. Mine, I trust, are not. My correspondent has not grasped that fact yet; when he does he will realize that to be 'practical' is the last thing I aim at.

I would remind him that the Socialist Party of St. Louis, the Socialist Party of Missouri, and the National organization have each issued platforms which answer his questions, and recommend him to secure copies for his enlightenment. He tells me he wants it answered in the *Harp*, but I desire him to understand that the *Harp* desires only to treat of the general principles of Socialism as a revolutionary movement, and not with any patching up of the old social order.

Personally, I believe that the fact that we still have long platforms and programs is one of the signs of the comparatively backward state of the Socialist movement, of our unripeness for Social Revolution. On the day that we have so far conquered the mind of the workers that we can safely abolish our platforms and concentrate and express our whole fighting principle in one simple phrase capable of being remembered by the average school boy, we will then, and then only, cease to be a propagandist association and become a revolutionary army.

At least so thinks

SPAILPÍN[21]

---

[21] A *spailpín* was an Irish travelling rural labourer, from the seventeenth to the twentieth centuries.

Chapter 3

Labour in Irish History

Connolly's years in America produced his most important single piece of writing, the short book *Labour in Irish History*. The work on the book pre-dated Connolly's emigration to the United States, and it was then halted while he was fully engaged in American activism and debate. Despite the diffuse conditions of its production, the book is a clearly-written, pungent essay in historical and historiographic polemic. It is not a fully scholarly treatise. It is not a history of Irish working people, nor of the labour movement. Nor is it an exercise in Marxist historical interpretation. But it remains a lodestone for any effort to produce a radical history of Ireland and, in the eyes of major radical scholars of our own times such as David Lloyd and Robert Young, it anticipates much in the most advanced contemporary 'postcolonial' historiography. As such it remains of enduring interest.

Foreword

In her great work, *The Making of Ireland and its Undoing*, the only contribution to Irish history we know of which conforms to the methods of modern historical science, the authoress, Mrs. Stopford Green, dealing with the effect upon Ireland of the dispersion of the Irish race in the time of Henry VIII and Elizabeth, and the consequent destruction of Gaelic culture, and rupture with Gaelic tradition and law, says that the Irishmen educated in schools abroad abandoned or knew nothing of the lore of ancient Erin, and had no sympathy with the spirit of the Brehon Code, nor with the social order of which it was the juridical expression.[1] She says they 'urged the theory, *so antagonistic to the immemorial law*

---

[1] Alice Stopford Green (1847–1929), Irish nationalist historian. Published *The Making of Ireland and its Undoing* (1908) and numerous other works. Opposed British policy in the Boer War, and admirer of Roger Casement's exposure of Belgian crimes

of Ireland, that only from the polluted sinks of heretics could come the idea that the people might elect a ruler, and confer supreme authority on whomsoever pleased them'. In other words the new Irish, educated in foreign standards, had adopted as their own the feudal-capitalist system of which England was the exponent in Ireland, and urged it upon the Gaelic Irish. As the dispersion of the clans, consummated by Cromwell, finally completed the ruin of Gaelic Ireland, all the higher education of Irishmen thenceforward ran in this foreign groove, and was coloured with this foreign colouring.[2]

In other words, the Gaelic culture of the Irish chieftainry was rudely broken off in the seventeenth century, and the continental Schools of European despots implanted in its place in the minds of the Irish students, and sent them back to Ireland to preach a fanatical belief in royal and feudal prerogatives, as foreign to the genius of the Gael as was the English ruler to Irish soil. What a light this sheds upon Irish history of the seventeenth, eighteenth, and nineteenth centuries! And what a commentary it is upon the real origin of that so-called 'Irish veneration for the aristocracy', of which the bourgeois charlatans of Irish literature write so eloquently! That veneration is seen to be as much of an exotic, as much of an importation, as the aristocratic caste it venerated. Both were

'... foul foreign blossoms
Blown hither to poison our plains'[3]

But so deeply has this insidious lie about the aristocratic tendencies of the Irish taken root in Irish thought, that it will take a long time to eradicate it from the minds of the people, or to make the Irish realise that the whole concept of orthodox Irish history for the last 200 years was a betrayal and abandonment of the best traditions of the Irish race. Yet such is undoubtedly the case. Let us examine this a little more closely!

Just as it is true that a stream cannot rise above its source, so it is true that a national literature cannot rise above the moral level of the

---

in the Congo. Took pro-Treaty side in Irish Civil War. Served as a Senator in the Irish Free State.

[2] Oliver Cromwell (1599–1658), English political and military leader, major figure in England's Civil War on the anti-royalist side, later Lord Protector of England, Scotland and Ireland. A hero of liberty to many in England, but considered a perpetrator of genocide in Ireland.

[3] A quotation from a ballad by John Banim (1798–1842), *He Said That He Was Not Our Brother*. With his brother Michael, Banim was a popular novelist, dramatist, poet and essayist.

social conditions of the people from whom it derives its inspiration. If we would understand the national literature of a people, we must study their social and political status, keeping in mind the fact that their writers were a product thereof, and that the children of their brains were conceived and brought forth in certain historical conditions. Ireland, at the same time as she lost her ancient social system, also lost her language as the vehicle of thought of those who acted as her leaders. As a result of this twofold loss, the nation suffered socially, nationally and intellectually from a prolonged arrested development. During the closing years of the seventeenth century, all the eighteenth, and the greater part of the nineteenth, the Irish people were the lowest helots in Europe, socially and politically. The Irish peasant, reduced from the position of a free clansman owning his tribeland and controlling its administration in common with his fellows, was a mere tenant-at-will subject to eviction, dishonour and outrage at the hands of an irresponsible private proprietor. Politically he was non-existent, legally he held no rights, intellectually he sank under the weight of his social abasement, and surrendered to the downward drag of his poverty. He had been conquered, and he suffered all the terrible consequences of defeat at the hands of a ruling class and nation who have always acted upon the old Roman maxim of 'Woe to the vanquished.'

To add to his humiliation, those of his name and race who had contrived to escape the general ruin, and sent their children to be educated in foreign schools, discovered, with the return of those 'wild geese' to their native habitat, that they who had sailed for France, Italy or Spain, filled with hatred of the English Crown and of the English landlord garrison in Ireland, returned as mere Catholic adherents of a pretender to the English throne, using all the prestige of their foreign schooling, to discredit the Gaelic ideas of equality and democracy, and instead, instilling into the minds of the growing generation feudal ideas of the divine right of kings to rule, and of subjects to unquestioningly obey. The Irish students in the universities of the Continent were the first products of a scheme which the Papacy still pursues with its accustomed skill and persistence – a persistence which recks little of the passing of centuries – a scheme which looks upon Catholic Ireland simply as a tool to be used for the spiritual re-conquest of England to Catholicity. In the eighteenth century this scheme did its deadliest work in Ireland. It failed ridiculously to cause a single Irish worker in town or country to strike a blow for the Stuart cause in the years of the Scottish Rebellions in 1715 and 1745, but it prevented them from striking any blows for their own cause, or from taking advantage of the civil feuds of their enemies.[4] It did more. It killed Gaelic Ireland; an Irish-speaking Catholic was of no value as a missionary of Catholicism in England, and an Irish peasant who treasured the tongue of his fathers might also have some reverence for the principles of the social polity and civilisation under which his forefathers had lived and prospered for unnumbered years. And such principles were even more distasteful to French, Spanish or Papal patrons of Irish schools of learning on the Continent than they were to English monarchs. Thus the poor Irish were not only pariahs in the social system of their day, but they were also precluded from hoping for a revival of intellectual life through the achievements of their children. Their children were taught to despise the language and traditions of their fathers.

It was at or during this period, when the Irish peasant had been crushed to the very lowest point, when the most he could hope for was to be pitied as animals are pitied; it was during this period Irish literature in English was born. Such Irish literature was not written for Irishmen as a real Irish literature would be, it was written by Irishmen, about Irishmen, but for English or Anglo-Irish consumption.

Hence the Irishman in English literature may be said to have been born with an apology in his mouth. His creators knew nothing of the free and independent Irishman of Gaelic Ireland, but they did know the conquered, robbed, slave-driven, brutalised, demoralised Irishman, the product of generations of landlord and capitalist rule, and him they seized upon, held up to the gaze of the world, and asked the nations to accept as the true Irish type.

If he crouched before a representative of royalty with an *abject* submission born of a hundred years of political outlawry and training in foreign ideas, his abasement was pointed to proudly as an instance of the 'ancient Celtic fidelity to hereditary monarchs'; if, with the memory of perennial famines, evictions, jails, hangings, and tenancy-at-will beclouding his brain, he humbled himself before the upper-class, or attached himself like a dog to their personal fortunes, his sycophancy was cited as a manifestation of 'ancient Irish veneration for the aristocracy', and if long-continued insecurity of life begat in him a fierce desire for the ownership of a piece of land to safe-guard his loved ones in a

---

[4] In the early eighteenth century, after the Glorious Revolution of 1688, when the Protestant William of Orange gained the British throne, the sons and grandsons of James II fought the Crown as Roman Catholic 'pretenders', resulting in rebellions in Scotland in 1715 and 1745.

system where land was life, this new-born land-hunger was triumphantly trumpeted forth as a proof of the 'Irish attachment to the principle of private property'. Be it understood we are not talking now of the English slanderers of the Irishman, but of his Irish apologists. The English slanderer never did as much harm as did these self-constituted delineators of Irish characteristics. The English slanderer lowered Irishmen in the eyes of the world, but his Irish middle-class teachers and writers lowered him in his own eyes by extolling as an Irish virtue every sycophantic vice begotten of generations of slavery. Accordingly, as an Irishman, peasant, labourer, or artisan, banded himself with his fellows to strike back at their oppressors in defence of their right to live in the land of their fathers, the 'respectable' classes, who had imbibed the foreign ideas publicly deplored his act, and unctuously ascribed it to the 'evil effects of English misgovernment upon the Irish character;' but when an occasional Irishman, abandoning all the traditions of his race, climbed up upon the backs of his fellows to wealth or position, his career was held up as a sample of what Irishmen could do under congenial or favourable circumstances. The seventeenth, eighteenth and nineteenth centuries were, indeed, the Via Dolorosa of the Irish race. In them the Irish Gael sank out of sight, and in his place the middle-class politicians, capitalists and ecclesiastics laboured to produce a hybrid Irishman, assimilating a foreign social system, a foreign speech, and a foreign character. In the effort to assimilate the first two the Irish were unhappily too successful, so successful that to-day the majority of the Irish do not know that their fathers ever knew another system of ownership, and the Irish Irelanders are painfully grappling with their mother tongue with the hesitating accent of a foreigner. Fortunately the Irish character has proven too difficult to press into respectable foreign moulds, and the recoil of that character from the deadly embrace of capitalist English conventionalism, as it has already led to a revaluation of the speech of the Gael, will in all probability also lead to a re-study and appreciation of the social system under which the Gael reached the highest point of civilisation and culture in Europe.

In the re-conversion of Ireland to the Gaelic principle of common ownership by a people of their sources of food and maintenance, the worst obstacles to overcome will be the opposition of the men and women who have imbibed their ideas of Irish character and history from Anglo-Irish literature. That literature, as we have explained, was born in the worst agonies of the slavery of our race; it bears all the birth-marks of such origin upon it, but irony of ironies, these birth-marks of slavery are hailed by our teachers as 'the native characteristics of the Celt'.

One of these slave birth-marks is a belief in the capitalist system of society; the Irishman frees himself from such a mark of slavery when he realises the truth that the capitalist system is the most foreign thing in Ireland.

Hence we have had in Ireland for over 250 years the remarkable phenomenon of Irishmen of the upper and middle classes urging upon the Irish toilers, as a sacred national and religious duty, the necessity of maintaining a social order against which their Gaelic forefathers had struggled, despite prison cells, famine, and the sword, for over 400 years. Reversing the procedure of the Normans settled in Ireland, who were said to have become 'more Irish than the Irish', the Irish propertied classes became more English than the English, and so have continued to our day.[5]

Hence we believe that this book, attempting to depict the attitude of the dispossessed masses of the Irish people in the great crisis of modern Irish history, may justly be looked upon as part of the literature of the Gaelic revival. As the Gaelic language, scorned by the possessing classes, sought and found its last fortress in the hearts and homes of the 'lower orders', to re-issue from thence in our own time to what the writer believes to be a greater and more enduring place in civilisation than of old, so in the words of Thomas Francis Meagher, the same 'wretched cabins have been the holy shrines in which the traditions and the hopes of Ireland have been treasured and transmitted'.[6]

The apostate patriotism of the Irish capitalist class, arising as it does upon the rupture with Gaelic tradition, will, of course, reject this conception, and saturated with foreignism themselves, they will continue to hurl the epithet of 'foreign ideas' against the militant Irish democracy. But the present Celtic revival in Ireland, leading as it must to a reconsideration and more analytical study of the laws and social structure of Ireland before the English Invasion, amongst its other good results, will have this one also, that it will confirm and establish the truth of this conception. Hitherto the study of the social structure of Ireland in the past has been marred by one great fault. For a description and interpretation of Irish social life and customs the student depended entirely upon the description and interpretation of men who were entirely lacking in

---

[5] Anglo-Norman influence in Ireland began in 1169, when the ousted King of Leinster Dermot MacMurragh sought Norman assistance in the recovery of his throne.

[6] Thomas Francis Meagher (1823–1867), Irish nationalist, leader of the Young Ireland movement, participant in the Young Ireland rebellion of 1848, and later Governor of Montana in the United States.

knowledge of, and insight into, the facts and spirit of the things they attempted to describe. Imbued with the conception of feudalistic or capitalistic social order, the writers perpetually strove to explain Irish institutions in terms of an order of things to which those institutions were entirely alien. Irish titles, indicative of the function in society performed by their bearers, the writers explained by what they supposed were analogous titles in the feudal order of England, forgetful of the fact that as the one form of society was the antithesis of the other, and not its counterpart, the one set of titles could not possibly convey the same meaning as the other, much less be a translation.

Much the same mistake was made in America by the early Spanish conquistadores in attempting to describe the social and political systems of Mexico and Peru, with much the same results of introducing almost endless confusion into every attempt to comprehend life as it actually existed in those countries before the conquest. The Spanish writers could not mentally raise themselves out of the social structure of continental Europe, and hence their weird and wonderful tales of despotic Peruvian and Mexican 'Emperors' and 'Nobles' where really existed the elaborately organised family system of a people not yet fully evolved into the political state. Not until the publication of Morgan's monumental work on *Ancient Society*, was the key to the study of American native civilisation really found and placed in the hands of the student.[7] The same key will yet unlock the doors which guard the secrets of our native Celtic civilisation, and make them possible of fuller comprehension for the multitude.

Meanwhile we desire to place before our readers the two propositions upon which this book is founded – propositions which we believe embody alike the fruits of the experience of the past, and the matured thought of the present, upon the points under consideration.

First, that in the evolution of civilisation the progress of the fight for national liberty of any subject nation must, perforce, keep pace with the progress of the struggle for liberty of the most subject class in that nation, and that the shifting of economic and political forces which accompanies the development of the system of capitalist society leads inevitably to the increasing conservatism of the non-working-class element, and to the revolutionary vigour and power of the working class.

---

[7] Lewis H. Morgan (1818–1881), pioneering American anthropologist, author of *Ancient Society; or Researches in the Lines of Human Progress from Savagery through Barbarism to Civilization* (1877), a work influential on Marx and Engels, and also discussed by Darwin and Freud.

Second, that the result of the long drawn out struggle of Ireland has been, so far, that the old chieftainry has disappeared, or, through its degenerate descendants, has made terms with iniquity, and become part and parcel of the supporters of the established order; the middle class, growing up in the midst of the national struggle, and at one time, as in 1798, through the stress of the economic rivalry of England almost forced into the position of revolutionary leaders against the political despotism of their industrial competitors, have now also bowed the knee to Baal, and have a thousand economic strings in the shape of investments binding them to English capitalism as against every sentimental or historic attachment drawing them toward Irish patriotism; only the Irish working class remain as the incorruptible inheritors of the fight for freedom in Ireland.[8]

To that unconquered Irish working class this book is dedicated by one of their number
James Connolly

Chapter I: The Lessons of History

'What is History but a fable agreed upon.'
– Napoleon I

It is in itself a significant commentary upon the subordinate place allotted to labour in Irish politics that a writer should think it necessary to explain his purpose before setting out to detail for the benefit of his readers the position of the Irish workers in the past, and the lessons to be derived from a study of that position in guiding the movement of the working class today. Were history what it ought to be, an accurate literary reflex of the times with which it professes to deal, the pages of history would be almost entirely engrossed with a recital of the wrongs and struggles of the labouring people, constituting, as they have ever done, the vast mass of mankind. But history, in general treats the working class as the manipulator of politics treats the working man – that is to say, with contempt when he remained passive, and with derision, hatred and misrepresentation whenever he dares evince a desire to throw off the yoke of political or social servitude. Ireland is no exception to the rule. Irish history has ever been written by the master class – in the interests of the master class.

---

[8] 1798 was the year of the rebellion against British rule in Ireland by the Enlightenment revolutionary Society of United Irishmen. 'Baal' is an ancient Semitic name for God.

Whenever the social question cropped up in modern Irish history, whenever the question of labour and its wrongs figured in the writings or speeches of our modern Irish politicians, it was simply that they might be used as weapons in the warfare against a political adversary, and not at all because the person so using them was personally convinced that the subjection of labour was in itself a wrong. This book is intended primarily to prove that contention. To prove it by a reference to the evidence – documentary and otherwise – adduced, illustrating the state of the Irish working class in the past, the almost total indifference of our Irish politicians to the sufferings of the mass of the people, and the true inwardness of many of the political agitations which have occupied the field in the eighteenth and nineteenth centuries. Special attention is given to the period preceding the Union and evidence brought forward relative to the state of Ireland before and during the continuance of Grattan's Parliament; to the condition of the working people in the town and country, and the attitude towards labour taken up by politicians of all sides, whether patriot or ministerialist.[9] In other words, we propose to do what in us lies to repair the deliberate neglect of the social question by our historians; and to prepare the way in order that other and abler pens than our own may demonstrate to the reading public the manner in which economic conditions have controlled and dominated our Irish history.

But as a preliminary to this essay on our part it becomes necessary to recapitulate here some of the salient facts of history we have elsewhere insisted upon as essential to a thorough grasp of the 'Irish Question'.

Politically, Ireland has been under the control of England for the past 700 years, during the greater part of which time the country has been the scene of constant wars against her rule upon the part of the native Irish. Until the year 1649, these wars were complicated by the fact that they were directed against both the political and *social* order recognised by the English invader. It may surprise many readers to learn that up to the date above-mentioned the basis of society in Ireland except within the Pale (a small strip of territory around the Capital city, Dublin), rested

---

[9] The Act of Union (1800) united the United Kingdom and the Kingdom of Ireland to create the United Kingdom of Great Britain and Ireland. Before this, Ireland was technically a lordship of the monarchs of England. Most significantly, the Union abolished the Irish Parliament in Dublin; henceforth Irish members sat in the Westminster Parliament. Henry Grattan (1746–1820) was an Irish parliamentarian. He campaigned for the autonomy of the Irish Parliament from that of Westminster. He opposed the Union but later took his seat at Westminster. 'Patriots' were Irish supporters of the English Whigs in the eighteenth century.

upon communal or tribal ownership of land. The Irish chief, although recognised in the courts of France, Spain, and Rome, as the peer of the reigning princes of Europe, in reality held his position upon the sufferance of his people, and as an administrator of the tribal affairs of his people, while the land or territory of the clan was entirely removed from his private jurisdiction. In the parts of Ireland where for 400 years after the first conquest (so-called) the English governors could not penetrate except at the head of a powerful army, the social order which prevailed in England – feudalism – was unknown, and as this comprised the greater portion of the country, it gradually came to be understood that the war against the foreign oppressor was also a war against private property in land. But with the forcible break up of the clan system in 1649, the social aspect of the Irish struggle sank out of sight, its place being usurped by the mere political expressions of the fight for freedom. Such an event was, of course, inevitable in any case. Communal ownership of land would undoubtedly have given way to the privately owned system of capitalist-landlordism, even if Ireland had remained an independent country, but coming as it did in obedience to the pressure of armed force from without, instead of by the operation of economic forces within, the change has been bitterly and justly resented by the vast mass of the Irish people, many of whom still mix with their dreams of liberty longings for a return to the ancient system of land tenure – now organically impossible. The dispersion of the clans, of course, put an end to the leadership of the chiefs, and in consequence, the Irish aristocracy *being all of foreign or traitor origin*, Irish patriotic movements fell entirely into the hands of the middle class, and became, for the most part, simply idealised expressions of middle-class interest.

Hence the spokesmen of the middle class, in the Press and on the platform, have consistently sought the emasculation of the Irish National movement, the distortion of Irish history, and, above all, the denial of all relation between the social rights of the Irish toilers and the political rights of the Irish nation. It was hoped and intended by this means to create what is termed 'a real National movement' – i.e. a movement in which each class would recognise the rights of other classes and laying aside their contentions, would unite in a national struggle against the common enemy – England. Needless to say, the only class deceived by such phrases was the working class. When questions of 'class' interests are eliminated from public controversy a victory is thereby gained for the possessing, conservative class, whose only hope of security lies in such elimination. Like a fraudulent trustee, the bourgeois dreads nothing so much as an impartial and rigid inquiry into the validity of his title deeds.

Hence the bourgeois press and politicians incessantly strive to inflame the working-class mind to fever heat upon questions outside the range of their own class interests. War, religion, race, language, political reform, patriotism – apart from whatever intrinsic merits they may possess – all serve in the hands of the possessing class as counter-irritants, whose function it is to avert the catastrophe of social revolution by engendering heat in such parts of the body politic as are the farthest removed from the seat of economic enquiry, and consequently of class consciousness on the part of the proletariat. The bourgeois Irishman has long been an adept at such manoeuvring, and has, it must be confessed, found in his working-class countrymen exceedingly pliable material. During the last hundred years every generation in Ireland has witnessed an attempted rebellion against English rule. Every such conspiracy or rebellion has drawn the majority of its adherents from the lower orders in town and country; yet, under the inspiration of a few middle class doctrinaires, the social question has been rigorously excluded from the field of action to be covered by the rebellion if successful; in hopes that by such exclusion it would be possible to conciliate the upper classes and enlist them in the struggle for freedom. The result has in nearly every case been the same. The workers, though furnishing the greatest proportion of recruits to the ranks of the revolutionists, and consequently of victims to the prison and the scaffold, could not be imbued *en masse* with the revolutionary fire necessary to seriously imperil a dominion rooted for 700 years in the heart of their country. They were all anxious enough for freedom, but realising the enormous odds against them, and being explicitly told by their leaders that they *must not expect any change in their condition of social subjection, even if successful*, they as a body shrank from the contest, and left only the purest-minded and most chivalrous of their class to face the odds and glut the vengeance of the tyrant – a warning to those in all countries who neglect the vital truth that successful revolutions are not the product of our brains, but of ripe material conditions.

The upper class also turned a contemptuously deaf ear to the charming of the bourgeois patriot. They (the upper class) naturally clung to their property, landed and otherwise; under the protecting power of England they felt themselves secure in the possession thereof, but were by no means assured as to the fate which might befall it in a successful revolutionary uprising. The landlord class, therefore remained resolutely loyal to England, and while the middle-class poets and romanticists were enthusing on the hope of a 'union of class and creeds', the aristocracy were pursuing their private interests against their tenants with a relentlessness which threatened to depopulate the country, and led even an

English Conservative newspaper, the London *Times*, to declare that 'the name of an Irish landlord stinks in the nostrils of Christendom'.

It is well to remember, as a warning against similar foolishness in future, that the generation of Irish landlords which had listened to the eloquent pleadings of Thomas Davis was the same as that which in the Famine years 'exercised its rights with a rod of iron and renounced its duties with a front of brass'.[10]

The lower middle class gave to the National cause in the past many unselfish patriots, but, on the whole, while willing and ready enough to please their humble fellow country-men, and to compound with their own conscience by shouting louder than all others their untiring devotion to the cause of freedom, they, as a class, unceasingly strove to divert the public mind upon the lines of constitutional agitation for such reforms as might remove irritating and unnecessary officialism, while leaving untouched the basis of national and economic subjection. This policy enabled them to masquerade as patriots before the unthinking multitude, and at the same time lent greater force to their words when as 'patriot leaders' they cried down any serious revolutionary movement that might demand from them greater proofs of sincerity than could be furnished by the strength of their lungs, or greater sacrifices than would be suitable to their exchequer. '48 and '67, the Young Ireland and the Fenian Movements, furnish the classic illustrations of this policy on the part of the Irish middle class.[11]

Such, then, is our view of Irish politics and Irish history. Subsequent chapters will place before our readers the facts upon which such a view is based.

Chapter II: The Jacobites and the Irish People

If there was a time when it behoved men in public stations to be explicit, if ever there was a time when those scourges of the human race called politicians should lay aside their duplicity and finesse, it is the present moment. Be assured that the people of this country will no longer bear that their

---

[10] Thomas Osborne Davis (1814–45), Irish writer and a leader of Young Ireland, a political, social and cultural movement which promoted an Anglophone Irish culture through its newspaper, *The Nation*.

[11] 'Fenian' was a name both for the Fenian Brotherhood and the Irish Republican Brotherhood, revolutionary republican groupings in both Ireland and America in the later nineteenth century and the early twentieth century. The Young Ireland group launched an unsuccessful rebellion against British rule in Ireland in 1845. Irish Fenians similarly failed in an uprising in 1867.

welfare should be the sport of a few family factions; be assured they are convinced their true interest consists in putting down men of self creation, who have no object in view but that of aggrandising themselves and their families at the expense of the public, and in setting up men who shall represent the nation, who shall be accountable to the nation, and who shall do the business of the nation'.
– **Arthur O'Connor** in Irish House of Commons, May 4, 1795[12]

Modern Irish History, properly understood, may be said to start with the close of the Williamite Wars in the year 1691.[13] All the political life of Ireland during the next 200 years draws its colouring from, and can only be understood in the light of that conflict between King James of England and William, Prince of Orange. Our Irish politics, even to this day and generation, have been and are largely determined by the light in which the different sections of the Irish people regarded the prolonged conflict which closed with the surrender of Sarsfield and the garrison of Limerick to the investing forces of the Williamite party.[14] Yet never, in all the history of Ireland, has there been a war in which the people of Ireland had less reason to be interested either on one side or the other. It is unfortunately beyond all question that the Irish Catholics of that time did fight for King James like lions. It is beyond all question that the Irish Catholics shed their blood like water, and wasted their wealth like dirt, in an effort to retain King James upon the throne. But it is equally beyond all question that the whole struggle was no earthly concern of theirs; that King James was one of the most worthless representatives of a worthless race that ever sat upon a throne; that the 'pious glorious and immortal' William was a mere adventurer fighting for his own hand, and his army recruited from the impecunious swordsmen of Europe who cared as little for Protestantism as they did for human life; and that neither army had the slightest claim to be considered as a patriot army combating for the freedom of the Irish race. So far from the paeans of praise lavished upon Sarsfield and the Jacobite army being justified, it

---

[12] Arthur O'Connor (1763–1852), Irish politician and revolutionary. MP in Irish Parliament 1790–1795. Member of Society of United Irishmen. Later served in the French Army under Napoleon I.

[13] The 'Williamite War' in Ireland, also known as the Jacobite War in Ireland, 1688–1691. In the wake of the Glorious Revolution of 1688 in England, which saw the deposition of the Roman Catholic James II by the Protestant William III, James sought to mobilise his supporters in Catholic Ireland in order to recover his throne. Because he was supported by France, the Jacobite War can also be seen as part of a wider European struggle, the Nine Years' War.

[14] Patrick Sarsfield, 1st Earl of Lucan (1660–1693), Irish military leader in the Jacobite cause. Died in the service of Louis XIV of France.

is questionable whether a more enlightened or patriotic age than our own will not condemn them as little better than traitors for their action in seducing the Irish people from their allegiance to the cause of their country's freedom, to plunge them into a war on behalf of a foreign tyrant – a tyrant who, even in the midst of their struggles on his behalf, opposed the Dublin Parliament in its efforts to annul the supremacy of the English Parliament. The war between William and James offered a splendid opportunity to the subject people of Ireland to make a bid for freedom while the forces of their oppressors were rent in a civil war. The opportunity was cast aside, and the subject people took sides on behalf of the opposing factions of their enemies. The reason is not hard to find. The Catholic gentlemen and nobles who had the leadership of the people of Ireland at the time were, one and all, men who possessed considerable property in the country, property to which they had, notwithstanding their Catholicity, *no more right or title than the merest Cromwellian or Williamite adventurer*. The lands they held were lands which in former times belonged to the Irish people – in other words, they were tribe-lands. As such, the peasantry – then reduced to the position of mere tenants-at-will – were the rightful owners of the soil, whilst the Jacobite chivalry of King James were either the descendants of men who had obtained their property in some former confiscation as the spoils of conquest; of men who had taken sides with the oppressor against their own countrymen and were allowed to retain their property as the fruits of treason; or finally, of men who had consented to seek from the English Government a grant giving them a personal title to the lands of their clansmen. From such a combination no really national action could be expected, and from first to last of their public proceedings they acted as an English faction, and as an English faction only. In whatever point they might disagree with the Williamites, they were at least in perfect accord with them on one point – viz., that the Irish people should be a subject people; and it will be readily understood that even had the war ended in the complete defeat of William and the triumph of James, the lot of the Irish, whether as tillers of the soil or as a nation, would not have been substantially improved. The undeniable patriotism of the rank and file does not alter the truthfulness of this analysis of the situation. They saw only the new enemy from England, the old English enemy settled in Ireland they were generously, but foolishly, ready to credit with all the virtues and attributes of patriotic Irishmen.

To further illustrate our point regarding the character of the Jacobite leaders in Ireland we might adduce the result of the great land settlement of Ireland in 1675. Eleven million acres had been surveyed at the time, of which four million acres were in the possession of Protestant settlers as the result of previous confiscations.

Lands so held were never disturbed, but the remainder were distributed as follows:

	ACRES
To soldiers who had served in the Irish Wars	2,367,715
To 49 officers	497,001
To adventurers (who had lent money)	707,321
To provisors (to whom land had been promised)	477,873
To Duke of Ormond and Colonel Butler	257,518
To Duke of York	169,436
To Protestant Bishops	31,526

The lands left to the Catholics were distributed among the Catholic gentlemen as follows:

	ACRES
To those who were declared 'innocent', that is to say, those who fought for freedom, but had sided with the Government	1,176,750
To provisors (land promised)	497,001
Nominees in possession	68,260
Restitutions	55,396
To those transferred to Connaught, under James I	541,330

It will be thus seen that with the exception of the lands held in Connacht, all the lands held by the Catholic gentry throughout Ireland were lands gained in the manner we have before described – as spoils of conquest or the fruits of treachery. Even in that province the lands of the gentry were held under a feudal tenure from the English Crown, and therefore their owners had entered into a direct agreement with the invader to set aside the rights of the clan community in favour of their own personal claims. Here then was the real reason for the refusal of the Irish leaders of that time to raise the standard of the Irish nation instead of the banner of an English faction. They fought, not for freedom for Ireland, nor for the restitution of their rights to the Irish people, but rather to secure that the class who then enjoyed the privilege of robbing the Irish people should not be compelled to give way in their turn to a fresh horde of land thieves. Much has been made of their attempt to repeal Poynings' Law and in other ways to give greater legislative force to the resolutions of the Dublin Parliament, as if such acts were a proof of their sincere desire to free the country, and not merely to make certain their own tenure of power.[15] But such claims, on the part of some writers, are only another proof of the difficulty of comprehending historical occurrences without having some central principle to guide and direct the task.

For the benefit of our readers we may here set forth the Socialist key to the pages of history, in order that it may be the more readily understood why in the past the governing classes have ever and always aimed at the conquest of political power as the guarantee for their economic domination – or, to put it more plainly, for the social subjection of the masses – and why the freedom of the workers, even in a political sense, must be incomplete and insecure until they wrest from the governing classes the possession of the land and instruments of wealth production. This proposition, or key to history, as set forth by Karl Marx, the greatest of modern thinkers and first of scientific Socialists, is as follows: –

> That in every historical epoch the prevailing method of economic production and exchange, and the social organisation necessarily following from it, forms the basis upon which alone can be explained the political and intellectual history of that epoch.[16]

In Ireland at the time of the Williamite war the 'prevailing method of economic production and exchange' was the feudal method, based upon the private ownership of lands stolen from the Irish people, and all the political struggles of the period were built upon the material interests of one set of usurpers who wished to retain, and another set who wished to obtain, the mastery of those lands – in other words, the application of such a key as the above to the problem furnished by the Jacobite Parliament of King James, at once explains the reason of the so-called patriotic efforts of the Catholic gentry. Their efforts were directed to the conservation of their own rights of property, as against the right of the English Parliament to interfere with or regulate such rights. The so-called Patriot Parliament was in reality, like every other Parliament that ever sat in Dublin, merely a collection of land thieves and their

---

[15] Poynings' Law, sometimes called The Statute of Drogheda, was a 1494 Act of the Irish Parliament which ruled that that parliament could not meet until its proposed legislation had been approved by Ireland's Lord Deputy and Privy Council, and England's monarch and Privy Council. It was a target of Irish 'patriot' politics in the eighteenth century, amended under Grattan's Parliament of 1782, effectively set aside by the Act of Union of 1800, and repealed in 1878.

[16] A quotation from Friedrich Engels' introduction to the 1888 English edition of *The Communist Manifesto*.

lackeys; their patriotism consisted in an effort to retain for themselves the lands of the native peasantry; the English influence against which they protested was the influence of their fellow thieves in England, hungry for a share of the spoil; and Sarsfield and his followers did not become patriots because of their fight against King William's government any more than an Irish Whig out of his office becomes a patriot because of his hatred to the Tories who are in. The forces which battled beneath the walls of Derry or Limerick were not the forces of England and Ireland, but the forces of two English political parties fighting for the possession of the powers of government; and the leaders of the Irish Wild Geese on the battle field of Europe were not shedding their blood because of their fidelity to Ireland, as our historians pretend to believe, but because they had attached themselves to the defeated side in English politics.[17] This fact was fully illustrated by the action of the old Franco-Irish at the time of the French Revolution. They in a body volunteered into the English army to help to put down the new French Republic, and as a result Europe witnessed the spectacle of the new republican Irish exiles fighting for the French Revolution, and the sons of the old aristocratic Irish exiles fighting under the banner of England to put down that Revolution. It is time we learned to appreciate and value the truth upon such matters, and to brush from our eyes the cobwebs woven across them by our ignorant or unscrupulous history-writing politicians.

On the other hand, it is just as necessary to remember that King William, when he had finally subdued his enemies in Ireland, showed by his actions that he and his followers were animated throughout by the same class feeling and considerations as their opponents. When the war was over William confiscated a million and a half acres, and distributed them among the aristocratic plunderers who followed him, as follows: – He gave Lord Bentinck, 135,300 acres; Lord Albemarle, 103,603; Lord Coningsby, 59,667; Lord Romney, 49,517; Lord Galway, 36,142; Lord Athlone, 26,840; Lord Rochford, 49,512; Dr. Leslie, 16,000; Mr. F. Keighley, 12,000; Lord Mountjoy, 12,000; Sir T. Prendergast, 7,083; Colonel Hamilton, 5,886 acres.

These are a few of the men whose descendants some presumably sane Irishmen imagine will be converted into 'nationalists' by preaching 'a union of classes'.

It must not be forgotten, also, if only as proof of his religious sincerity, that King William bestowed 95,000 acres, plundered from the Irish

---

[17] The 'Wild Geese' were Irish soldiers, usually loyal to the Jacobite cause, who fled to continental Europe after defeat, particularly after the Williamite war in 1691.

people, upon his paramour, Elizabeth Villiers, Countess of Orkney. But the virtuous Irish Parliament interfered, took back the land, and distributed it amongst their immediate friends, the Irish Loyalist adventurers.

Chapter III: Peasant Rebellions

> '*To permit a small class, whether alien or native, to obtain a monopoly of the land is an intolerable injustice; its continued enforcement is neither more nor less a robbery of the hard and laborious earnings of the poor*'.
> – **Irish People** (*Organ of the Fenian Brotherhood*) July 30, 1864[18]

In the preceding chapter we pointed out that the Williamite war in Ireland, from Derry to Limerick, was primarily a war for mastery over the Irish people, and that all questions of national or industrial freedom were ignored by the leaders on both sides as being presumably what their modern prototypes would style 'beyond the pale of practical politics'.

When the nation had once more settled down to the pursuits of peace, and all fear of a Catholic or Jacobite rising had departed from the minds of even the most timorous squireen, the unfortunate tenantry of Ireland, whether Catholic or Protestant, were enlightened upon how little difference the war had made to their position as a subject class. The Catholic who had been so foolish as to adhere to the army of James could not, in the nature of things, expect much consideration from his conquerors – and he received none – but he had the consolation of seeing that the rank and file of his Protestant enemies were treated little, if at all, better than himself. When the hungry horde of adventurers who had brought companies to the service of William had glutted themselves with the plunder for which they had crossed the Channel, they showed no more disposition to remember the claims of the common soldier – by the aid of whose sword they had climbed to power – than do our present rulers when they consign to the workhouse the shattered frames of the poor fools who, with murder and pillage, have won for their masters empire in India or Africa.

Before long the Protestant and Catholic tenants were suffering one common oppression. The question of political supremacy having been finally decided, the yoke of economic slavery was now laid unsparingly upon the backs of the labouring people. All religious sects suffered equally from this cause. The Penal Laws then in operation against the Catholics did indeed make the life of the propertied Catholics more inse-

---

[18] The *Irish People* was a Fenian newspaper, published in Dublin between 1863 and 1865.

cure than would otherwise have been the case; but to the vast mass of the population the misery and hardship entailed by the working out of economic laws were fraught with infinitely more suffering than it was at any time within the power of the Penal Laws to inflict.[19] As a matter of fact, the effect of the latter code in impoverishing wealthly Catholics has been much overrated. The class interests, which at all times unite the propertied section of the community, operated, to a large extent, to render impossible the application of the power of persecution to its full legal limits. Rich Catholics were quietly tolerated, and generally received from the rich Protestants an amount of respect and forbearance which the latter would not at any time extend to their Protestant tenantry or work-people. So far was this true that, like the Jew, some Catholics became notorious as moneylenders, and in the year 1763 a bill was introduced into the Irish House of Commons to give greater facilities to Protestants wishing to borrow money from Catholics. The bill proposed to enable Catholics to become mortgagees of the landed estates in order that Protestants wishing to borrow money could give a mortgage upon their lands as security to the Catholic leader. The bill was defeated, but its introduction serves to show how little the Penal Laws had operated to prevent the accumulation of wealth by the Catholic propertied classes.

But the social system thus firmly rooted in the soil of Ireland – and accepted as righteous by the ruling class irrespective of religion – was a greater enemy to the prosperity and happiness of the people than any legislation religious bigotry could devise. Modern Irish politicians, inspired either by a blissful unconsciousness of the facts of history, or else sublimely indifferent to its teachings, are in the habit of tracing the misery of Ireland to the Legislative Union as its source, but the slightest possible acquaintance with ante-Union literature will reveal a record of famine, oppression, and injustice, due to economic causes, unsurpassed at any other stage of modern Irish history. Thus Dean Swift, writing in 1729, in that masterpiece of sarcasm entitled *A Modest Proposal for Preventing the Children of the Poor People in Ireland from becoming a Burden on their Parents or Country, and for making them Beneficial to the Public*, was so moved by the spectacle of poverty and wretchedness

---

[19] The Penal Laws were a series of laws imposed in Ireland chiefly after the Jacobite War, which tried to compel Roman Catholics and Protestant Dissenters (mostly Presbyterians) to accept the domination of the Anglican Church of England and Ireland. The laws worked mostly by exclusion – exclusion from public office, from holding firearms, from membership of Parliament, from entering Trinity College Dublin, from owning certain kinds of property. The laws were gradually relaxed, chiefly with Catholic Emancipation in 1829.

that, although having no love for the people, for whom, indeed, he had no better name than 'the savage old Irish', he produced the most vehement and bitter indictment of the society of his day, and the most striking picture of hopeless despair, that literature has yet revealed.[20] Here is in effect his *Proposal*:

> 'It is a melancholy object to those who walk through this great town, or travel in the country, when they see the streets, the roads, and cabin doors crowded with beggars of the female sex, followed by three, four, or six children all in rags, and importuning every passenger for an alms . . . I, do, therefore, offer it to public consideration that of the hundred and twenty thousand children already computed, twenty thousand may be reserved for breed . . . that the remaining hundred thousand may at a year old be offered in sale to the persons of quality and fortune through the kingdom, always advising the mother to let them suck plentifully in the last month so as to render them plump and fat for a good table. A child will make two dishes at an entertainment for friends, and when the family dines alone the fore or hind quarters will make a reasonable dish, and seasoned with a little pepper or salt, will be very good boiled on the fourth day, especially in winter . . . I have already computed the charge of nursing a beggar's child (in which list I reckon *all cottagers, labourers, and four-fifths of the farmers*), to be about two shillings per annum, rags included; and I believe no gentleman would refuse to give ten shillings for the carcase of a good, fat child, which, as I have said, will make four dishes of excellent, nutritious meat.'

Sarcasm, truly, but how terrible must have been the misery which made even such sarcasm permissible! Great as it undoubtedly was, it was surpassed twelve years later in the famine of 1740, when no less a number than 400,000 are estimated to have perished of hunger or of the diseases which follow in the wake of hunger.[21] This may seem an exaggeration, but the statement is amply borne out by contemporary evidence. Thus Bishop Berkeley, of the Anglican Church, writing to Mr. Thomas Prior, of Dublin, in 1741, mentions that 'The other day I heard one from the county of Limerick say that whole villages were entirely dispeopled. About two months since I heard Sir Richard Cox say that five hundred were dead in the parish, though in a country, I believe, not

---

[20] Jonathan Swift (1667–1745), Irish writer and Church of Ireland clergyman. A pamphleteer, poet and essayist, famous as the author of *Gulliver's Travels* (1726), reckoned one of the greatest satirists in English.

[21] In 1740–1741, Ireland was affected by a very severe famine, estimated to have been proportionately more lethal than the more famous (and better-documented) Great Famine of 1845–1852.

very populous.'²² And a pamphlet entitled *The Groans of Ireland*, published in 1741, asserts 'the universal scarcity was followed by fluxes and malignant fevers, which swept off multitudes of all sorts, so that whole villages were laid waste'.²³

This famine, be it remarked, like all modern famine, was solely attributable to economic causes; the poor of all religions and politics were equally sufferers; the rich of all religions and politics were equally exempt. It is also noteworthy, as illustrating the manner in which the hireling scribes of the propertied classes have written history, while a voluminous literature has arisen round the Penal Laws – a subject of merely posthumous interest – a matter of such overwhelming importance, both historically and practically, as the predisposing causes of Irish famine can, as yet, claim no notice except scanty and unavoidable references in national history.

The country had not recovered from the direful effects of this famine when a further economic development once more plunged the inhabitants into blackest despair. Disease having attacked and destroyed great quantities of cattle in England, the aristocratic rulers of that country – fearful lest the ensuing high price of meat should lead to a demand for higher wages on the part of the working class in England – removed the embargo off Irish cattle, meat, butter and cheese at the English ports, thus partly establishing free trade in those articles between the two countries. The immediate result was that all such provisions brought such a price in England that tillage farming in Ireland became unprofitable by comparison, and every effort was accordingly made to transform arable lands into sheep-walks or grazing lands. The landlord class commenced evicting their tenants; breaking up small farms, and even seizing upon village common lands and pasture grounds all over the country with the most disastrous results to the labouring people and cottiers generally. Where a hundred families had reaped as sustenance from their small farms, or by hiring out their labour to the owners of large farms, a dozen shepherds now occupied their places. Immediately there sprung up throughout Ireland numbers of secret societies in which the dispossessed people strove by lawless acts and violent methods to restrain the greed of their masters, and to enforce their own right to life. They

---

²² George Berkeley (1685–1753), Irish philosopher and Church of Ireland Bishop of Cloyne, and promulgator of the theory of subjective idealism. Thomas Prior (1680–1751), lifelong friend of Berkeley and founder of the Royal Dublin Society.

²³ *The Groans of Ireland*, a pamphlet on the trade in wool, published by and for George Faulkner, 1741.

met in large bodies, generally at midnight, and proceeded to tear down enclosures; to hough cattle; to dig up and so render useless the pasture lands; to burn the houses of the shepherds; and in short, to terrorise their social rulers into abandoning the policy of grazing in favour of tillage, and to give more employment to the labourers and more security to the cottier. These secret organisations assumed different names and frequently adopted different methods, and it is now impossible to tell whether they possessed any coherent organisation or not. Throughout the South they were called Whiteboys, from the practice of wearing white shirts over their clothes when on their nocturnal expeditions.[24] About the year 1762 they posted their notices on conspicuous places in the country districts – notably, Cork, Waterford, Limerick, and Tipperary – threatening vengeance against such persons as had incurred their displeasure as graziers, evicting landlords, etc.

These proclamations were signed by an imaginary female, sometimes called the 'Sive Oultagh' sometimes 'Queen Sive', sometimes they were in the name of 'Queen Sive and Her Subjects'. Government warred upon these poor wretches in the most vindictive manner: hanging, shooting, transporting without mercy; raiding villages at dead of night for suspected Whiteboys, and dragging the poor creatures before magistrates who never condescended to hear any evidence in favour of the prisoners, but condemned them to whatever punishments their vindictive class spirit or impaired digestion might prompt.

The spirit of the ruling class against those poor slaves in revolt may be judged by two incidents exemplifying how Catholic and Protestant proprietors united to fortify injustice and preserve their privileges, even at a time when we have been led to believe that the Penal Laws formed an insuperable barrier against such Union. In the year 1762 the Government offered the sum of £100 for the capture of the first five Whiteboy Chiefs. The Protestant inhabitants of the city of Cork offered in addition £300 for the Chief, and £50 for each of his first five accomplices arrested. Immediately the wealthy Catholics of the same city added to the above sums a promise of £200 for the chief and £40 for each of his first five subordinates. This was at a time when an English governor, Lord Chesterfield, declared that if the military had killed half as many landlords as they did Whiteboys they would have contributed more effectually to restore quiet, a remark which conveys some slight

---

[24] Whiteboyism was a form of secret illegal agrarian agitation and radicalism in Ireland in the eighteenth century, which defended the rights of subsistence farmers against their landlords.

idea of the carnage made among the peasantry.[25] Yet, Flood, the great Protestant 'patriot,' he of whom Davis sings

> 'Bless Harry Flood, who nobly stood
> By us through gloomy years'[26]

in the Irish House of Commons of 1763 fiercely denounced the Government for not killing enough of the Whiteboys. He had called it 'clemency'.[27]

Chapter IV: Social Revolts and Political Kites and Crows

'When the aristocracy come forward the people fall backward; when the people come forward the aristocracy, fearful of being left behind, insinuate themselves into our ranks and rise into timid leaders of treacherous auxiliaries'.
– Secret Manifesto of Projectors of United Irish Society, 1791[28]

In the North of Ireland the secret organisations of the peasantry were known variously as Oakboys and the Hearts of Steel or Steelboys.[29] The former directed their efforts mainly against the system of compulsory road repairing, by which they were required to contribute their unpaid labour for the upkeep of the county roads; a system, needless to say, offering every opportunity to the county gentry to secure labour gratuitously for the embellishment of their estates and private roads on the pretext of serving public ends. The Oakboy organisation was particularly strong in the counties of Monaghan, Armagh, and Tyrone. In a pamphlet published about the year 1762, an account is given of a 'rising' of the peasantry in the first-named county and of the heroic exploits of the officer in command of the troops engaged in suppressing said rising, in a manner which irresistibly recalls the present accounts in the English newspapers

---

[25] Philip Stanhope (1694–1773), 4th Earl of Chesterfield, served as Viceroy of Ireland 1745–1746; a liberal and a reformer.
[26] Quoted from Thomas Davis's ballad, *Song of the Volunteers of 1782*.
[27] Henry Flood (1732–1791), Irish politician and patriot, associated with Henry Grattan.
[28] Quotation from a private pamphlet 'Idem, sentire, dicere, agere' by William Drennan (1754–1820), physician, poet, and a founder of the Society of the United Irishmen. In this pamphlet, privately circulated in Dublin in 1791, Drennan called for the foundation of a Masonic secret society to be called the Irish Brotherhood.
[29] As Connolly suggests, the Hearts of Oak (Oakboys) and Hearts of Steel (Steelboys) were the approximate equivalent of the Whiteboys in eighteenth-century Ulster: agrarian radicals, dedicated to asserting the rights of poor tenants, particularly in regard to rents and tithes.

of the punitive expeditions of the British army against the 'marauding' hill tribes of India or Dacoits of Burmah. The work is entitled *True and Faithful Account of the Late Insurrections in the North, with a narrative Colonel Coote's Campaign amongst the Oakboys in County Monaghan, etc.* The historian tells how, on hearing of the 'rising', the brave British officer set off with his men to the town of Castleblayney; how on his way thither he passed numerous bodies of the peasantry proceeding in the same direction, each with an oak bough or twig stuck in his hat as a sign of his treasonable sympathies; how on entering Castleblayney he warned the people to disperse, and only received defiant replies, and even hostile manifestations; how he then took refuge in the Market House and prepared to defend it if need be; and how, after occupying that stronghold all night, he found the next morning the rebels had withdrawn from the town. Next, there is an account of the same valiant General's entry into the town of Ballybay. Here he found all the houses shut against him, each house proudly displaying an oak bough in its windows and all the people seemingly prepared to resist to the uttermost. Apparently determined to make an example, and so to strike terror, the valiant soldier and his men proceeded to arrest the ringleader, and, after a severe struggle, did succeed in breaking into some one of the cabins of the poor people, and arresting some person, who was accordingly hauled off to the town of Monaghan, there to be dealt with according to the forms of the law from which every consideration of justice was rigorously excluded. In the town of Clones, we are informed, the people withstood the Royal forces in the market place, but were, of course defeated. The Monaghan Oakboys were then driven across the borders of their own county into Armagh, where they made a last stand, but were attacked and defeated in a 'pitched battle', the severity of which may be gauged from the fact that no casualties were reported on the side of the troops.

But the general feeling of the people was so pronouncedly against the system of compulsory and unpaid labour on the roads the Government subsequently abolished the practice, and instituted a road rate providing for payment for such necessary labour by a tax upon owners and occupiers of property in the district. Needless to say, the poor peasants who were suffering martyrdom in prison for their efforts to remedy what the Government had by such remedial legislation admitted to be an injustice, were left to rot in their cells – the usual fate of pioneers of reform.

The Steelboys were a more formidable organisation, and had their strongholds in the counties of Down and Antrim. They were for the most part Presbyterian or other dissenters from the Established Church, and, like the Whiteboys, aimed at the abolition or reduction of tithes and the restriction of the system of consolidating farms for grazing purposes. They frequently appeared in arms, and moved with a certain degree of discipline, coming together from widely separated parts in obedience, apparently, to the orders of a common centre. In the year 1722 six of their number were arrested and lodged in the town jail of Belfast. Their associates immediately mustered in thousands, and in the open day marched upon that city, made themselves masters thereof, stormed the jail, and released their comrades. This daring action excited consternation in the ranks of the governing classes, troops were despatched to the spot, and every precaution taken to secure the arrest of the leaders. Out of the numerous prisoners made, a batch were selected for trial, but whether as a result of intimidation or because of their sympathy with the prisoners it is difficult to tell, the jury in Belfast refused to convict, and when the trial was changed to Dublin, the Government was equally unfortunate. The refusal of the juries to convict was, probably, in a large measure due to the unpopularity of the Act then just introduced to enable the Government to put persons accused of agrarian offences on trial in a different county to their own. When this Act was repealed the convictions and executions went on as merrily as before. Many a peasant's corpse swung on the gibbet, and many a promising life was doomed to blight and decay in the foul confines of the prison hell, to glut the vengeance of the dominant classes. Arthur Young, in his *Tour of Ireland*, thus describes the state of matters against which those poor peasants revolted.

> 'A landlord in Ireland can scarcely invent an order which a servant, labourer, or cottier dares to refuse to execute ... Disrespect, or anything tending towards sauciness he may punish with his cane or his horsewhip with the most perfect security. A poor man would have his bones broken if he offered to lift a hand in his own defence ... Landlords of consequence have assured me that many of their cottiers would think themselves honoured by having their wives and daughters sent for to the bed of their master – a mark of slavery which proves the oppression under which people must live.'[30]

It will be observed by the attentive student that the 'patriots' who occupied the public stage in Ireland during the period we have been dealing with never once raised their voices in protest against such social injustice. Like their imitators to-day, they regarded the misery of the Irish people as a convenient handle for political agitation; and, like their

---

[30] Arthur Young (1741–1820), English agriculturalist and campaigner for farmworkers' rights. Published *A Tour in Ireland* in 1780.

imitators to-day, they were ever ready to outvie even the Government in their denunciation of all those who, more earnest than themselves, sought to find a radical cure for such misery.

Of the trio of patriots – Swift, Molyneux and Lucas – it may be noted that their fight was simply a repetition of the fight waged by Sarsfield and his followers in their day – a change of persons and of stage costume truly, but no change of character; a battle between the kites and the crows.[31]

They found themselves members of a privileged class, living upon the plunder of the Irish people; but early perceived, to their dismay, that they could not maintain their position as a privileged class without the aid of the English Army; and in return for supplying that army the English ruling class were determined to have the lion's share of the plunder. The Irish Parliament was essentially an English institution; nothing like it existed before the Norman Conquest. In that respect it was on the same footing as landlordism, capitalism, and their natural-born child – pauperism. England sent a swarm of adventurers to conquer Ireland; having partly succeeded, these adventurers established a Parliament to settle disputes among themselves, to contrive measures for robbing the natives, and to prevent their fellow-tyrants who had stayed in England, from claiming the spoil. But in course of time the section of land-thieves resident in England did claim a right to supervise the doings of the adventurers in Ireland, and consequently to control their Parliament. Hence arose Poynings' Law, and the subordination of Dublin Parliament to London Parliament. Finding this subordinate position of the Parliament enabled the English ruling class to strip the Irish workers of the fruits of their toil, the more far-seeing of the privileged class in Ireland became alarmed lest the stripping process should go too far, and leave nothing for them to fatten upon.

At once they became patriots, anxious that Ireland – which, in their phraseology, meant the ruling class in Ireland – should be free from the control of the Parliament of England. Their pamphlets, speeches, and all public pronouncements were devoted to telling the world how much nicer, equitable, and altogether more delectable it would be for the Irish people to be robbed in the interests of a native-born aristocracy than to witness the painful spectacle of that aristocracy being compelled to divide the plunder with its English rival. Perhaps Swift, Molyneux, or Lucas did not confess even to themselves that such was the basis of their

---

[31] William Molyneux (1656–1698), Irish philosopher. Published *The Case for Ireland's being Bound by Acts of Parliament in England, Stated* in 1698. Charles Lucas (1713–1771), Irish physician and politician, and Member of Parliament for Dublin.

political creed. The human race has at all times shown a proneness to gloss over its basest actions with a multitude of specious pretences, and to cover even its iniquities with the glamour of a false sentimentality. But we are not dealing with appearances but realities, and, in justice to ourselves, we must expose the flimsy sophistry which strives to impart to a sordid, self-seeking struggle the appearance of a patriotic movement. In opposition to the movements of the people, the patriot politicians and Government alike were an undivided mass.

In their fight against the tithes the Munster peasantry, in 1786, issued a remarkable document, which we here reprint as an illustration of the thought of the people of the provinces of that time. This document was copied into many papers at the time, and was also reprinted as a pamphlet in October of that year.

LETTER ADDRESSED TO THE MUNSTER PEASANTRY

'To obviate the bad impression made by the calumnies of our enemies, we beg leave to submit to you our claim for the protection of a humane gentry and humbly solicit yours, if said claim shall appear to you founded in justice and good policy.

'In every age, country, and religion the priesthood are allowed to have been artful, usurping, and tenacious of their ill-acquired prerogatives. Often have their jarring interests and opinions deluged with Christian blood this long-devoted isle.

'Some thirty years ago our unhappy fathers – galled beyond human sufferance – like a captive lion vainly struggling in the toils, strove violently to snap their bonds asunder, but instead rivetted them more tight. Exhausted by the bloody struggle, the poor of this province submitted to their oppression, and fattened with their vitals each decimating leech.

'The luxurious parson drowned in the riot of his table the bitter groans of those wretches that his proctor fleeced, and the poor remnant of the proctor's rapine was sure to be gleaned by the rapacious priest; but it was blasphemy to complain of him; Heaven, we thought, would wing its lightning to blast the wretch who grudged the Holy Father's share. Thus plundered by either clergy, we had reason to wish for our simple Druids again.

'At last, however, it pleased pitying Heaven to dispel the murky cloud of bigotry that hovered over us so long. Liberality shot her cheering rays, and enlightened the peasant's hovel as well as the splendid hall. O'Leary told us, plain as friar could, that a God of a universal love would not confine His salvation to one sect alone, and that the subject's election was the best title to the crown.

'Thus improved in our religion and our politics ... we resolve to evince on every occasion the change in our sentiments and hope to succeed in our sincere attempts. We examined the double causes of our grievances, and debated long how to get them removed, until at length our resolves terminated in this general peaceful remonstrance.

'Humanity, justice, and policy enforce our request. Whilst the tithe farmer enjoys the fruit of our labours, agriculture must decrease, and while the griping priest insists on more for the bridegroom than he is worth, population must be retarded.

'Let the legislature befriend us now, and we are theirs forever. Our sincerity in the warmth of our attachment when once professed was never questioned, and we are bold to say no such imputation will ever fall on the Munster peasantry.

'At a very numerous and peaceable meeting of the delegates of the Munster peasantry, held on Thursday, the 1st day of July, 1786, the following resolutions were unanimously agreed to, viz.: –

'Resolved – That we will continue to oppose our oppressors by the most justifiable means in our power, either until they are glutted with our blood or until humanity raises her angry voice in the councils of the nation to protect the toiling peasant and lighten his burden.

'Resolved – That the fickleness of the multitude makes it necessary for all and each of us to swear not to pay voluntarily priest or parson more than as follows: –

'Potatoes, first crop, 6s. per acre; do., second crop, 4s.; wheat, 4s.; barley, 4s.; oats, 3s.; meadowing, 2s. 8d.; marriage, 5s.; baptism, 1s. 6d.; each family confession, 2s.; Parish Priest's Sun. Mass, 1s.; any other, 1s. Extreme Unction, 1s.
'Signed by order, WILLIAM O'DRISCOL,
General to the Munster Peasantry'[32]

Chapter V: Grattan's Parliament

'Dynasties and thrones are not half so important as workshops, farms and factories. Rather we may say that dynasties and thrones, and even provisional governments, are good for anything exactly in proportion as they secure fair play, justice and freedom to those who labour.'
– **John Mitchel**, 1848[33]

We now come to the period of the Volunteers. In this year, 1778, the

---

[32] Cited in Alice Stopford Green, *Irish Nationality* (1911).

[33] John Mitchel (1815–1875), Irish nationalist political writer and campaigner. Member both of Young Ireland and the Irish Confederation. Charged with sedition in 1848 and transported. His *Jail Journal* (1854) is one of the most important tracts of Irish nationalism.

people of Belfast, alarmed by rumours of intended descents of French privateers, sent to the Irish Secretary of State at Dublin Castle asking for a military force to protect their town. But the English Army had long been drafted off to the United States – then rebel American colonies of England – and Ireland was practically denuded of troops. Dublin Castle answered Belfast in the famous letter which stated that the only force available for the North would be 'a troop or two of horse, or part of a company of invalids'.

On receipt of this news the people began arming themselves and publicly organising Volunteer corps throughout the country. In a short time Ireland possessed an army of some 80,000 citizen soldiers, equipped with all the appurtenances of war; drilled, organised, and in every way equal to any force at the command of a regular Government. All the expenses of the embodiment of this Volunteer army were paid by subscriptions of private individuals. As soon as the first alarm of foreign invasion had passed, the Volunteers turned their attention to home affairs and began formulating certain demands for reform – demands which the Government was not strong enough to resist. Eventually, after a few years' agitation on the Volunteer side, met by intrigue on the part of the Government, the 'patriot' party, led by Grattan and Flood, and supported by the moral pressure of a Volunteer review outside the walls of the Parliament House, succeeded in obtaining from the legislature a temporary abandonment of the claim set up by the English Parliament to force laws upon the assembly at College Green. This and the concession of Free Trade (enabling Irish merchants to trade on equal terms with their English rivals) inaugurated what is known in Irish History as Grattan's Parliament. At the present day our political agitators never tire of telling us with the most painful iteration that the period covered by Grattan's Parliament was a period of unexampled prosperity for Ireland, and that, therefore, we may expect a renewal of this same happy state with a return of our 'native legislature' as they somewhat facetiously style that abortive product of political intrigue – Home Rule.

We might, if we choose, make a point against our political historians by pointing out that prosperity such as they speak of is purely capitalistic prosperity – that is to say, prosperity gauged merely by the *volume* of wealth produced, and entirely ignoring the manner in which the wealth is distributed amongst the workers who produce it. Thus in a previous chapter we quoted a manifesto issued by the Munster Peasantry in 1786 in which – four years after Grattan's Parliament had been established – they called upon the legislature to help them, and resolved if such help was not forthcoming – and it was not forthcoming – to 'resist our oppressors until they are glutted with our blood', an expression which would seem to indicate that the 'prosperity' of Grattan's Parliament had not penetrated far into Munster. In the year 1794 a pamphlet published at 7 Capel Street, Dublin, stated that the average wage of a day labourer in the County Meath reached only 6d. per day in Summer, and 4d. per day in Winter; and in the pages of the *Dublin Journal*, a ministerial organ, and the *Dublin Evening Post*, a supporter of Grattan's Party, for the month of April, 1796, there is to be found an advertisement of a charity sermon to be preached in the Parish Chapel, Meath Street, Dublin, in which advertisement there occurs the statement that in *three streets* of the Parish of St. Catherine's 'no less than 2,000 souls had been found in a starving condition'. Evidently 'prosperity' had not much meaning to the people of St. Catherine's.

But this is not the ground we mean at present to take up. We will rather admit, for the purpose of our argument, that the Home Rule capitalistic definition of 'prosperity' is the correct one, and that Ireland was prosperous under Grattan's Parliament, but we must emphatically deny that such prosperity was in any but an infinitesimal degree produced by Parliament. Here again the Socialist philosophy of history provides the key to the problem – points to the economic development as the true solution. The sudden advance of trade in the period in question was almost solely due to the introduction of mechanical power, and the consequent cheapening of manufactured goods. It was the era of the Industrial Revolution when the domestic industries we had inherited from the Middle Ages were finally replaced by the factory system of modern times. The warping frame, invented by Arkwright in 1769; the spinning jenny, patented by Hargreaves in 1770; Crampton's mechanical mule, introduced in 1779; and the application in 1778 of the steam-engine to blast-furnaces, all combined to cheapen the cost of production, and so to lower the price of goods in the various industries affected. This brought into the field fresh hosts of customers, and so gave an immense impetus to trade in general in Great Britain as well as in Ireland. Between 1782 and 1804 the cotton trade more than trebled its total output; between 1783 and 1796 the linen trade increased nearly threefold; in the eight years between 1788 and 1796 the iron trade doubled in volume. The latter trade did not long survive this burst of prosperity. The invention of smelting by coal instead of wood in 1750, and the application of steam to blast-furnaces, already spoken of, placed the Irish manufacturer at an enormous disadvantage in dealing with his English rival, but in the halcyon days of brisk trade – between 1780 and 1800. – this was not very acutely felt. But, when trade once more assumed its normal aspect of keen competition, Irish manufacturers, without a native coal supply, and almost entirely dependent on imported English coal, found it impossible to compete with their trade rivals in the sister country who, with abundant supplies of coal at their own door, found it very easy, before the days of railways, to undersell and ruin the unfortunate Irish. The same fate, and for the same reason, befell the other important Irish trades. The period marked politically by Grattan's Parliament was a period of commercial inflation due to the introduction of mechanical improvements into the staple industries of the country. As long as such machinery was worked by hand, Ireland could hold her place on the markets, but with this application of steam to the service of industry, which began on a small scale in 1785, and the introduction of the power-loom, which first came into general use about 1813, the immense natural advantage of an indigenous coal supply finally settled the contest in favour of English manufacturers.

A native Parliament might have hindered the subsequent decay, as an alien Parliament may have hastened it; but in either case, under capitalistic conditions, the process itself was as inevitable as the economic evolution of which it was one of the most significant signs. How little Parliament had to do with it may be gauged by comparing the positions of Ireland and Scotland. In the year 1799, Mr. Foster in the Irish Parliament stated that the production of linen was twice as great in Ireland as in Scotland. The actual figures given were for the year 1796 – 23,000,000 yards for Scotland as against 46,705,319 for Ireland. This discrepancy in favour of Ireland he attributed to the native Parliament.[34] But by the year 1830, according to *McCulloch's Commercial Dictionary*, the one port of Dundee in Scotland exported more linen than all Ireland.[35] Both countries had been deprived of self-government. Why had Scottish manufacture advanced whilst that of Ireland had decayed? Because Scotland possessed a native coal supply, and every facility for industrial pursuits which Ireland lacked.

The 'prosperity' of Ireland under Grattan's Parliament was almost as little due to that Parliament as the dust caused by the revolutions of the coach-wheel was due to the presence of the fly who, sitting on the coach, viewed the dust, and fancied himself the author thereof. And, therefore,

---

[34] John Foster, 1st Baron Oriel (1740–1828), Irish politician, Member of Parliament for Louth and last Speaker of the Irish Parliament.

[35] John Ramsay McCulloch (1789–1864), Scottish economist and author. *A Dictionary, Practical, Theoretical and Historical of Commerce and Commercial Navigation* was published in 1832.

true prosperity cannot be brought to Ireland except by measures somewhat more drastic than that Parliament ever imagined.

Chapter VI: Capitalist Betrayal of the Irish Volunteers

> 'Remember still, through good and ill,
> How vain were prayers and tears.
> How vain were words till flashed the swords
> Of the Irish Volunteers'.
>
> Thomas Davis[36]

The theory that the fleeting 'prosperity' of Ireland in the time we refer to was caused by the Parliament of Grattan is only useful to its propagators as a prop to their argument that the Legislative Union between Great Britain and Ireland destroyed the trade of the latter country, and that, therefore, the repeal of that Union placed all manufactures on a paying basis. The fact that the Union placed all Irish manufactures upon an absolutely equal basis legally with the manufactures of England is usually ignored, or, worse, still, is so perverted in its statement as to leave the impression that the reverse is the case. In fact many thousands of our countrymen still believe that English laws prohibit mining in Ireland after certain minerals, and the manufacture of certain articles.

A moment's reflection should remove such an idea. An English capitalist will cheerfully invest his money in Timbuctoo or China, or Russia, or anywhere that he thinks he can secure a profit, even though it may be in the territory of his mortal enemy. He does not invest his money in order to give employment to his workers, but to make a profit, and hence it would be foolish to expect that he would allow his Parliament to make laws prohibiting him from opening mines or factories in Ireland to make a profit out of the Irish workers. And there are not, and have not been since the Union, any such laws.

If a student desires to continue the study of this remarkable controversy in Irish history, and to compare this Parliamentarian theory of Irish industrial decline with that we have just advanced – the Socialist theory outlined in our previous chapter – he has an easy and effective course to pursue in order to bring this matter to the test. Let him single out the most prominent exponents of Parliamentarianism and propound the following question:

---

[36] Thomas Davis, *Song of the Volunteers of 1782*, first published in the Young Ireland paper, *The Nation*, in 1845.

Please explain the process by which the removal of Parliament from Dublin to London – a removal absolutely unaccompanied by any legislative interference with Irish industry – prevented the Irish capitalistic class from continuing to produce goods for the Irish market?

He will get no logical answer to his question – no answer that any reputable thinker on economic questions would accept for one moment. He will instead undoubtedly be treated to a long enumeration of the number of tradesmen and labourers employed at manufactures in Ireland before the Union, and the number employed at some specific period, 20 or 30 years afterwards. This was the method adopted by Daniel O'Connell, the Liberator, in his first great speech in which he began his Repeal agitation, and has been slavishly copied and popularised by all his imitators since.[37] *But neither O'Connell nor any of his imitators have ever yet attempted to analyse and explain the process by which those industries were destroyed.* The nearest approach to such an explanation ever essayed is the statement that the Union led to absentee landlordism and the withdrawal of the custom of these absentees from Irish manufacturers. Such an explanation is simply no explanation at all. It is worse than childish. Who would seriously contend that the loss of a few thousand aristocratic clients killed, for instance, the leather industry, once so flourishing in Ireland and now scarcely existent. The district in the city of Dublin which lies between Thomas Street and the South Circular Road was once a busy hive of men engaging in the tanning of leather and all its allied trades. Now that trade has almost entirely disappeared from this district. Were the members of Irish Parliament and the Irish landlords the only wearers of shoes in Ireland? – the only persons for whose use leather was tanned and manufactured? If not, how did their emigration to England make it impossible for the Irish manufacturer to produce shoes or harness for the millions of people still left in the country after the Union? The same remark applies to the weavers, once so flourishing a body in the same district, to the woollen trade, to the fishing trade, and so down along the line. The people of Ireland still wanted all these necessaries of life after the Union just as much as before, yet the superficial historian tells us that the Irish manufacturer was unable to cater to their demand, and went out of business accordingly. Well, we Irish are credited with being gifted with a strong sense of humour, but one is almost

---

[37] Daniel O'Connell (1775–1847), Irish politician, Member of Parliament, and campaigner for the repeal of the Penal Laws – 'Catholic Emancipation' – and for the repeal of the Act of Union. Emancipation was won in 1829.

inclined to doubt it in the face of gravity with which the Parliamentary theory has been accepted by the masses of the Irish people.

It surely is an amusing theory when we consider that it implies that the Irish manufacturers were so heartbroken, grieving over losing the trade of a few thousand rack-renting landlords, that they could not continue to make a profit by supplying the wants of the millions of Irish people at their doors. The English and the Scotch, the French and the Belgian manufacturers, miners, merchants, and fishermen could and did wax fat prosperous by supplying the wants of the Irish commonalty, but the Irish manufacturer could not. He had to shut up shop and go to the poorhouse because my Lord Rackrent of Castle Rackrent, and his immediate personal following, had moved to London.[38]

If our Parliamentarian historians had not been the most superficial of all recorders of history; if their shallowness had not been so phenomenal that there is no equal to it to be found except in the bigotry and stupidity of their loyalist rivals, they might easily have formulated from the same set of facts another theory equally useful to their cause, and more in consonance with the truth. That other theory may be stated thus: –

That the Act of Union was made possible because Irish manufacture was weak, and, consequently, Ireland had not an energetic capitalist class with sufficient public spirit and influence to prevent the Union.

Industrial decline having set in, the Irish capitalist class was not able to combat the influence of the corruption fund of the English Government, or to create and lead a party strong enough to arrest the demoralisation of Irish public life. This we are certain is the proper statement of the case. Not that the loss of the Parliament destroyed Irish manufacture, but that the decline of Irish manufacture, due to causes already outlined, made possible the destruction of the Irish Parliament. Had a strong enterprising and successful Irish capitalist class been in existence in Ireland, a Parliamentary reform investing the Irish masses with the suffrage would have been won under the guns of the Volunteers without a drop of blood being shed; and with a Parliament elected under such conditions the Act of Union would have been impossible. But the Irish capitalist class used the Volunteers to force commercial reforms from the English Government and then, headed by Henry Grattan, forsook

---

[38] 'Rack-renting' was the charging of an extortionate rent by landlords in Britain and Ireland in the eighteenth and nineteenth centuries. Maria Edgeworth's novel *Castle Rackrent* (1800) was a notable parody and critique of the Anglo-Irish landlord class, and is often held to be the inaugural Irish novel.

and denounced the Volunteers when that body sought, by reforming the representative system, to make it more responsive to the will of the people, and thus to secure in peace what they had won by the threat of violence. An Ireland controlled by popular suffrage would undoubtedly have sought to save Irish industry, while it was yet time, by a stringent system of protection which would have imposed upon imported goods a tax heavy enough to neutralise the advantages accruing to the foreigner from his coal supply, and such a system might have averted that decline of Irish industry which, as we have already stated, was otherwise inevitable. But the only hope of realising that Ireland lay then in the armed force of the Volunteers; and as the capitalist class did not feel themselves strong enough as a class to hold the ship of state against the aristocracy on the one hand and the people on the other, they felt impelled to choose the only alternative – viz., to elect to throw in their lot with one or other of the contending parties. They chose to put their trust in the aristocracy, abandoned the populace, and as a result were deserted by the class whom they had trusted, and went down into bankruptcy and slavery with the class they had betrayed.

A brief glance at the record of the Volunteer movement will illustrate the far-reaching treachery with which the capitalist class of Ireland emulated their aristocratic compatriots who

> sold for place or gold,
> Their country and their God.

but, unlike them, contrived to avoid the odium their acts deserved.

At the inception of this movement Ireland was under the Penal Laws. Against the Roman Catholic, statutes unequalled in ferocity were still upon the statute books. Those laws, although ostensibly designed to convert Catholics to the Protestant Faith, were in reality chiefly aimed at the conversion of Catholic-owned property into Protestant-owned property. The son of a Catholic property-holder could dispossess his own father and take possession of his property simply by making affidavit that he, the son, had accepted the Protestant religion. Thenceforth the father would be by law a pensioner upon the son's bounty. The wife of a Catholic could deprive her husband of all control over his property by simply becoming a Protestant. A Catholic could not own a horse worth more than £5. If he did, any Protestant could take his horse from him in the light of day and give him £5 in full payment of all rights in the horse. On the head of a Catholic schoolmaster or a Catholic priest the same price was put as on the head of a wolf. Catholics were eligible to no public office, and were debarred from most of the professions.

In fact the Catholic religion was an illegal institution. Yet it grew and flourished, and incidentally it may be observed it secured a hold upon the affections and in the hearts of the Irish people as rapidly as it lost the same hold in France and Italy, where the Catholic religion was a dominant state institution – a fact worth noting by those Catholics who are clamouring for the endowment of Catholic institutions out of public funds.

It must be remembered by the student, however, that the Penal Laws, although still upon the statute book, had been largely inoperative before the closing quarter of the eighteenth century. This was not due to any clemency on the part of the English Government, but was the result of the dislike of those laws felt by the majority of intelligent Irish Protestants. The latter simply refused to take advantage of them even to their personal aggrandisement, and there are very few cases on actual record where the property of Catholics was wrested from them by their Protestant neighbours as a result of the Penal Laws in the generations following the close of the Williamite war. These laws were in fact too horrible to be enforced, and in this matter public opinion was far ahead of legislative enactment. All historians agree upon this point.

Class lines, on the other hand, were far more strictly drawn than religious lines, as they always were in Ireland since the break up of the clan system, and as they are to this day. We have the words of such an eminent authority as Archbishop Whately in this connection, which coming, as they do, from the pen of a supporter of the British Government and of the Protestant Establishment, are doubly valuable as witness to the fact that Irish politics and divisions turn primarily around questions of property and only nominally around questions of religion.[39] He says:

> 'Many instances have come to my knowledge of the most furious Orangemen stripping their estates of a Protestant tenantry who had been there for generations and letting their land to Roman Catholics ... at an advance of a shilling an acre.'[40]

These Protestants so evicted, be it remembered, were the men and women whose fathers had saved Ireland for King William and Protestantism, as against King James and Catholicity, and the evictions

---

[39] Richard Whately (1787–1863), English economist and theologian, Church of Ireland Archbishop of Dublin, and professor of political economy at Trinity College Dublin.

[40] Quoted from Elizabeth Jane Whately, *The Life and Correspondence of Richard Whately, Late Archbishop of Dublin* (1866).

here recorded were the rewards of their father's victory and their own fidelity. In addition to this class line on the economic field the political representation of the country was the exclusive property of the upper class.

A majority of the members of the Irish Parliament sat as the nominees of certain members of the aristocracy who owned the estates on which the boroughs which they 'represented' were situated. Such boroughs were called 'Pocket Boroughs' from the fact that they were as much under the control of the landed aristocrat as if he carried them in his pocket. In addition to this, throughout the entire island the power of electing members of Parliament was the exclusive possession of a privileged few. The great mass of the Catholic and Protestant population were voteless.

This was the situation when the Volunteer movement arose. There were thus three great political grievances before the Irish public. The English Parliament had prohibited Irish trade with Europe and America except through an English port, thus crippling the development of Irish capitalism; representation in the House of Commons in Dublin was denied alike to Protestant and Catholic workers, and to all save a limited few Protestant capitalists, and the nominees of the aristocracy; and finally all Catholics were suffering under religious disabilities. As soon as the Volunteers (all of whom were Protestants) had arms in their hands they began to agitate for the removal of all these grievances.

On the first all were unanimous, and accordingly when they paraded the streets of Dublin on the day of the assembling of Parliament, they hung upon the mouths of their cannon placards bearing the significant words:

FREE TRADE OR ELSE

– and the implied threat from a united people in arms won their case. Free Trade was granted. And at that moment an Irish Republic could have been won as surely as Free Trade. But when the rank and file of the Volunteers proceeded to outline their demands for the removal of their remaining political grievances – to demand popular representation in Parliament – all their leaders deserted. They had elected aristocrats, glib-tongued lawyers and professional patriots to be their officers, and all higher ranks betrayed them in their hour of need. After the granting of Free Trade a Volunteer convention was summoned to meet in Dublin to consider the question of popular representation in Parliament. Lord Charlemont, the commander-in-chief of the body, repudiated the convention; his example was followed by all the lesser fry of the aristocratic officers, and finally when it did meet, Henry Grattan, whose political and personal fortunes the Volunteers had made, denounced them in Parliament as 'an armed rabble'.[41]

The convention, after some fruitless debate, adjourned in confusion, and on a subsequent attempt to convene another Convention the meeting was prohibited by Government proclamation and the signers of the call for the assembly were arrested and heavily fined. The Government, having made peace in America, with the granting of American independence, had been able to mass troops in Ireland and prepare to try conclusions with the Volunteers. Its refusal to consider the demand for popular representation was its gage of battle, and the proclamation of the last attempt at a Convention was the sign of its victory. The Volunteers had, in fact, surrendered without a blow. The responsibility for this shameful surrender rests entirely upon the Irish capitalist class. Had they stood by the reformers, the defection of the aristocracy would have mattered little, indeed it is certain that the radical element must have foreseen and had been prepared for that defection. But the act of the merchants in throwing in their lot with the aristocracy could not have been foreseen; it was too shameful an act to be anticipated by any but its perpetrators. It must not be imagined, moreover, that these reactionary elements made no attempt to hide their treason to the cause of freedom.

On the contrary, they were most painstaking in keeping up the appearance of popular sympathies and in endeavouring to divert public attention along other lines than those on which the real issues were staked. There is a delicious passage in the *Life of Henry Grattan*, edited by his son, describing the manner in which the Government obtained possession of the arms of the various corps of Dublin Volunteers, which presents in itself a picture in microcosm of very many epochs of Irish history and illustrates the salient characteristics of the classes and the part they play in Irish public life.[42]

Dublin is Ireland in miniature; nay, Dublin is Ireland in concentrated essence. All that makes Ireland great or miserable, magnificent or squalid, ideally revolutionary or hopelessly reactionary, grandly unselfish or vilely treacherous, is stronger and more pronounced in Dublin than elsewhere in Ireland. Thus the part played by Dublin in any National crisis is sure to be simply a metropolitan setting for the role played by the same passions throughout the Irish provinces. Hence

---

[41] James Caulfeild, 1st Earl of Charlemont (1728–1799), Irish politician and patriot, first President of the Royal Irish Academy.

[42] *Memoirs of the Life and Times of the Rt. Hon. Henry Grattan, by his son*, 5 vols. (1839–46).

the value of the following unconscious contribution to the study of Irish history from the pen of the son of Henry Grattan.

In Dublin there were three divisions of Volunteers – corresponding to the three popular divisions of the 'patriotic' forces. There was the Liberty Corps, recruited exclusively from the working class; the Merchants Corps, composed of the capitalist class, and the Lawyers Corps, the members of the legal fraternity. Henry Grattan, Jr., telling of the action of the Government after the passage of the *Arms and Gunpowder Bill* requiring the Volunteers to give up their arms to the authorities for safe keeping, says the Government 'seized the artillery of the Liberty Corps, made a private arrangement by which it got possession of that belonging to the Merchant Corps; they induced the lawyers to give up theirs, first making a public procession before they were surrendered'.

In other words and plainer language, the Government had to use force to seize the arms of the working men, but the capitalists gave up theirs secretly as the result of a private bargain, the terms of which we are not made acquainted with; and the lawyers took theirs through the streets of Dublin in a public parade to maintain the prestige of the legal fraternity in the eyes of the credulous Dublin workers, and then, whilst their throats were still husky from publicly cheering the 'guns of the Volunteers', privately handed those guns over to the enemies of the people.

The working men fought, the capitalists sold out, and the lawyers bluffed.

Then, as ever in Ireland, the fate of the country depended upon the issue of the struggle between the forces of aristocracy and the forces of democracy. The working class in town and the peasantry in the country were enthusiastic over the success of the revolutionary forces in America and France, and were burning with a desire to emulate their deeds in Ireland. But the Irish capitalist class dreaded the people more than they feared the British Government; and in the crisis of their country's fate their influence and counsels were withdrawn from the popular side. Whilst this battle was being fought out with such fatal results to the cause of freedom, there was going on elsewhere in Ireland a more spectacular battle over a mock issue. And as is the wont of things in Ireland this sham battle engrosses the greatest amount of attention in Irish history. We have already alluded to the Henry Flood who made himself conspicuous in the Irish Parliament by out-Heroding Herod in his denunciation of the Government for failing to hang enough peasants to satisfy him. Mr. Henry Grattan we have also introduced to our readers. These two men were the Parliamentary leaders of the 'patriot party' in the House of Commons – the 'rival Harries', as the Dublin crowd sarcastically described them. When the threat of the Volunteers compelled the English authorities to formally renounce all its rights to make laws binding the Irish parliament, these two patriots quarrelled, and, we are seriously informed by the grave historians and learned historians, the subject of their quarrel divided all Ireland. In telling of what that subject was we hope our readers will not accuse us of fooling; we are not, although the temptation is almost irresistible. We are soberly stating the historical facts. The grave and learned historians tell us that Grattan and Flood quarrelled because Flood insisted that England should be required to promise that it would never again interfere to make laws governing the Irish Parliament, and Grattan insisted that it would be an insult to the honour of England to require any such promise.

As we have said, the grave and learned historians declare that all Ireland took sides in this quarrel, even such a hater of England as John Mitchel in his *History of Ireland* seemingly believes this to be the case.[43] Yet we absolutely refuse to give any credence to the story. We are firmly convinced that while Grattan and Flood were splitting the air with declamations upon this subject, if an enquirer had gone down into any Irish harvest field and asked the first reaper he met his opinion of the matter, the said reaper would have touched the heart of the question without losing a single swing of his hook. He would have said truly: –

'An' sure, what does it matter what England promises? Won't she break her promise, anyway as soon as it suits her, and she is able to?'

It is difficult to believe that either Grattan or Flood could have seriously thought that any promise would bind England, a country which even then was notorious all over the world for broken faith and dishonoured treaties. Today the recital of facts of this famous controversy looks like a poor attempt at humour, but in view of the tragic setting of the controversy we must say that it bears the same relation to humour that a joke would in a torture chamber. Grattan and Flood in this case were but two skilful actors indulging in oratorical horse-play at the death-bed of the murdered hopes of a people. Were any other argument, outside of the absurdity of the legal hairsplitting on both sides, needed to prove how little such a sham battle really interested the great mass of the people the record of the two leaders would suffice. Mr. Flood was not only known to be an enemy of the oppressed peasantry and a hater

---

[43] John Mitchel, *The History of Ireland: From the Treaty of Limerick to the Present Time* (1869).

of the Catholics – that is to say, of the great mass of the inhabitants of Ireland – but he had also spoken and voted in the Irish Parliament in favour of a motion to pay the expenses of an army of 10,000 British soldiers to be sent to put down the Revolution in America, and Mr. Grattan on his part had accepted a donation of £50,000 from the Government for his 'patriotic' services, and afterwards, in excess of gratitude for this timely aid, repaid the Government by betraying and denouncing the Volunteers.

On the other great questions of the day they were each occupying an equivocal position, playing fast and loose. For instance: –

Mr. Flood believed in Democracy – amongst Protestants, but opposed religious freedom.

Mr. Grattan believed in religious freedom – amongst property owners, but opposed all extension of the suffrage to the working class.

Mr. Flood would have given the suffrage to all Protestants, rich or poor, and denied it to all Catholics, rich or poor.

Mr. Grattan would have given the vote to every man who owned property, irrespective of religion, and he opposed its extension to any propertyless man. In the Irish House of Commons he bitterly denounced the United Irishmen, of whom we will treat later, for proposing universal suffrage, which he declared would ruin the country and destroy all order.

It will be seen that Mr. Grattan was the ideal capitalist statesman; his spirit was the spirit of the bourgeoisie incarnate. He cared more for the interests of property than for human rights or for the supremacy of any religion.

His early bent in that direction is seen in a letter he sent to his friend, a Mr. Broome, dated November 3, 1767, and reproduced by his son in his edition of the life and speeches of his father. The letter shows the eminently respectable, anti-revolutionary, religious Mr. Henry Grattan to have been at heart, a free thinker, free-lover, and epicurean philosopher, who had early understood the wisdom of not allowing these opinions to be known to the common multitude whom he aspired to govern. We extract: –

> 'You and I, in this as in most other things, perfectly agree; we think marriage is an artificial, not a natural, institution, and imagine women too frail a bark for so long and tempestuous a voyage as that of life . . . I have become an epicurean philosopher; consider this world as our *ne plus ultra*, and happiness as our great object in it . . . Such a subject is too extensive and too dangerous for a letter; in our privacy we shall dwell upon it more copiously.'

This, be it noted, is perhaps not the Grattan of the poet Moore's rhapsody, but it is the real Grattan.[44]

Small wonder that the Dublin mob stoned this Grattan on his return from England, on one occasion, after attending parliament in London. His rhetoric and heroics did not deceive them, even if they did bewitch the historians. His dramatic rising from a sick bed to appear before the purchased traitors who sold their votes to carry the Union, in order to appeal to them not to fulfil their bargain, makes indeed a fine tableau for romantic historians to dwell upon, but it was a poor compensation to the common people for the Volunteers insulted and betrayed, and the cause of popular suffrage opposed and misrepresented.

A further and, to our mind, conclusive proof of the manner in which the 'Parliament of '82' was regarded by the real Nationalists and progressive thinkers of Ireland is to be found in the extract below from the famous pamphlet written by Theobald Wolfe Tone and published September, 1791, entitled *An Argument on behalf of the Catholics of Ireland*[45] It is interesting to recall that this biting characterisation of the 'glorious revolution of 1782' from the pen of the most far-seeing Irishman of his day, has been so little to the liking of our historians and journalists that it was rigidly boycotted by them all until the present writer reprinted it in 1897, in Dublin, in a series of *'98 Readings* containing also many other forgotten and inconvenient documents of the same period. Since then it has several times been republished exactly as we reprinted the extract, but to judge by the manner in which some of our friends still declare they 'stand upon the constitution of '82' it has been published in vain for some people.

WOLFE TONE ON GRATTAN'S PARLIAMENT

(Extract from the famous pamphlet, *An Argument on behalf of the Catholics of Ireland*, published September, 1791)

I have said that we have no National Government. Before the year 1782 it was not pretended that we had, and it is at least a curious, if not a useful, speculation to examine how we stand in that regard now. And I have little dread of being confuted, when I assert that all we got by what we are pleased to dignify with the name of Revolution was simply the means of doing good according to law, without recurring to the

---

[44] Thomas Moore (1779–1852), Irish poet and songwriter, famous for ballads such as *The Minstrel Boy*.
[45] Theobald Wolfe Tone (1763–1798), Irish politician and revolutionary, a founder of the Society of United Irishmen, and father of Irish republicanism.

great rule of nature, which is above all positive Statutes; whether we have done good or not, why we have omitted to do good is a serious question. The pride of the nation, the vanity of individuals concerned, the moderation of some honest men, the corruption of knaves, I know may be alarmed when I assert that the revolution of 1782 was the most bungling, imperfect business that ever threw ridicule on a lofty epithet, by assuming it unworthily. It is not pleasant to any Irishman to make such a concession, but it cannot be helped if truth will have it so. It is much better to delude ourselves or be gulled by our enemies with praises which we do not deserve, or imaginary blessings which we do not enjoy.

I leave to the admirers of that era to vent flowing declamations on its theoretical advantages, and its visionary glories; it is a fine subject, and peculiarly flattering to my countrymen, many of whom were actors, and almost all spectators of it. Be mine the unpleasing task to strip it of its plumage and its tinsel, and show the naked figure. The operation will be severe, but if properly attended to may give us a strong and striking lesson of caution and of wisdom.

The Revolution of 1782 was a Revolution which enabled Irishmen to sell at a much higher price their honour, their integrity, and the interests of their country; it was a Revolution which, while at one stroke it doubled the value of every borough-monger in the kingdom, left three-fourths of our countrymen slaves as it found them, and the government of Ireland in the base and wicked and contemptible hands who had spent their lives in degrading and plundering her; nay, some of whom had given their last vote decidedly, though hopelessly, against this, our famous Revolution. Who of the veteran enemies of the country lost his place or his pension? Who was called forth to station or office from the ranks of opposition? Not one. The power remained in the hands of our enemies, again to be exerted for our ruin, with this difference, that formerly we had our distress, our injuries, and our insults gratis at the hands of England; but now we pay very dearly to receive the same with aggravation, through the hands of Irishmen – yet this we boast of and call a Revolution!

And so we close this chapter on the Volunteers – a chapter of great opportunities lost, of popular confidence betrayed. A few extracts from some verses written at the time in Dublin serve as an epitome of the times, even if they do seem a little bitter.

> Who aroused the people?
> The rival Harries rose
> And pulled each other's nose.
> And said they aroused the people.

> What did the Volunteers?
> They mustered and paraded
> Until their laurels faded.
> Thus did the Volunteers.
>
> How died the Volunteers?
> The death that's fit for slaves.
> They slunk into their graves.

Chapter VII: The United Irishmen

'Our freedom must be had at all hazards. If the men of property will not help us they must fall; we will free ourselves by the aid of that large and respectable class of the community – the men of no property.'[46]
– Theobald Wolfe Tone

Contemporaneously with the betrayal and fall of the Volunteers, Ireland witnessed the rise and progress of the Society of United Irishmen. This organisation was at first an open, peaceful association, seeking to utilise the ordinary means of political agitation in order to spread its propaganda among the masses and so prepare them for the accomplishment of its greater end – viz., the realisation in Ireland of a republic on the lines of that established in France at the Revolution. Afterwards, unable to maintain its public character in face of the severe persecution by the British Government of anything savouring in the least of a democratic nature, the organisation assumed the veil and methods of secrecy, and in that form attained to such proportions as enabled it to enter into negotiations with the Revolutionary Directory of France on the basis of an equal treaty making national power.[47] As the result of this secret treaty between Revolutionary France and Revolutionary Ireland against the common enemy, aristocratic England, various fleets and armies were dispatched from the Continent to assist the Irish Republicans, but all of those expeditions were disastrous in their outcome. The first, under the command of Grouchy and Hoche, was dispersed by a storm, some of the ships being compelled to return to France for repairs, and when the remainder, including the greater part of the army, reached Bantry Bay, on the Irish coast, the French commander exhibited to the full all that hesitation, indecision and lack of initiative which he afterwards was to show with equally fatal results to Napoleon on the eve of the

---

[46] Quoted from William Theobald Wolfe Tone, *Life of Theobald Wolfe Tone* (1826).
[47] The Directory was the government of revolutionary France in the period 1795–1799. A committee of five members, it was overthrown by Napoleon.

battle of Waterloo.[48] Finally, despite the desperate protests of the Irish Revolutionists on board, he weighed anchor and returned to France without striking a blow or landing a corporal's guard. Had he been a man equal to the occasion and landed his expedition, Ireland would almost undoubtedly have been separated from England and become mistress of her own national destinies.

Another expedition, fitted out by the Dutch Republic in alliance with France, was detained by contrary winds in the harbour until the British fleet had time to come upon the scene, and then the Dutch commander chivalrously but foolishly accepted the British challenge to fight, and, contending under unequal and adverse conditions, was defeated.

An unauthorised but gallant attempt was made under another French officer, General Humbert, and this actually landed in Ireland, proclaimed the Irish Republic at Killala, in Connacht, armed large numbers of the United Irishmen amongst the inhabitants, and in conjunction with these latter fought and utterly routed a much superior British force at Castlebar, and penetrated far into the country before it was surrounded and compelled to surrender to a force more than ten times its own in number.[49] The numbers of the French expedition in this case were insufficient for the purposes of making a stand long enough to permit of the people reaching it and being armed and organised efficiently, and hence its failure. But had Humbert possessed the number commanded by Grouchy, or Grouchy possessed the dash and daring of Humbert, the Irish Republic would have been born, for weal or woe, in 1798. It is a somewhat hackneyed observation, but so true that it compels repetition, that the elements did more for England than her armies. Indeed, whether in conflict with the French expeditionary force of Humbert, with the Presbyterians and Catholics of the United Irish Army under General Munro in the North, or with the insurgent forces of Wicklow, Wexford, Kildare and Dublin, the British army can scarcely be said to have any time justified its reputation, let alone covered itself with glory. All the glory was, indeed, on the other side, as was also most of the humanity, and all of the zeal for human freedom. The people were wretchedly armed, totally undrilled, and compelled to act without any systematic plan of campaign, because of the sudden arrest and imprisonment of their leaders. Yet they fought and defeated the British troops on a score of battlefields, despite the fact that the latter were thoroughly

---

[48] Emmanuel de Grouchy (1766–1847), French general. Louis Lazare Hoche (1768–1797), French general, also known for his defeat of Royalist forces in the Vendée.

[49] Jean Joseph Amable Humbert (1767–1823), French general.

disciplined, splendidly armed, and directed like a huge machine, from one common centre. To suppress the insurrection in the counties of Wicklow and Wexford alone required all the efforts of 30,000 soldiers; had the plans of the United Irishmen for a concerted uprising all over the island on a given date not failed, the task of coping with the Republican forces would have been too great for the Government to achieve. As it was, the lack of means of communication prevalent in those days made it possible for the insurrection in any one district to be almost fought and lost before news of its course had penetrated into other parts of the country.

While the forces of republicanism and of despotism were thus contending for supremacy upon the land, the victory was being in reality decided for the latter by its superiority upon the sea. The successes of the British fleet alone made it possible to keep the shores of England free of invading enemies, and to enable Pitt, the English Prime Minister, to subsidise and maintain the armies of the allied despots of Europe in their conflict with the forces of freedom and progress throughout the Continent.[50] In the face of this undoubted fact, it is somewhat humiliating to be compelled to record that the overwhelming majority of those serving upon that fleet were Irishmen. But, unlike those serving in the British army, the sailors and marines of the navy were there against their own will. During the coercive proceedings of the British Government in Ireland, in their attempt to compel the revolutionary movement to explode prematurely, the authorities suspended the Habeas Corpus Act (the guarantee of ordinary legal procedure) and instituted Martial Law and Free Quarters for the Military. Under the latter system the soldiery were forced as boarders upon the civilian population, each family being compelled to provide food and lodging for a certain number. For all attempts at resistance, or all protests arising out of the licentious conduct of the brutal soldiery, or all incautious expressions overheard by them during their unwelcome residence in the houses of the people, the authorities had one great sovereign remedy – viz., the transportation on board the British fleet.

Thousands of young men were seized all over the island and marched in chains to the various harbours, from thence taken on board the English men of war ships, and there compelled to fight for the Government that had broken up their homes, ruined their lives and desolated their

---

[50] William Pitt the Younger (1759–1806), British politician and prime minister (1783–1801 and 1804–1806), architect of the Act of Union; tried but failed to pass legislation for Catholic Emancipation.

country. Whenever any district was suspected of treasonable sympathies it was first put under Martial Law, then every promising young man was seized and thrown into prison on suspicion and without trial, and then those who were not executed or flogged to the point of death were marched on board the fleet. All over Ireland, but especially in Ulster and Leinster during the closing years of the 18th and the opening of the 19th century, the newspapers and private letters of the time are full of records of such proceedings, telling of the vast numbers everywhere sent on board the fleet as a result of the wholesale dragooning of the people. Great numbers of these were United Irishmen, sworn to an effort to overthrow the despotism under which the people of Ireland suffered, and as a result of their presence on board, every British ship soon became a nest of conspirators. The 'Jack Tars of Old England' were conspiring to destroy the British Empire, and any one at all acquainted with the facts relative to their treatment by their superiors and the authorities cannot wonder at their acts. The subject is not loved by the jingo historians of the English governing classes, and is consequently usually complacently lied about, but, as a cold matter of fact 'the wooden walls of England', so beloved of the poets of that country, were in reality veritable floating hells to the poor sailors and marines.

Flogging for the most trivial offences was inflicted, upon the unsupported word of the most petty officer; the quarters in which the men were compelled to sleep and eat below decks were of the vilest and most unsanitary conditions; the food was of the filthiest, and every man had to pay tribute to a greedy quarter master in order to escape actual starvation, and the whole official life of the ship, from the captain down to the youngest midshipman, was based upon the wealth and rank and breathed hatred and contempt for anything belonging to the lower classes. Mutinies and attempts at mutiny were consequently of constant occurrence, and, therefore, the forcibly impressed United Irishmen found a fertile field for their operations. In the Government records of naval court-martials at that time, the charge of 'administering the secret oath of the United Irishmen' is one of the commonest against the accused, and the number of men shot and transported beyond seas for this offence is simply enormous. English and Scottish sailors were freely sworn into the ranks of the conspirators, and the numbers of those disaffected grew to such an extent that on one occasion – the mutiny of the Nore – the sailors were able to revolt, depose their officers, and take command of the fleet. The wisest heads amongst them, the original United Irishmen, proposed to sail the ships into a French port and turn them over to the French Government, and for a time they had great hopes of accomplishing this purpose, but finally they were compelled to accede to a proposal to attempt to win over the sailors on some other ships in the port of London before sailing to France. This they did, and even threatened to bombard the city; but the delay had enabled the Government to rally its loyal ships, and also enabled the 'loyal' slaves still on board the revolting ships to play upon the 'patriotic' feelings of the waverers among the British mutineers by representing to them the probability of their being confined in French prisons instead of welcomed as allies. In the end the admiral and officers, by promising a 'redress of their just grievances' succeeded in winning over a sufficient number on each ship to paralyse any chance of resistance, and the mutiny was quenched. The usual tale of shootings, floggings, and transportations followed, but the conditions of life on board ship were long in being altered for the better. It may be wondered that the men forcibly impressed, and the conspirators against a tyrannical Government could fight for that Government as did those unfortunates under Nelson, but it must be borne in mind that once on board a war vessel and that vessel brought into action with an enemy in the open sea, there was no possibility of escape or even of co-operation with the enemy; the necessity of self-preservation compelled the rebellious United Irishmen or the discontented mutineers to fight as loyally for the ship as did the soulless slaves amongst whom they found themselves. And being better men, with more manhood they undoubtedly fought better.

In concluding this brief summary of this aspect of that great democratic upheaval we desire to quote from the *Press*, the organ of the United Irishmen, published in Dublin, the following short news item of the period, which we trust will be found highly illustrative of the times in question, as well as a confirmation of the points we have set forth above: –

ROASTING

'Near Castle Ward, a northern hamlet, a father and son had their heads roasted on their own fire to extort a confession of concealed arms. The cause was that the lock of a gun was found in an old box belonging to the wife of the elder man. It is a fact that the above old couple had two sons serving on board the British fleet, one under Lord Bridgport, the other under Lord St. Vincent'.

Chapter VIII: United Irishmen as Democrats and Internationalists

'Och, Paddies, my hearties, have done wid your parties,
Let min of all creeds and professions agree,
If Orange and Green, min, no longer were seen, min,
Och, naboclis, how aisy ould Ireland we'd free.'
Jamie Hope, 1798[51]

As we have pointed out elsewhere (*Erin's Hope: the End and the Means*) native Irish civilisation disappeared, for all practical purposes, with the defeat of the Insurrection of 1641 and the break-up of the Kilkenny Confederation.[52] This great Insurrection marked the last appearance of the Irish clan system, founded upon common property and a democratic social organisation, as a rival to the politico-social order of capitalist feudalism founded upon the political despotism of the proprietors, and the political and the social slavery of the actual producers. In the course of this Insurrection the Anglo-Irish noblemen, who held Irish tribelands as their private property under the English feudal system, did indeed throw in their lot with the native Irish tribesmen, but the union was never a cordial one, and their presence in the councils of the insurgents was at all times a fruitful source of dissension, treachery and incapacity. Professing to fight for Catholicity, they, in reality, sought only to preserve their right to the lands they held as the result of previous confiscations, from the very men, or the immediate ancestors of the men, by whose side they were fighting. They feared confiscation from the new generation of Englishmen if the insurrection was defeated, and they feared confiscation at the hands of the insurgent clansmen if the insurrection was successful.

In the vacillation and treachery arising out of this state of mind can be found the only explanation for the defeat of this magnificent movement of the Irish clans, a movement which had attained to such proportions

---

[51] James 'Jemmy' Hope (1764–1847), a senior figure amongst the United Irishmen, of particularly radical and anti-bourgeois leanings. Took part in the rebellions of 1798 and 1803.

[52] The 1641 Rebellion was an uprising against English rule by the residual Catholic Irish aristocracy, in the wake of the Tudor and Stuart colonisations. It helped to initiate the English Civil War, and contributed to a series of wars in Ireland in the 1650s, culminating in defeat by Oliver Cromwell and the English New Model Army. The Kilkenny Confederation, also known as the Catholic Confederation, was the de facto government of Ireland between 1642 and 1649, composed of Irish Catholic nobles, soldiers and clergy.

that it held sway over and made laws for the greater part of Ireland, issued its own coinage, had its own fleet, and issued letters of marque to foreign privateers, made treaties with foreign nations, and levied taxes for the support of its several armies fighting under its flag.[53] The fact that it had enrolled under its banner the representatives of two different social systems contained the germs of its undoing. Had it been all feudal it would have succeeded in creating an independent Ireland, albeit with a serf population like that of England at the time; had it been all composed of the ancient septs it would have crushed the English power and erected a really free Ireland, but as it was but a hybrid, composed of both, it had all the faults of both and the strength of neither, and hence went down in disaster. With its destruction, and the following massacres, expropriations and dispersion of the native Irish, the Irish clans disappear finally from history.

Out of these circumstances certain conditions arose, well worthy of the study of every student who would understand modern Irish history.

One condition which thus arose was, that the disappearance of the clan as a rallying point for rebellions and possible base of freedom made it impossible thereafter to localise an insurrectionary effort, or to give it a smaller or more circumscribed aim than that of the Irish Nation. When, before the iron hand of Cromwell, the Irish clans went down into the tomb of a common subjection, the only possible reappearance of the Irish idea henceforth lay through the gateway of a National resurrection. And from that day forward, the idea of common property was destined to recede into the background as an avowed principle of action, whilst the energies of the nation were engaged in a slow and painful process of assimilating the social system of the conqueror; of absorbing the principles of that political society based upon ownership, which had replaced the Irish clan society based upon a common kinship.

Another condition ensuing upon the total disappearance of the Irish Social Order was the growth and accentuation of class distinctions amongst the conquerors. The indubitable fact that from that day forward the ownership of what industries remained in Ireland was left in the hands of the Protestant element, is not to be explained as sophistical anti-Irish historians have striven to explain it, by asserting that it arose from the greater enterprise of Protestants as against Catholics; in reality it was due to the state of social and political outlawry in which the Catholics were henceforth placed by the law of the land. According

---

[53] A letter of marque and reprisal was a licence issued by a government to a private vessel permitting it to attack and capture enemy vessels. This practice was used in Europe from the Middle Ages into the nineteenth century.

to the English Constitution as interpreted for the benefit of Ireland, the Irish Catholics were not presumed to exist, and hence the practical impossibility of industrial enterprise being in their hands, or initiated by them. Thus, as the landed property of the Catholic passed into the ownership of the Protestant adventurers, so also the manufacturing business of the nation fell out of the stricken grasp of the hunted and proscribed 'Papists' into the clutches of their successful and remorseless enemies. Amongst these latter there were two elements – the fanatical Protestant, and the mere adventurer trading on the religious enthusiasm of the former. The latter used the fanaticism of the former in order to disarm, subjugate and rob the common Catholic enemy, and having done so, established themselves as a ruling landed and commercial class, leaving the Protestant soldier to his fate as tenant or artisan. Already by the outbreak of the Williamite war in the generation succeeding Cromwell, the industries of the North of Ireland had so far developed that the 'Prentice Boys' of Derry were the dominating factor in determining the attitude of that city towards the contending English Kings, and, with the close of that war, industries developed so quickly in the country as to become a menace to the capitalists of England, who accordingly petitioned the King of England to restrict and fetter their growth, which he accordingly did.[54] With the passing of this restrictive legislation against Irish industries, Irish capitalism became discontented and disloyal without, as a whole, the power or courage to be revolutionary. It was a re-staging of the ever-recurring drama of English invasion and Anglo-Irish disaffection, with the usual economic background. We have pointed out in a previous chapter how each generation of English adventurers, settling upon the soil as owners, resented the coming of the next generation, and that their so-called Irish patriotism was simply inspired by the fear that they should be dispossessed in their turn as they had dispossessed others. What applies to the land-owning 'patriots' applies also to the manufacturers. The Protestant capitalists, with the help of the English, Dutch, and other adventurers, dispossessed the native Catholics and became prosperous; as their commerce grew it became a serious rival to that of England, and accordingly the English capitalists compelled legislation against it, and immediately the erstwhile 'English Garrison in Ireland' became an Irish 'patriot' party.

---

[54] During the Williamite wars, the city of Derry was laid siege in 1688 by Catholic forces. The city gates were closed by thirteen apprentices. In 1814, a Protestant society, the Apprentice Boys of Derry, was founded to commemorate the siege and the Protestant resistance it embodied.

From time to time many weird and fanciful theories have been evolved to account for the transformation of English settlers of one generation into Irish patriots in the next. We have been told it was the air, or the language, or the religion, or the hospitality, or the lovableness of Ireland; and all the time the naked economic fact, the material reason, was plain as the alleged reason was mythical or spurious. But there are none so blind as those who will not see, yet the fact remains that, since English confiscations of Irish land ceased, no Irish landlord body has become patriotic or rebellious, and since English repressive legislation against Irish manufacturers ceased, Irish capitalists have remained valuable assets in the scheme of English rule in Ireland. So it would appear that since the economic reason ceased to operate, the air, and the language, and the religion, and the hospitality, and the lovableness of Ireland have lost all their seductive capacity, all their power to make an Irish patriot out of an English settler of the propertied classes.

With the development of this 'patriotic' policy amongst the Irish manufacturing class, there had also developed a more intense and aggressive policy amongst the humbler class of Protestants in town and country. In fact, in Ireland at that time, there were not only two nations divided into Catholics and non-Catholics, but each of those two nations in turn was divided into another two: the rich and the poor. The development of industry had drawn large numbers of the Protestant poor from agricultural pursuits into industrial occupations, and the suppression of those latter in the interest of English manufacturers left them both landless and workless. This condition reduced the labourers in town and country to the position of serfs. Fierce competition for farms and for jobs enabled the master class to bend both Protestant and Catholic to its will, and the result was seen in the revolts we have noticed earlier in our history. The Protestant workman and tenant was learning that the Pope of Rome was a very unreal and shadowy danger compared with the social power of his employer or landlord, and the Catholic tenant was awakening to a perception of the fact that under the new social order the Catholic landlord represented the Mass less than the rent-roll. The times were propitious for a union of the two democracies of Ireland. They had travelled from widely different points through the valleys of disillusion and disappointment to meet at last by the unifying waters of a common suffering.

To accomplish this union, and make it a living force in the life of the nation, there was required the activity of a revolutionist with statesmanship enough to find a common point upon which the two elements could unite, and some great event, dramatic enough in its character, to arrest the attention of all and fire them with a common feeling. The first, the

Man, revolutionist and statesman, was found in the person of Theobald Wolfe Tone, and the second, the Event, in the French Revolution. Wolfe Tone had, although a Protestant, been secretary for the Catholic Committee for some time, and in that capacity had written the pamphlet quoted in a previous chapter, but eventually had become convinced that the time had come for more comprehensive and drastic measures than the Committee could possibly initiate, even were it willing to do so.[55] The French Revolution operated alike upon the minds of the Catholic and Protestant democracies to demonstrate this fact, and prepare them for the reception of it. The Protestant workers saw in it a revolution of a great Catholic nation, and hence wavered in the belief so insidiously instilled into them that Catholics were willing slaves of despotism; and the Catholics saw in it a great manifestation of popular power – a revolution of the people against the aristocracy, and, therefore, ceased to believe that aristocratic leadership was necessary for their salvation.

Seizing this propitious moment, Tone and his associates proposed the formation of a society of men of every creed for the purpose of securing an equal representation of all the people in Parliament.

This was, as Tone's later words and works amply prove, intended solely as a means of unity. Knowing well the nature of the times and political oligarchy in power, he realised that such a demand would be resisted with all the power of government; but he wisely calculated that such resistance to a popular demand would tend to make closer and more enduring the union of the democracy, irrespective of religion. And that Tone had no illusions about the value of the aristocracy is proven in scores of passages in his autobiography. We quote one, proving alike this point, and also the determining effect of the French Revolution upon the popular mind in Ireland: –

> 'As the Revolution advanced, and as events expanded themselves, the public spirit of Ireland rose with a rapid acceleration. *The fears and animosities of the aristocracy rose in the same or a still higher proportion.* In a little time the French Revolution became the test of every man's political creed, and the nation was fairly divided into great parties – the aristocrats and democrats borrowed from France, who have ever since been measuring each other's strength and carrying on a kind of smothered war, which the course of events, it is highly probable, may soon call into energy and action.'

---

[55] The Catholic Committee, founded in 1782, was an organisation dedicated to seeking Catholic emancipation, or the repeal of the Penal Laws. It drew on both Irish, and English Catholic support.

It will be thus seen that Tone built up his hopes upon a successful prosecution of a Class War, although those who pretend to imitate him to-day raise up their hands in holy horror at the mere mention of the phrase.

The political wisdom of using a demand for equal representation as a rallying cry for the democracy of Ireland is evidenced by a study of the state of the suffrage at the time. In an *Address from the United Irishmen of Dublin to the English Society of the Friends of the People*, dated Dublin, October 26, 1792, we find the following description of the state of representation: –

> 'The state of Protestant representation is as follows: – seventeen boroughs have no resident elector; sixteen have but one; ninety out of thirteen electors each; ninety persons return for 106 rural boroughs – that is 212 members out of 300 – the whole number; fifty-four members are returned by five noblemen and four bishops; and borough influence has given landlords such power in the counties as to make them boroughs also ... yet the Majesty of the People is still quoted with affected veneration; and if the crown be ostensibly placed in a part of the Protestant portion it is placed there in mockery, for it is encircled with thorns.
>
> 'With regard to the Catholics, the following is the simple and sorrowful fact: – Three millions, every one of whom has an interest in the State, and collectively give it its value, are taxed without being represented, and bound by laws to which they have not given consent.'

The above Address, which is signed by Thomas Wright as secretary, contains one sentence which certain Socialists and others in Ireland and England might well study to advantage, and is also useful as illustrating the thought of the time. It is as follows: –

> 'As to any union between the two islands, believe us when we assert that *our union rests upon our mutual independence. We shall love each other if we be left to ourselves*. It is the union of mind which ought to bind these nations together.'

This, then, was the situation in which the Society of United Irishmen was born. That society was initiated and conducted by men who realised the importance of all those principles of action upon which latter-day Irish revolutionists have turned their backs. Consequently it was as effective in uniting the democracy of Ireland as the 'patriots' of our day have been in keeping it separated into warring religious factions. It understood that the aristocracy was necessarily hostile to the principle and practice of Freedom; it understood that the Irish fight for liberty was but a part of the world-wide upward march of the human race, and hence it allied itself with the revolutionists of Great Britain as well as with those of France, and it said little about ancient glories, and much about modern misery. The *Report of the Secret Committee of the House of Lords* reprinted in full the *Secret Manifesto to the Friends of Freedom in Ireland*, circulated throughout the country by Wolfe Tone and his associates, in the month of June, 1791.[56] As this contains the draft of the designs of the revolutionary association known to history as the Society of United Irishmen, we quote a few passages in support of our contentions, and to show the democratic views of its founders. The manifesto is supposed to have been written by Wolfe Tone in collaboration with Samuel Neilson and others:[57]

> 'It is by wandering from the few plain and simple principles of Political Faith that our politics, like our religion, has become preaching, not practice; words not works. A society such as this will disclaim those party appellations which seem to pale the human hearts into petty compartments, and parcel out into sects and sections common sense, common honesty, and common weal.
>
> 'It will not be an aristocracy, affecting the language of patriotism, the rival of despotism for its own sake, nor its irreconcilable enemy for the sake of us all. It will not, by views merely retrospective, stop the march of mankind or force them back into the lanes and alleys of their ancestors.
>
> 'This society is likely to be a means the most powerful for the promotion of a great end. What end? *The Rights of Man in Ireland*.[58] The greatest happiness of the greatest number in this island, the inherent and indefeasible claim of every free nation to rest in this nation – the will and the power to be happy to pursue the common weal as an individual pursues his private welfare, and to stand in insulated independence, an imperatorial people.
>
> 'The greatest happiness of the Greatest Number. – On the rock of this principle let this society rest; by this let it judge and determine every political question, and whatever is necessary for this end let it not be accounted hazardous, but rather our interest, our duty, our glory and our common religion. The Rights of Man are the Rights of God, and to vindicate the one is to maintain the other. We must be free in order to serve Him whose service is perfect freedom.

---

[56] This manifesto and the previously quoted Address from the United Irishmen of Dublin are listed in the *Reports from the Committees of the House of Commons, printed by order of the House 1715–1801*, published in London 1803–1806.

[57] Samuel Neilson (1761–1803), a founder of the United Irishmen, and founder of the organisation's main newspaper, the *Northern Star*.

[58] The reference here is both to the Declaration of the Rights of Man and the Citizen, promulgated by the French National Constituent Assembly in 1789, and to Thomas Paine's famous book, *Rights of Man*, published in two parts in 1791 and 1792 – the most widely-read political tract in eighteenth century Ireland.

'The external business of this society will be – first, publication, in order to propagate their second principles and effectuate their ends. Second, communications with the different towns to be assiduously kept up and every exertion used to accomplish a National Convention of the People of Ireland, who may profit by past errors and by many unexpected circumstances which have happened since this last meeting. Third, communications with similar societies abroad – as the Jacobin Club of Paris, the Revolutionary Society in England, the Committee for Reform in Scotland.[59] *Let the nations go abreast.* Let the interchange of sentiments among mankind concerning the Rights of Man be as immediate as possible.

'When the aristocracy come forward, the people fall backward; when the people come forward, the aristocracy, fearful of being left behind, insinuate themselves into our ranks and rise into timid leaders or treacherous auxiliaries. They mean to make us their instruments; let us rather make them our instruments. One of the two must happen. The people must serve the party, or the party must emerge in the mightiness of the people, and Hercules will then lean upon his club. On the 14th of July, the day which shall ever commemorate the French Revolution, let this society pour out their first libation to European liberty, eventually the liberty of the world, and, their eyes raised to Heaven in His presence who breathed into them an ever-living soul, let them swear to maintain the rights and prerogatives of their nature as men, and the right and prerogative of Ireland as an independent people.

'Dieu et mon Droit (God and my right) is the motto of kings. Dieu et la liberté (God and liberty), exclaimed Voltaire when he beheld Franklin, his fellow citizen of the world.[60] Dieu et nos Droits (God and our rights), let every Irishman cry aloud to each other, the cry of mercy, of justice, and of victory.'

It would be hard to find in modern Socialist literature anything more broadly International in its scope and aims, more definitely of a class character in its methods, or more avowedly democratic in its nature than this manifesto, yet, although it reveals the inspiration and methods of a revolutionist acknowledged to be the most successful organiser of revolt in Ireland since the days of Rory O'More, all his present-day professed followers constantly trample upon and repudiate every one of these principles, and reject them as a possible guide to their political activity.

---

[59] The Society of the Friends of the Constitution, better known as the Jacobin Club, was the most important and influential political organisation involved in the French Revolution. It was founded in 1789 and dissolved in 1795.

[60] François-Marie Arouet (1694–1778), French man of letters and philosopher better known by his pen-name Voltaire, and one of the greatest figures of the French Enlightenment. Benjamin Franklin (1706–1790), American political theorist, scientist, statesman, and the first ambassador of the United States to France.

The Irish Socialist alone is in line with the thought of this revolutionary apostle of the United Irishmen.⁶¹

The above quoted manifesto was circulated in June, 1791, and in July of the same year the townspeople and volunteer societies of Belfast met to celebrate the anniversary of the Fall of the Bastille, a celebration recommended by the framer of the manifesto as a means of educating and uniting the real people of Ireland – the producers.⁶² From the *Dublin Chronicle* of the time we quote the following passages from the *Declaration of the Volunteers and Inhabitants at Large of the town and neighbourhood of Belfast on the subject of the French Revolution.* As Belfast was then the hot-bed of revolutionary ideas in Ireland, and became the seat of the first society of United Irishmen, and as all other branches of the society were founded upon this original, it will repay us to study the sentiments here expressed.

COLONEL SHERMAN, President

Neither on marble, nor brass, can the rights and duties of men be so durably registered as on their memories and on their hearts. We therefore meet this day to commemorate the French Revolution, that the remembrance of this great event may sink deeply into our hearts, warmed not merely with the fellow-feeling of townsmen, but with a sympathy which binds us to the human race in a brotherhood of interest, of duty and affection.

Here then we take our stand, and if we be asked what the French Revolution is to us, we answer, much. Much as men. It is good for human nature that the grass grows where the Bastille stood. We do rejoice at an event that means the breaking up of civil and religious bondage, when we behold this misshapen pile of abuses, cemented merely by customs, and raised upon the ignorance of a prostrate people, tottering to its base to the very level of equal liberty and commonwealth. We do really rejoice in this resurrection of human nature, and we congratulate our brother-man coming forth from the vaults of ingenious torture and from the cave of death. We do congratulate the Christian World that there is in it one great nation which has renounced all ideas of conquest, and has published the first glorious manifesto of humanity, of union, and of peace. In return we pray to God that peace may rest in their land, and that it may never be in power of royalty, nobility, or a priesthood to disturb the harmony of a good people, consulting about those laws which must ensure their own happiness and that of unborn millions.

---

⁶¹ Rory O'More (d.1578), Irish Gaelic chieftain and rebel against encroaching English rule.

⁶² The Bastille Sainte-Antoine, a major fortress and prison in Paris. Construction began in 1357. Stormed by revolutionaries on 14 July 1789, it was demolished shortly afterwards.

Go on, then – great and gallant people; to practise the sublime philosophy of your legislation, to force applause from nations least disposed to do you justice, and by conquest but by the omnipotence of reason, to convert and liberate the world – a world whose eyes are fixed on you, whose heart is with you, who talks of you with all her tongues; you are in very truth the hope of this world, of all except a few men in a few cabinets who thought the human race belonged to them, not them to the human race; but now are taught by awful example, and tremble, and not dare confide in armies arrayed against you and your cause.

Thus spoke Belfast. It will be seen that the ideas of the publishers of the secret manifesto were striking a responsive chord in the hearts of the people. A series of meetings of the Dublin Volunteer Corps were held in October of the same year, ostensibly to denounce a government proclamation offering a reward for the apprehension of Catholics under arms, but in reality to discuss the political situation. The nature of the conclusions arrived at may be judged by a final paragraph in the resolution, passed 23rd October, 1791, and signed amongst others by James Napper Tandy, on behalf of the Liberty Corps of Artillery.[63] It reads:

'While we admire the philanthropy of that great and enlightened nation, who have set an example to mankind, both of political and religious wisdom, we cannot but lament that distinctions, injurious to both, have too long disgraced the name of Irishmen; and we most fervently wish that our animosities were entombed with the bones of our ancestors; and that we and our Roman Catholic brethren would unite like citizens, *and claim the Rights of Man.*'

This was in October. In the same month Wolfe Tone went to Belfast on the invitation of one of the advanced Volunteer Clubs, and formed the first club of United Irishmen. Returning to Dublin he organised another. From the minutes of the Inauguration Meeting of this First Dublin Society of United Irishmen, held at the Eagle Inn, Eustace Street, 9th November, 1791, we make the following extracts, which speak for the principles of the original members of those two parent clubs of a society destined in a short time to cover all Ireland, and to set in motion the fleets of two foreign auxiliaries.

For the attainment then of this great and important object – the removal of absurd and ruinous distinctions – and for promoting a complete coalition of the people, a club has been formed composed of all religious persuasions who have adopted for their name The Society of

---

[63] James Napper Tandy (1740–1803), senior member of the United Irishmen.

United Irishmen of Dublin, and have taken as their declaration that of a similar society in Belfast, which is as follows: –

In the present great era of reform, when unjust governments are falling in every quarter of Europe, when religious persecution is compelled to abjure her tyranny over conscience; *when the Rights of Man are ascertained in Theory, and that Theory substantiated by Practice*; when antiquity can no longer defend absurd and oppressive forms against the common sense and common interests of mankind; when all government is acknowledged to originate from the people, and to be so far only obligatory as it protects their rights and promotes their welfare; we think it our duty as Irishmen to come forward and state what we feel to be our heavy grievance, and what we know to be its effectual remedy.

We have no National Government; we are ruled by Englishmen and the servants of Englishmen, whose object is the interest of another country; whose instrument is corruption; whose strength is the weakness of Ireland; and these men have the whole of the power and patronage of the country as means to seduce and subdue the honesty and the spirit of her representatives in the legislature. Such an extrinsic power, acting with uniform force in a direction too frequently opposite to the true line of our obvious interests, can be resisted with effect solely by unanimity, decision, and spirit in the people, qualities which may be exerted most legally, constitutionally, and efficaciously by that great measure essential to the prosperity and freedom of Ireland – an equal Representation of all the People in Parliament . . .

We have gone to what we conceive to be the root of the evil; we have stated what we conceive to be the remedy – with a Parliament thus reformed everything is easy; without it nothing can be done.

Here we have a plan of campaign indicated on the lines of those afterwards followed so successfully by the Socialists of Europe – a revolutionary party openly declaring their revolutionary sympathies, but limiting their first demand to a popular measure such as would enfranchise the masses, upon whose support their ultimate success must rest. No one can read the manifesto we have just quoted without realising that these men aimed at nothing less than a social and political revolution such as had been accomplished in France, or even greater, because the French Revolution did not enfranchise all the people, but made a distinction between active and passive citizens, taxpayers and non-taxpayers. Nor yet can an impartial student fail to realise that it was just this daring aim that was the secret of their success as organisers, as it is the secret of the political effectiveness of the Socialists of our day. Nothing less would have succeeded in causing Protestant and Catholic masses to shake hands over the bloody chasm of religious hatreds, nothing less will accomplish the same result in our day among the Irish workers. It must be related to the credit of the leaders of the United Irishmen that they remained true to their principles, even when moderation might have secured a mitigation of their lot. When examined before the Secret Committee of the House of Lords at the prison of Fort George, Scotland, Thomas Addis Emmet did not hesitate to tell his inquisitors that if successful they would have inaugurated a very different social system to that which then prevailed.[64]

Few movements in history have been more consistently misrepresented, by open enemies and professed admirers, than that of the United Irishmen. The *suggestio falsi*, and the *suppressio veri* have been remorselessly used. The middle class 'patriotic' historians, orators, and journalists of Ireland have ever vied with one another in enthusiastic descriptions of their military exploits on land and sea, their hair-breadth escapes and heroic martyrdom, but have resolutely suppressed or distorted their writings, songs and manifestoes. We have striven to reverse the process, to give publicity to their literature, believing that this literature reveals the men better than any partisan biographer can do. Dr. Madden, a most painstaking and conscientious biographer, declares in his volume of *The Literary Remains of the United Irishmen*, that he has suppressed many of their productions because of their 'trashy' republican and irreligious tendencies.[65]

This is to be regretted, as it places upon other biographers and historians the trouble (a thousand times more difficult now) of searching for anew, and re-collecting the literary material from which to build a proper appreciation of the work of those pioneers of democracy in Ireland. And as Irish men and women progress to a truer appreciation of correct social and political principles, perhaps it will be found possible to say, without being in the least degree blasphemous or irreverent, that the stones rejected by the builders of the past have become the corner-stones of the edifice.

---

[64] Thomas Addis Emmet (1764–1827), Irish and American lawyer and revolutionary politician. A senior member of the United Irishmen, he later served as Attorney-General of the State of New York. Elder brother of Robert Emmet.

[65] Richard Madden (1798–1886), Irish physician and abolitionist. His *Literary Remains of the United Irishmen* was published in 1887.

Chapter IX: The Emmet Conspiracy

'The Rich always betray the Poor'.
Henry Joy M'Cracken's *Letter to his Sister*, 1798[66]

The Emmet Conspiracy – the aftermath of the United Irish movement of 1798, was even more distinctly democratic, international and popular in its sympathies and affiliations.[67] The treacherous betrayal of the United Irish chiefs into the hands of the Government, had removed from the scene of action practically all the middle-class supporters of the revolutionary movement; and left the rank and file to their own resources and to consult their own inclinations. It was, accordingly, with these humble workers in town and country Emmet had to deal, when he essayed to reorganise the scattered forces of freedom for a fresh grapple with the despotic power of the class government then ruling Ireland and England. All students who have investigated the matter are as one in conceding that Emmet's conspiracy was more of a working-class character than its predecessors. Indeed it is a remarkable fact that this conspiracy, widespread throughout Ireland, England, and France, should have progressed so rapidly, and with such elaborate preparations for armed revolt, amongst the poorer section of the populace, right up to within a short time of the date for the projected rising, without the alert English Government or its Irish Executive being able to inform themselves of the matter.

Probably the proletarian character of the movement – the fact that it was recruited principally amongst the working class of Dublin and other large centres, as well as amongst the labouring element of the country districts, was the real reason why it was not so prolific of traitors as its forerunner. After the conspiracy had fallen through, the Government, of course, pretended that it had known of it all along – indeed the British Government in Ireland always pretends to be omniscient – but nothing developed during the trial of Emmet to justify such a claim. Nor has anything developed since, although searchers of the Government documents of the time, the Castlereagh papers, the records of the secret service and other sources of information, have been able to reveal in

---

[66] Henry Joy M'Cracken (1767–1798), Irish revolutionary and founder-member of the United Irishmen.

[67] 67. Robert Emmet (1778–1803), Irish revolutionary and republican, brother of Thomas Addis Emmet. Leader of the failed United Irishmen's rebellion of 1803, and famous for his 'Speech from the Dock', delivered in court after he was condemned to death.

their true colours of infamy many who had posed in the limelight for more than a generation as whole-souled patriots and reformers. Thus Leonard McNally, barrister-at-law, and legal defender of the United Irishmen, who acted for all the chiefs of that body at their trials, was one of the Catholic Committee and elected as Catholic delegate to England in 1811, looked up to and revered as a fearless advocate of Catholic rights, and champion of persecuted Nationalists, was discovered to have been all the time in the pay of the Government, acting the loathsome part of an informer, and systematically betraying to the Government the inmost secrets of the men whose cause he was pretending to champion in the court-room.[68] But this secret was kept for half a century. Francis Magan, another worthy, received a secret pension of £200 per year from the Government for the betrayal of the hiding-place of Lord Edward Fitzgerald, and lived and died revered as an honest, unoffending citizen.[69] A body of the Royal Meath Militia stationed at Mallow, County Cork, had conspired to seize the artillery stationed there, and with that valuable arm, join the insurgents in a body. One of their number mentioned the plot in his confessions to the Rev. Thomas Barry, parish priest of Mallow, and was by him ordered to reveal it to the military authorities. The leader of the plotters, Sergeant Beatty, seeing by the precautions suddenly taken that the plot was discovered, fought his way out of the barracks with nineteen men, but was subsequently captured and hanged in Dublin. Father Barry (how ironical the title sounds) received £100 per year pension from the Government, and drew this blood-money in secret for a lifetime before his crime was discovered. It is recorded that the great Daniel O'Connell at one time turned pale when shown a receipt for this blood-money signed by Father Barry, and yet it is known now that O'Connell himself, as a member of the lawyers' Yeomanry Corps of Dublin, was turned out on duty to serve against the rebels on the night of Emmet's insurrection, and in Daunt's *Recollections* he relates that O'Connell pointed out to him a house in James's Street which he (O'Connell) had searched for 'Croppies' (patriots).[70]

The present writer has seen in Derrynane, O'Connell's ancestral home

---

[68] Leonard McNally (1752–1820), Irish writer and barrister, founder-member of the United Irishmen. He represented Tone and Emmet at their trials for treason. He was later revealed to have been an informer and British spy, who betrayed Edward Fitzgerald and Emmet to the Dublin authorities.

[69] Francis Magan (1772–1843), Irish barrister, member of the United Irishmen, British informant.

[70] William Joseph Daunt O'Neill (1807–1894), Irish novelist, historian and Member of Parliament. Published *Personal Recollections of the Late Daniel O'Connell* in 1848.

in County Kerry, a brass-mounted blunderbuss, which we were assured by a member of the family was procured at a house in James's Street, Dublin, by O'Connell from the owner, a follower of Emmet, a remark that recalled to our mind that 'search for Croppies' of which Daunt speaks, and gave rise to a conjecture that possibly the blunderbuss in question owed its presence in Derrynane to that memorable raid.[71]

But although latter-day investigators have brought to light many such treasons against liberty as those recorded, and have revealed depths of corruption in quarters long unsuspected, nothing has yet been demonstrated to dim the glory or sully the name of the men and women of the working class, who carried the dangerous secret of Emmet's conspiracy and guarded it so well and faithfully to the end. It must be remembered in this connection, that at that period the open organisation of labourers for any purpose was against the law, that consequently the trade unions which then flourished amongst the working class were all illegal organisations, whose members were in constant danger of arrest and transportation for the crime of organising, and that, therefore, a proposal to subvert the oppressive governing class and establish a republic founded upon the votes of all citizens, as Emmet planned, was one likely to appeal alike to the material requirements and imagination of the Irish toilers. And, as they were already trained to secrecy in organisation, they naturally made splendid material for the revolutionary movement. It is significant that the only serious fight on the night of the ill-fated insurrection took place in the Coombe district of the Liberties of Dublin, a quarter inhabited exclusively by weavers, tanners, and shoemakers, the best organised trades in the city, and that a force of Wicklow men brought into Dublin by Michael Dwyer, the insurgent chieftain, were sheltered on the quays amongst the dock-labourers; and eventually managed to return home without any traitor betraying their whereabouts to the numerous Government spies over-running the city.[72]

The ripeness of the labouring element in the country at large for any movement that held out hopes of social emancipation may be gauged by the fact that a partial rebellion had already taken place in 1802 in Limerick, Waterford, and Tipperary, where, according to Haverty's

---

[71] A blunderbuss is a muzzle-loaded gun with a short large-calibre barrel, akin to a short shotgun.

[72] The Liberties of Dublin is one the oldest parts of the city, taking its name from townlands adjacent to the city in the period of the Middle Ages, but of independent jurisdiction (hence 'liberty'). Michael Dwyer (1772–1825), Irish revolutionary and a leader of the United Irishmen in Co. Wicklow during the 1798 Rebellion. He later led a guerrilla struggle in the Wicklow highlands until 1803.

History of Ireland, 'the alleged grounds for rebellion were the dearness of the potatoes', and 'the right of the old tenants to retain possession of their farms'.[73]

Such were the domestic materials upon which the conspiracy of Emmet rested – working-class elements fired with the hope of political and social emancipation. Abroad he sought alliance with the French Republic – the incarnation of the political, social, and religious unrest and revolution of the age, and in Great Britain he formed alliance with the 'Sassenach' reformers who were conspiring to overthrow the English monarchy. On November 13, 1802, one Colonel Despard, with nineteen others, was arrested in London charged with the crime of high treason; they were tried on the charge of conspiracy to murder the King; although no evidence in support of such a charge was forthcoming, Despard and seven others were hanged.[74] According to the Castlereagh papers Emmet and Despard were preparing for a simultaneous uprising, a certain William Dowdall, of Dublin, described as one of the most determined of the society of United Irishmen, being the confidential agent who acted for both.[75] Mr. W.J. Fitzpatrick in his books *Secret Service Under Pitt* and *The Sham Squire* brings out many of these facts, as a result of an extensive and scholarly investigation of Government records and the papers of private families, yet, although these books were published half a century ago, every recurring Emmet anniversary continues to bring us its crop of orators who know all about Emmet's martyrdom, and nothing about his principles. Even some of the more sympathetic of his panegyrists do not seem to realise that they dim his glory when they represent him as the victim of a protest against an injustice local to Ireland, instead of as an Irish apostle of a world-wide movement for liberty, equality and fraternity. Yet this latter was indeed the character and position of Emmet, and as such the democracy of the future will revere him. He fully shared in the international sympathies of that Dublin Society of United Irishmen who had elected a Scottish reformer to be a United Irishman upon hearing that the Government had sentenced him to transportation for attending a reform convention

---

[73] Martin Haverty, *The History of Ireland, Ancient and Modern* (1860).

[74] Edward Despard (1751–1803), Irish revolutionary and soldier.

[75] Robert Stewart, 2nd Marquis of Londonderry (1769–1822), Irish politician and diplomat, better known as Lord Castlereagh; Chief Secretary of Ireland during the 1798 rebellion. *Memoirs and Correspondence of Viscount Castlereagh*, edited by his brother Charles Vane, was published 1848–1853. William John Fitzpatrick, *The Sham Squire, and the Informers of 1798, with a View of their Contemporaries* (1866) and *Secret Service under Pitt* (1892).

in Edinburgh. He believed in the brotherhood of the oppressed, and in the community of free nations, and died for his ideal.

Emmet is the most idolised, the most universally praised of all Irish martyrs; it is, therefore, worthy of note that in the proclamation he drew up to be issued in the name of the 'Provisional Government of Ireland' the first article decrees the wholesale confiscation of church property and the nationalising of the same, and the second and third decrees forbid and declare void the transfer of all landed property, bonds, debentures, and public securities, until the national government is established and the national will upon them is declared.

Two things are thus established – viz., that Emmet believed the 'national will' was superior to property rights, and could abolish them at will; and also that he realised that the producing classes could not be expected to rally to the revolution unless given to understand that it meant their freedom from social as well as from political bondage.

Chapter X: The First Irish Socialist: A Forerunner of Marx[76]

'It is a system which in its least repulsive aspects compels thousands and tens of thousands to fret and toil, to live and die in hunger and rags and wretchedness, in order that a few idle drones may revel in ease and luxury.'
– *Irish People*, July 9, 1864[77]

For Ireland, as for every part of Europe, the first quarter of the nineteenth century was a period of political darkness, or unbridled despotism and reaction. The fear engendered in the heart of the ruling classes by the French Revolution had given birth to an almost insane hatred of reform, coupled with a wolfish ferocity in hunting down even the mildest reformers. The triumph of the allied sovereigns over Napoleon was followed by a perfect saturnalia of despotism all over Europe, and every form of popular organisation was ruthlessly suppressed or driven under the surface. But driving organisations under the surface does not remove the causes of discontent, and consequently we find that, as rapidly as reaction triumphed above ground, its antagonists spread their secret conspiracies underneath. The popular discontent

---

[76] It is not completely clear whether or how much Connolly read Marx's writings on Ireland, though in August 1902, *The Workers' Republic* published a letter written by Marx to Ludwig Kugelmann in 1869, on the importance of Irish independence to radical class politics in England.

[77] The *Irish People* was a paper of the Irish Republican Brotherhood, published from 1863 to 1865.

was further increased by the fact that the return home of the soldiers disbanded from the Napoleonic wars had a serious economic effect. It deprived the agriculturists of a market for their produce, and produced a great agricultural and industrial crisis. It threw out of employment all the ships employed in provisioning the troops, all the trades required to build, equip and repair them, all the industries engaged in making war material; and in addition to suspending the work and flooding the labour market with the men and women thus disemployed, it cast adrift scores of thousands of able-bodied soldiers and sailors, to compete with the civilian workers who had fed, clothed and maintained them during the war. In Ireland especially the results were disastrous, owing to the inordinately large proportion of Irish amongst the disbanded soldiers and sailors. Those returning home found the labour market glutted with unemployed in the cities, and in the rural districts the landlords engaged in a fierce war of extermination with their tenantry, who, having lost their war market and war prices, were unable to meet the increasing exactions of the owners of the soil. It was at this period the great Ribbon conspiracy took hold upon the Irish labourer in the rural districts, and although the full truth relative to that movement has never yet been unearthed, sufficient is known to indicate that it was in effect a secret agricultural trades union of labourers and cottier farmers – a trades union which undertook, in its own wild way, to execute justice upon the evictor, and vengeance upon the traitor to his fellows.[78] Also at this time Irish trade unionism, although secret and illegal, attained to its maximum of strength and compact organisation. In 1824 the chief constable of Dublin, testifying before a committee of the House of Commons, declared that the trades of Dublin were perfectly organised, and many of the employers were already beginning to complain of the 'tyranny of the Irish trades unions'. Under such circumstances it is not to be wondered at, that the attention which in the eighteenth century had been given to political reforms and the philosophy thereof, gave way in the nineteenth to solicitude for social amelioration.

In England, France, and Germany a crop of social philosophers sprang up, each with his scheme of a perfect social order, each with a plan by which the regeneration of society could be accomplished, and poverty and all its attendant evils abolished. For the most part these theorists had no complaint to make against the beneficiaries of the social

---

[78] Ribbonism was a movement of agrarian radicalism in early nineteenth century Ireland, not unlike Whiteboyism in the eighteenth century. Ribbonmen campaigned for tenant rights, and against tithes.

system of the day; their complaint was against the results of the social system. Indeed they, in most cases, believed that the governing and possessing classes would themselves voluntarily renounce their privileges and property and initiate the new order once they were convinced of its advantages. With this belief it was natural that the chief direction taken by their criticism of society should be towards an analysis of the effects of competition upon buyer and seller, and that the relation of the labourer as producer to the proprietor as appropriator of the thing produced should occupy no part of their examination. One result of this one sided view of social relations necessarily was a complete ignoring of historical development as a factor in hastening the attainment of their ideal; since the new order was to be introduced by the governing class, it followed that the stronger that class became the easier would be the transition, and consequently, everything which would tend to weaken the social bond by accentuating class distinction, or impairing the feelings of reverence held by the labourer for his masters, would be a hindrance to progress.

Those philosophers formed socialist sects, and it is known that their followers, when they lost the inspiring genius of their leaders, degenerated into reactionaries of the most pronounced type, opposed to every forward move of labour.

The Irish are not philosophers as a rule, they proceed too rapidly from thought to action.

Hence it is not to be wondered at, that the same period which produced the Utopian Socialists before alluded to in France, England, and Germany produced in Ireland an economist more thoroughly Socialist in the modern sense than any of his contemporaries – William Thompson, of Clonkeen, Roscarbery, County Cork – a Socialist who did not hesitate to direct attention to the political and social subjection of labour as the worst evil of society; nor to depict, with a merciless fidelity to truth, the disastrous consequences to political freedom of the presence in society of a wealthy class.[79] Thompson was a believer in the possibility of realising Socialism by forming co-operative colonies on the lines of those advocated by Robert Owen, and to that extent may be classed

---

[79] 'Utopian socialism' is a derogatory term used by Marx and Engels and later socialists to refer to the first generation of European socialists of the early nineteenth century. Leading figures in this early flowering of socialism included Henri de Saint-Simon (1760–1825) and Charles Fourier (1772–1837) in France, and Robert Owen (1771–1858) in England. For Marx and Engels, the thinking of the early socialists was insufficiently grounded in the material circumstances of their activism.

as a Utopian.[80] On the other hand he believed that such colonies must be built by the labourers themselves, and not by the governing class. He taught that the wealth of the ruling class was derived from the plunder of labour, and he advocated, as a necessary preliminary to Socialism, the conquest of political representation on the basis of the adult suffrage of both sexes. He did not believe in the State as a basis of Socialist society, but he insisted upon the necessity of using political weapons to destroy all class privileges founded in law, and to clear the ground of all obstacles which the governing class might desire to put in the way of the growth of Socialist communities.

Lest it may be thought that we are exaggerating the merits of Thompson's work as an original thinker, a pioneer of Socialist thought, superior to any of the Utopian Socialists of the Continent, and long ante-dating Karl Marx in his insistence upon the subjection of labour as the cause of all social misery, modern crime and political dependence, as well as in his searching analysis of the true definition of capital, we will quote a passage from his most important work, published in 1824: *An Inquiry into the principles of the distribution of Wealth most conducive to Human Happiness as applied to the newly-proposed System of the Voluntary Equality of Wealth*. Third edition.[81]

> 'What, then, is the most accurate idea of capital? It is that portion of the product of labour which, whether of a permanent nature or not, is capable of being made the instrument of profit. Such seem to be the real circumstances which mark out one portion of the products of labour as capital. On such distinctions, however, have been founded the insecurity and oppression of the productive labourer – the real parent, under the guidance of knowledge, of all wealth – and the enormous usurpation, over the productive forces and their fellow-creatures, of those who, under the name of capitalists, or landlords, acquired the possession of those accumulated products – the yearly or permanent supply of the community. Hence the opposing claims of the capitalist and the labourer. The capitalist, getting into his hands, under the reign of insecurity and force, the consumption of many labourers for the coming year, the tools or machinery necessary to make their labour productive, and the dwellings in which they must

---

[80] Thompson (1775–1833) was actually quite critical of Owen's elitism and occasional authoritarianism. The two clashed at the Third Cooperative Congress of 1832, Owen arguing the necessity of government support and financing of new communities and Thompson countering that such ventures needed always to remain under worker control.

[81] William Thompson, *An Inquiry into the Principles of the Distribution of Wealth Most Conducive to Human Happiness, applied to the Newly Proposed System of Voluntary Equality of Wealth* (1824).

live, turned them to the best account, and bought labour and its future products with them as cheaply as possible. The greater the profit of capital, or the more the capitalist made the labourer pay for the advance of his food, the use of the implements or machinery and the occupation of the dwelling, the less of course remained to the labourer for the acquisition of any object of desire.'

Or again, see how, whilst advocating political reform as a means to an end, he depicts its inefficiency when considered as an end in itself: –

'As long as the accumulated capital of society remains in one set of hands, and the productive power of creating wealth remains in another, the accumulated capital will, while the nature of man continues as at present, be made use of to counter-act the natural laws of distribution, and to deprive the producers of the use of what their labour has produced. Were it possible to conceive that, under simple representative institutions, any such of the expedients of insecurity should be permitted to remain in existence as would uphold the division of capital and labour, such representative institutions (though all the plunder of political power should cease) would be of little further benefit to the real happiness of mankind, than as affording an easy means for the development of knowledge, and the ultimate abolition of all such expedients. As long as a class of mere capitalists exists, society must remain in a diseased state. Whatever plunder is saved from the hand of political power will be levied in another way, under the name of profit, by capitalists who, while capitalists, must be always lawmakers.'

Thompson advocated free education for all, and went into great detail to prove its feasibility, giving statistics to show that the total cost of such education could easily be borne by Ireland, without unduly increasing the burden of the producers. In this he was three generations ahead of his time – the reform he then advocated being only partially realised in our day. Living in a country in which a small minority imposed a detested religion by force upon a conquered people, with the result that a ferocious fanaticism disgraced both sides, he yet had courage and foresight enough to plead for secular education, and to the cry of the bigots who then as now declared that religion would die unless supported by the State, he answered: –

'Not only has experience proved that religion can exist without interfering with the natural laws of distribution by violation of security, but it has increased and flourished during centuries in Ireland, and in Greece, under and in spite of the forced abstraction of its own resources from its own communicants, to enrich a rival and hated priesthood, or to feed the force that enchained it.'

How different was the spirit of the Socialism preached by Thompson from the visionary sentimentalism of the Utopians of Continental Europe, or of Owen in his earlier days in England, with their constant appeals to the 'humanity' of the possessing classes, is further illustrated by the following passage which, although lengthy, we make no apology for reproducing. Because of its biting analysis of the attitude of the rich in the various stages of political society, and the lust for power which accompanies extreme wealth, the passage might have never been written by a Socialist of the twentieth century: –

'The unoccupied rich are without any active pursuit; an object in life is wanting to them. The means of gratifying the senses, the imagination even, of sating all wants and caprices they possess. The pleasures of power are still to be attained. It is one of the strongest and most unavoidable propensities of those who have been brought up in indulgence, to abhor restraint, to be uneasy under opposition, and therefore to desire power to remove these evils of restraint and opposition. How shall they acquire the power? First by the direct influence of their wealth, and the hopes and fears it engenders; then when these means are exhausted, or to make these means more effectual, they endeavour everywhere to seize on, to monopolise the powers of Government.

'Where despotism does exist, they endeavour to get entirely into their own hands, or in conjunction with the head of the State, or other bodies, they seize as large a portion as they can of the functions of legislation. Where despotism does not exist, or is modified, they share amongst themselves all the subordinate departments of Government; they monopolise, either directly or indirectly, the command of the armed force, the offices of judges, priests and all those executive departments which give the most power, require the least trouble, and render the largest pecuniary returns. Where despotism exists, the class of the excessively rich make the best terms they can with the despot, to share his power whether as partners, equals or mere slaves.

'If his situation is such as to give them a confidence in their strength, they make terms with the despot, and insist on what they call their rights; if they are weak they gladly crawl to the despot, and appear to glory in their slavishness to him for the sake of the delegated power of making slaves to themselves of the rest of the community. Such do the historians of all nations prove the tendencies of excessive wealth to be.'

In the English-speaking world the work of this Irish thinker is practically unknown, but on the Continent of Europe his position has long been established. Besides the work already quoted he wrote an *Appeal of One-half of the Human Race – Women – Against the Pretensions of the Other Half – Men – to Retain them in Political and Thence in Civil and Domestic Slavery* published in London in 1825. *Labour Rewarded, the Claims of Labour and Capital Conciliated; or, How to Secure to Labour the Whole Product of its Exertions*, published in 1827, and *Practical Directions for the Speedy and Economical Establishment of Communities*, published in London in 1830, are two other known works. He also left behind the manuscript of other books on the same subject, but they have never been published, and their whereabouts is now unknown. It is told of him that he was for twenty years a vegetarian and total abstainer, and in his will left the bulk of his fortune to endow the first co-operative community to be established in Ireland, and his body for the purpose of dissection in the interests of science. His relations successfully contested the will on the ground that 'immoral objects were included in its benefit'.

His position in the development of Socialism as a science lies, in our opinion, midway between the Utopianism of the early idealists and the historical materialism of Marx. He anticipated the latter in most of his analyses of the economic system, and foresaw the part that a democratisation of politics must play in clearing the ground of the legal privileges of the professional classes. In a preface to the English translation of the work of one of his German biographers, Anton Menger, the writer, H.S. Foxwell, M.A., says of his contribution to economic science:

> 'Thompson's fame will rest, not upon his advocacy of Owenite co-operation, devoted and public-spirited as that was, but upon the fact that *he was the first writer to elevate the question of the just distribution of wealth* to the supreme position it has since held in English political economy. Up to his time political economy had been rather commercial than industrial, indeed he finds it necessary to explain the very meaning of the term 'industrial', which he says, was from the French, no doubt adopted from Saint Simon'.[82]

If we were to attempt to estimate the relative achievements of Thompson and Marx we should not hope to do justice to either by putting them in contrast, or by eulogising Thompson in order to belittle Marx, as some Continental critics of the latter seek to do. Rather we should say that the relative position of this Irish genius and of Marx are best comparable to the historical relations of the pre-Darwinian evolutionists to Darwin; as Darwin systematised all the theories of his predecessors and gave a lifetime to the accumulation of the facts required to

---

[82] William Thompson, *An Inquiry into the Principles of the Distribution of Wealth Most Conducive to Human Happiness, Applied to the Newly Proposed System of Voluntary Equality of Wealth* (1824).

establish his and their position, so Marx found the true line of economic thought already indicated, and brought his genius and encyclopaedic knowledge and research to place it upon an unshakable foundation. Thompson brushed aside the economic fiction maintained by the orthodox economists and accepted by the Utopian, that profit was made in exchange, and declared that it was due to the subjection of labour and the resultant appropriation, by the capitalists and landlords, of the fruits of the labour of others. He does not hesitate to include himself as a beneficiary of monopoly. He declared, in 1827, that for about twelve years he had been 'living on what is called rent, the produce of the labour of others'. All the theory of the class war is but a deduction from this principle. But, although Thompson recognised this class war as a fact, he did not recognise it as a factor, as *the* factor in the evolution of society towards freedom. This was reserved for Marx, and in our opinion, is his chief and crowning glory. While Owen and the Continental Socialists were beseeching the favour of kings, Parliaments and Congresses, this Irishman was arraigning the rich, pointing out that lust of power for ever followed riches, that 'capitalists, while capitalists, would always be law-makers', but that 'as long as a class of mere capitalists exists, society must remain in a diseased state'. The fact that the daring Celt who preached this doctrine, arraigning alike the social and political rulers of society and society itself, also vehemently demanded the extension of the suffrage to the whole adult population, is surely explanation enough why his writings found no favour with the respectable classes of society, with those same classes who so frequently lionised the leaders of the Socialist sects of his day.

In our day another great Irishman, Standish O'Grady, perhaps the greatest litterateur in Ireland, has been preaching in the pages of *The Peasant* Dublin, 1908–9, against capitalist society, and urged the formation of co-operative communities in Ireland as an escape therefrom.[83] It is curiously significant how little Irishmen know of the intellectual achievements of their race, that O'Grady apparently is entirely unconscious of the work of his great forerunner in that field of endeavour. It is also curiously significant of the conquest of the Irish mind by English traditions, that Irish Nationalists should often be found fighting fiercely against Socialism as 'a German idea', although every social conception which we find in the flower in Marx, we can also find in the bud in

---

[83] Standish James O'Grady (1846–1928), Irish writer, historian and journalist, and a major influence on the Irish Literary Revival of the late nineteenth and early twentieth centuries.

Thompson, twenty-three years before the publication of the *Communist Manifesto*, forty-three years before the issue of *Das Kapital*.[84]

We will conclude this chapter by another citation from this Irish pioneer of revolutionary Socialism; we say of revolutionary Socialism advisedly, for all the deductions from his teachings lead irresistibly to the revolutionary action of the working class. As, according to the Socialist philosophy, the political demands of the working-class movement must at all times depend upon the degree of development of the age and country in which it finds itself, it is apparent that Thompson's theories of action were the highest possible expression of the revolutionary thought of his age.

'The productive labourers, stripped of all capital, of tools, houses, and materials to make their labour productive, toil from want, from the necessity of existence, their remuneration being kept at the lowest compatible figure with the existence of industrious habits.

'How shall the wretchedly poor be virtuous? Who cares about them? What character have they to lose? What hold has public opinion on their action? What care they for the delicate pleasures of reputation who are tormented by the gnawings of absolute want? How should they respect the property or rights of others who have none of their own to beget a sympathy for those who suffer from their privation? How can they feel for others' woes, for others' passing light complaints, who are tormented by their own substantial miseries? The mere mention of the trivial inconveniences of others insults and excites the indignation, instead of calling forth their complacent sympathies. Cut off from the decencies, the comforts, the necessaries of life, want begets ferocity. If they turn they find many in the same situation with themselves, partaking of their feelings of isolation from kindly sympathies with the happy. They become a public to each other, a public of suffering, of discontent and ignorance; they form a public opinion of their own in contempt of the public opinion of the rich, whom, and their laws, they look upon as the result of force alone. From whom are the wretched to learn the principle while they never see the practice of morality? Of respect for the security of others? From their superiors? From the laws? The conduct of their superiors, the operation of those laws have been one practical lesson to them of force, of restraint, of taking away without their consent, without any equivalent, the fruits of their labour. Of what avail are morals or principles or commands, when opposed, when belied by example? These can never supply motives of virtuous conduct. *Motives arise from things, from surrounding circumstances, not from the idleness*

---

[84] Karl Marx (1818–1883), German philosopher, economist, journalist and revolutionary socialist. Co-authored *The Manifesto of the Communist Party* (1848) and author of *Capital: Critique of Political Economy* (1867–1894).

of words and empty declamations. Words are only useful to convey and impress a knowledge of these things and circumstances. If these things do not exist, words are mere mockery.'

With this bit of economic determinist philosophy – teaching that morality is a thing of social growth, the outcome of things and circumstances – we leave this earliest Irish apostle of the social revolution. Fervent Celtic enthusiasts are fond of claiming, and the researches of our days seem to bear out the claim, that Irish missionaries were the first to rekindle the lamp of learning in Europe, and dispel the intellectual darkness following the downfall of the Roman Empire; may we not also take pride in the fact that an Irishman was the first to pierce the worse than Egyptian darkness of capitalist barbarism, and to point out to the toilers the conditions of their enslavement, and the essential prerequisites of their emancipation?

Chapter XI: An Irish Utopia

'Were the hand of Locke to hold from heaven a scheme of government most perfectly adapted to the nature and capabilities of the Irish nation, it would drop to the ground a mere sounding scroll were there no other means of giving it effect than its intrinsic excellence. All true Irishmen agree in what ought to be done, but how to get it done is the question.'
– *Secret Manifesto (Ireland)*, 1793

In our last chapter we pointed out how the close of the Napoleonic wars precipitated a commercial crisis in Great Britain and Ireland, and how in the latter country it also served to intensify the bitterness of the relations existing between landlord and tenant. During the continuance of the wars against Napoleon, agricultural prices had steadily risen owing to the demand by the British Government for provisions to supply its huge army and navy. With the rise in prices rents had also risen, but when the close of the war cut off the demand, and prices consequently fell, rents did not fall along with them. A falling market and a stationary or rising rent-roll could have but one result in Ireland – viz., agrarian war.

The landlords insisted upon their 'pound of flesh,' and the peasantry organised in secret to terrorise their oppressors and protect themselves. In the year 1829 a fresh cause of popular misery came as a result of the Act granting Catholic Emancipation. Until that year no Catholic had the right to sit in the English House of Commons, to sit on the Bench as a Judge, or to aspire to any of the higher posts in the Civil, Military, or Naval services. As the culmination of a long fight against this iniquitous 'Protestant Ascendancy', after he had aroused the entire Catholic population to a pitch of frenzy against the injustices inherent in it, the Catholic leader, Daniel O'Connell, presented himself as a candidate for the representation in Parliament of the County Clare, declaring that if elected he would refuse to take the oath then required of a Member of Parliament, as it libelled the Catholic Religion. In Ireland at that time open voting prevailed, every elector having to declare openly before the clerks of the election and all others who chose to attend, the name of the candidate for whom he voted. In Ireland at that time also, most of the tenants were tenants-at-will, removable at the mere pleasure of the agent or landlord. Hence elections were a combination of farce and tragedy – a farce as far as a means of ascertaining the real wish of the electors was concerned, a tragedy whenever any of the tenants dared to vote against the nominee of the landlord. The suffrage had been extended to all tenants paying an annual rental of forty shillings, irrespective of religious belief, but the terrible power of life and death possessed by the landlord made this suffrage ordinarily useless for popular purposes. Yet when O'Connell appealed to the Catholic peasantry of Clare to brave the vengeance of their landed tyrants, and vote for him in the interests of religious liberty, they nobly responded. O'Connell was elected, and as a result Catholic Emancipation was soon afterwards achieved. But the ruling classes and the British Government took their revenge by coupling with this reform a Bill depriving the smaller tenants of the suffrage, and raising the amount of rent necessary to qualify for a vote to ten pounds.

Up till that time landlords had rather encouraged the growth of population on their estates, as it increased the number of their political adherents, but with the passage of this Act of Parliament this reason ceased to exist, and they immediately began the wholesale eviction of their tenantry and the conversion of the arable lands into grazing farms. The Catholic middle, professional and landed class by Catholic Emancipation had the way opened to them for all the snug berths in the disposal of the Government; the Catholics of the poorer class as a result of the same Act were doomed to extermination, to satisfy the vengeance of a foreign Government and an aristocracy whose power had been defied where it knew itself most supreme.

The wholesale eviction of the smaller tenants and the absorption of their farms into huge grazing ranches, thus closing up every avenue of employment to labour, meant death to the agricultural population, and hence the peasantry struck back by every means in their power. They formed lodges of the secret Ribbon Society, made midnight raids for arms upon the houses of the gentry, assembled at night in large bodies and ploughed up the grass lands, making them useless for grazing purposes, filled up ditches, terrorised graziers into surrendering their ranches, wounded and killed those who had entered the service of graziers or obnoxious landlords, assassinated agents, and sometimes, in sheer despair, opposed their unarmed bodies to the arms of the military. Civil war of the most sanguinary character was convulsing the country; in May, 1831, the Lord Lieutenant of Ireland and a huge military force accompanied by artillery marched through Clare to overawe the people, but as he did not stop evictions, nor provide employment for the labourers whom the establishment of grazing had deprived of their usual employment on the farm, the 'outrages' still continued. Nor were the professional patriots, or the newly emancipated Catholic rich, any more sympathetic to the unfortunate people. They had opened the way for themselves to place and preferment by using the labourer and cottier-farmer as a lever to overthrow the fortress of religious bigotry and ascendancy, and now when the fight was won, they abandoned these poor co-religionists of theirs to the tender mercies of their economic masters. To the cry of despair welling up from the hearts of the evicted families, crouching in hunger upon the road-side in sight of their ruined homes, to the heartbroken appeal of the labourer permanently disemployed by the destruction of his source of employment; to the wail of famishing women and children the politicians invariably had but one answer – 'Be law-abiding, and wait for the Repeal of the Union.' We are not exaggerating. One of the most ardent Repealers and closest friends of Daniel O'Connell, Mr. Thomas Steele, had the following manifesto posted up in the Market Place of Ennis and other parts of Clare, addressed to the desperate labourers and farmers: –

> 'Unless you desist, I denounce you as traitors to the cause of the liberty of Ireland . . . I leave you to the Government and the fire and bayonets of the military. Your blood be upon your own souls.'[85]

This language of denunciation was uttered to the heroic men and women who had sacrificed their homes, their security, and the hopes of food for their children to win the emancipation from religious tyranny of the well-fed snobs who thus abandoned them. It is difficult to see how a promised Repeal of the Union some time in the future could have been of any use to the starving men of Clare, especially when they knew that their fathers had been starved, evicted and tyrannised over *before* just as they were *after* the Union. At that time, however, it was deemed a

---

[85] Thomas Steele (1788–1848), Irish politician and engineer, close ally and supporter of O'Connell in the campaigns for Emancipation and Repeal of the Union.

highly patriotic act to ascribe all the ills that Irish flesh is heir to, to the Union. For example, Mr. O'Gorman Mahon, speaking in the House of Commons, London, on February 8, 1831, hinted that the snow-storm then covering Ireland was a result of the Legislative Union. He said: –

> 'Did the Hon. Members imagine that they could prevent the unfortunate men who were under five feet of snow from thinking they could better their condition by a Repeal of the Union. It might be said that England had not caused the snow, but the people had the snow on them, and they thought that their connection with England had reduced them to the state in which they now were.'[86]

Another patriot, destined in after years to don the mantle of an Irish rebel, William Smith O'Brien, at this time, 1830, published a pamphlet advocating emigration as the one remedy for Irish misery.[87]

On the other hand a Commission appointed by the House of Lords in 1839 to inquire into the causes of the unrest and secret conspiracies amongst the poorer class examined many witnesses in close touch with the life of the peasantry and elicited much interesting testimony tending to prove that the evil was much more deeply rooted than any political scheme of Government, and that its real roots were in the social conditions.[88] Thus examined as to the attitude of the labourers towards the Ribbon Association, one witness declared: –

> 'Many look to the Association for protection. They think they have no other protection'.
> Question: – 'What are the principal objects they have in view?'
> Answer: – 'To keep themselves upon their lands. I have often heard their conversation, when they say: –
>
> "What good did Emancipation do for us? Are we better clothed or fed, or are our children better clothed or fed? Are we not as naked as we were, and eating dry potatoes when we can get them? Let us notice the farmers to give us better food and better wages, and not give so much to the landlord, and more to the workman; we must not be letting them be turning the poor people off the ground."'

---

[86] Charles James Patrick Mahon (1800–1891), also known as the O'Gorman Mahon, Irish politician, journalist, Member of Parliament and sometime mercenary.

[87] William Smith O'Brien (1803–1864), Irish politician and leader of the Young Ireland group. Transported to Van Dieman's Land for his part in the 1848 Young Ireland rebellion.

[88] Quoted from *Report from the Select Committee of the House of Lords appointed to enquire into the state of Ireland in respect of crime and to report thereon to the House* (1839).

And a Mr. Poulett Scroope, M.P., declared in one of his writings upon the necessity for a Poor Law: 'The tithe question, the Church, the Grand Jury laws, the more or fewer Catholics appointed to the Shrievalty or Magistracy – these are all topics for political agitation among idle mobs; but the midnight massacre, the daily plunder, the frequent insurrection, the insecurity of life and property throughout agricultural districts of Ireland, these are neither caused by agitation, nor can be put down with agitation.'[89]

It will be thus seen that the opinion of the independent Member of Parliament coincided with that of the revolting labourers as to the relative unimportance to the toilers of Ireland of the subjects which then, as now, bulked most largely in the minds of politicians.

This was the state of things political and social in Ireland in the year 1831 and as it was in Clare the final effective blow had been struck for religious emancipation, so it also was Clare that was destined to see the first effort to discover a peaceful way of achieving that social Emancipation, without which all other freedom, religious or political, must ever remain as Dead Sea fruit to the palate of Labour.

In 1823 the great English socialist, Robert Owen, visited Ireland and held a number of meetings in the Rotunda, Dublin, for the purpose of explaining the principles of Socialism to the people of that city.[90] His audiences were mainly composed of the well-to-do inhabitants, as was, indeed, the case universally at that period when Socialism was the fad of the rich instead of the faith of the poor. The Duke of Leinster, the Catholic Archbishop Murray, Lord Meath, Lord Cloncurry, and others occupied the platform, and as a result of the picture drawn by Owen of the misery then existing, and the attendant insecurity of life and property amongst all classes, and his outline of the possibilities which a system of Socialist co-operation could produce, an association styling itself the Hibernian Philanthropic Society was formed to carry out his ideas. A sum of money was subscribed to aid the prospects of the society, a General Brown giving £1,000, Lord Cloncurry £500, Mr. Owen himself subscribing £1,000, and £100 being raised from other sources. The society was short-lived and ineffectual, but one of the members, Mr. Arthur Vandeleur, an Irish landlord, was so deeply impressed with all he had seen and heard

---

[89] George Julius Poulett Scrope (1797–1876), English politician, scientist and Member of Parliament.

[90] Robert Owen (1771–1858), Welsh social reformer, founder of the co-operative movement, and 'utopian' socialist, founder of the New Harmony utopian colony in Indiana, USA.

of the possibilities of Owenite Socialism, that in 1831, when crime and outrage in the country had reached its zenith, and the insecurity of life in his own class had been brought home to him by the assassination of the steward of his estate for unfeeling conduct towards the labourers, he resolved to make an effort to establish a Socialist colony upon his property at Ralahine, County Clare.[91] For that purpose he invited to Ireland a Mr. Craig, of Manchester, a follower of Owen, and entrusted him with the task of carrying the project into execution.

Though Mr. Craig knew no Irish, and the people of Ralahine, as a rule, knew no English – a state of matters which greatly complicated the work of explanation – an understanding was finally arrived at, and the estate was turned over to an association of the people organised under the title of The Ralahine Agricultural and Manufacturing Co-operative Association.

In the preamble to the Laws of the Association, its objects were defined as follows: –

- The acquisition of a common capital.
- The mutual assurance of its members against the evils of poverty, sickness, infirmity, and old age.
- The attainment of a greater share of the comforts of life than the working classes now possess.
- The mental and moral improvement of its adult members.
- The education of their children.

The following paragraphs selected from the Rules of the Association will give a pretty clear idea of its most important features: –

BASIS OF THE SOCIETY

That all the stock, implements of husbandry, and other property belong to and are the property of Mr. Vandeleur, until the Society accumulates sufficient to pay for them; they then become the joint property of the Society.

PRODUCTION

We engage that whatever talents we may individually possess, whether mental or muscular, agricultural, manufacturing, or scientific, shall be directed to the benefit of all, as well by their immediate exercise in all necessary occupations as by communicating our knowledge to each other, and particularly to the young.

---

[91] The Ralahine Commune was a co-operative community set up in Newmarket-on-Fergus in Co. Clare in 1831, on the estate of John Vandeleur, who sought in part to break the influence of Ribbonism in the community.

That, as far as can be reduced to practice, each individual shall assist in agricultural operations, particularly in harvest, it being fully understood that no individual is to act as steward, but all are to work.

That all the youth, male or female, do engage to learn some useful trade, together with agriculture and gardening, between the ages of nine and seventeen years.

That the committee meet every evening to arrange the business for the following day.

That the hours of labour be from six in the morning till six in the evening in summer, and from daybreak till dusk in winter, with the intermission of one hour for dinner.

That each agricultural labouring man shall receive eightpence, and every woman fivepence per day for their labour [these were the ordinary wages of the country, the secretary, storekeeper, smiths, joiners, and a few others received something more; the excess being borne by the proprietor] which it is expected will be paid out at the store in provisions, or any other article the society may produce or keep there; any other articles may be purchased elsewhere.

That no member be expected to perform any service or work but such as is agreeable to his or her feelings, or they are able to perform; but if any member thinks that any other member is not usefully employing his or her time, it is his or her duty to report it to the committee, whose duty it will be to bring that member's conduct before a general meeting, who shall have power, if necessary, to expel that useless member.

DISTRIBUTION AND DOMESTIC ECONOMY

That all the services usually performed by servants be performed by the youth of both sexes under the age of seventeen years, either by rotation or choice.

That the expenses of the children's food, clothing, washing, lodging, and education be paid out of the common funds of the society, from the time they are weaned till they arrive at the age of seventeen, when they shall be eligible to become members.

That a charge be made for the food and clothing, &c., of those children trained by their parents, and residing in their dwelling houses.

That each person occupying a house, or cooking and consuming their victuals therein, must pay for the fuel used.

That no charge be made for fuel used in the public room.

That it shall be a special object for the sub-committee of domestic economy, or the superintendent of that department, to ascertain and put in practice the best and most economical methods of preparing and cooking the food.

That all the washing be done together in the public washhouse; the expenses of soap, labour, fuel, &c., to be equally borne by all the adult members.

That each member pay the sum of one half-penny out of every shilling received as wages to form a fund to be placed in the hands of the committee, who shall pay the wages out of this fund of any member who may fall sick or meet with an accident.

Any damage done by a member to the stock, implements, or any other property belonging to the society to be made good out of the wages of the individual, unless the damage is satisfactorily accounted for to the committee.

EDUCATION AND FORMATION OF CHARACTER

We guarantee each other that the young children of any person dying whilst a member of this society, shall be equally protected, educated, and cherished with the children of the living members, and entitled, when they arrive at the age of seventeen, to all the privileges of members.

That each individual shall enjoy perfect liberty of conscience, and freedom of expression of opinion, and in religious worship.

That no spirituous liquors of any kind, tobacco, or snuff be kept in the store, or on the premises.

That if any of us should unfortunately have a dispute with any other person, we agree to abide by a decision of the majority of the members, or any person to whom the matter in question may be by them referred.

That any person wishing to marry another do sign a declaration to that effect one week previous to the marriage taking place, and that immediate preparations be made for the erection, or fitting-up of a suitable dwelling house for their reception.

That any person wishing to marry another person, not a member, shall sign a declaration according to the last rule; the person not a member shall then be balloted for, and, if rejected, both must leave the society.

That if the conduct of any member be found injurious to the well-being of the society, the committee shall explain to him or her in what respect his or her conduct shall continue to transgress the rules, such member shall be brought before a general meeting, called for the purpose, and if the complaint be substantiated, three-fourths of the members present shall have power to expel, by ballot, such refractory member.

GOVERNMENT

The society to be governed, and its business transacted, by a committee of nine members, to be chosen half-yearly, by ballot, by all the adult male and female members, the ballot list to contain at least four of the last committee.

The committee to meet every evening and their transactions to be regularly entered into a minute book, the recapitulation of which is to be given at the society's general meeting by the secretary.

That there be a general weekly meeting of the society; that the treasurer's accounts be audited by the committee, and read over to the society; that the *Suggestion Book* be also read at this meeting.

The colony did not use the ordinary currency of the country, but instead adopted a 'Labour Note' system of payment, all workers being paid in notes according to the number of hours worked, and being able to exchange the notes in the store for all the necessities of life. The notes were printed on stiff cardboard about the size of a visiting card, and represented the equivalent of a whole, a half, a quarter, an eighth, and a sixteenth of a day's labour. There were also special notes printed in red ink representing respectively the labours of a day and a half, and two days. In his account of the colony published under the title of *History of Ralahine*, by Heywood & Sons, Manchester (a book we earnestly recommend to all our readers), Mr. Craig says: – 'The labour was recorded daily on a "Labour Sheet", which was exposed to view during the following week. The members could work or not at their own discretion. If no work, no record, and, therefore, no pay. Practically the arrangement was of great use. There were no idlers.' Further on he comments: –

> 'The advantages of the labour notes were soon evident in the saving of members. They had no anxiety as to employment, wages, or the price of provisions. Each could partake of as much vegetable food as he or she could desire. The expenses of the children from infancy, for food or education, were provided for out of the common fund.
>
> 'The object should be to obtain a rule of justice, if we seek the law of righteousness. This can only be fully realised in that equality arising out of a community of property where the labour of one member is valued at the same rate as that of another member, and labour is exchanged for labour. It was not possible to attain to this condition of equality at Ralahine, but we made such arrangements as would impart a feeling of security, fairness and justice to all. The prices of provisions were fixed and uniform. A labourer was charged one shilling a week for as many vegetables and as much fruit as he chose to consume; milk was a penny per quart; beef and mutton fourpence, and pork two and one-half pence per pound. The married members occupying separate quarters were charged sixpence per week for rent, and twopence for fuel.'[92]

In dealing with Ireland no one can afford to ignore the question of the attitude of the clergy; it is therefore interesting to quote the words of an English visitor to Ralahine, a Mr. Finch, who afterwards wrote a series of fourteen letters describing the community, and offered to lay a special report before a Select Committee of the House of Commons upon the subject. He says: –

---

[92] Edward Thomas Craig, *An Irish Commune: The History of Ralahine* (1920).

'The only religion taught by the society was the unceasing practice of promoting the happiness of every man, woman, and child to the utmost extent in their power. Hence the Bible was not used as a school-book; no sectarian opinions were taught in the schools; no public dispute about religious dogmas or party political questions took place; nor were members allowed to ridicule each other's religion; nor were there any attempts at proselytism. Perfect freedom in the performance of religious duties and religious exercises was guaranteed to all. The teaching of religion was left to ministers of religion and to the parents; but no priest or minister received anything from the funds of the society. Nevertheless, both Protestant and Catholic priests were friendly to the system as soon as they understood it, and one reason was that they found these sober, industrious persons had now a little to give them out of their earnings, whereas formerly they had been beggars.'

Mr. Craig also states that the members of the community, after it had been in operation for some time, were better Catholics than before they began. He had at first considerable difficulty in warding off the attacks of zealous Protestant proselytisers, and his firmness in doing so was one of the chief factors in winning the confidence of the people as well as their support in insisting upon the absolutely non-sectarian character of the teaching.

All disputes between the members were settled by appeals to a general meeting in which all adults of both sexes participated, and from which all judges, lawyers, and other members of the legal fraternity were rigorously excluded.

To those who fear that the institution of common property will be inimical to progress and invention, it must be reassuring to learn that this community of 'ignorant' Irish peasants introduced into Ralahine the first reaping machine used in Ireland, and hailed it as a blessing at a time when the gentleman farmers of England were still gravely debating the practicability of the invention. From an address to the agricultural labourers of the County Clare, issued by the community on the introduction of this machine, we take the following passages, illustrative of the difference of effect between invention under common ownership and capitalist ownership: –

'This machine of ours is one of the first machines ever given to the working classes to lighten their labour, and at the same time increase their comforts. It does not benefit any one person among us exclusively, nor throw any individual out of employment. Any kind of machinery used for shortening labour – except used in a co-operative society like ours – must tend to lessen wages, and to deprive working men of employment, and finally either to starve them, force them into some other employment (and then reduce wages in that also) or compel them to emigrate. Now, if the working classes would cordially and peacefully unite to adopt our system, no power or party could prevent their success.'

This was published by order of the committee, 21st August, 1833, and when we observe the date we cannot but wonder at the number of things Clare – and the rest of Ireland – has forgotten since.

It must not be supposed that the landlord of the estate on which Ralahine was situated had allowed his enthusiasm for Socialism to run away with his self-interest. On the contrary, when turning over his farms to the community he stipulated for the payment to himself of a very heavy rental in kind. We extract from *Brotherhood*, a Christian Socialist Journal published in the north of Ireland in 1891, a statement of the rental, and a very luminous summing-up of the lesson of Ralahine, by the editor, Mr. Bruce Wallace, long a hard and unselfish worker for the cause of Socialism in Ireland: –

'The Association was bound to deliver annually, either at Ralahine, Bunratty, Clare, or Limerick, as the landlord might require, free of expense –

Wheat	320 brls.
Barley	240 brls.
Oats	50 brls.
Butter	10 cwt.
Pork	30 cwt.
Beef	70 cwt.

'At the prices then prevailing, this amount of produce would be equivalent to about, £900, £700 of rent for the use of natural forces and opportunities, and £200 of interest upon capital. It was thus a pretty stiff tribute that these poor Irish toilers had to pay for the privilege of making a little bit of their native soil fruitful. This tribute was, of course, so much to be deducted from the means of improving their sunken condition. In any future efforts that may be made to profit by the example of Ralahine and to apply again the principles of co-operation in farming, there ought to be the utmost care taken to reduce to a mininum the tribute payable to non-workers, and if possible to get rid of it altogether. If, despite this heavy burden of having to produce a luxurious maintenance for loungers, the condition of the toilers at Ralahine, as we shall see, was marvellously raised by the introduction of the co-operative principle amongst them, how much more satisfactorily would it have been raised had they been free of that depressing dead weight?'[93]

---

[93] John Bruce Wallace, Presbyterian and mystic, issued *The Brotherhood* starting in 1889 in Limavady in Co. Londonderry.

Such is the lesson of Ralahine. Had all the land and buildings belonged to the people, had all other estates in Ireland been conducted on the same principles, and the industries of the country also so organised, had each of them appointed delegates to confer on the business of the country at some common centre as Dublin, the framework and basis of a free Ireland would have been realised. And when Ireland does emerge into complete control of her own destinies she must seek the happiness of her people in the extension on a national basis of the social arrangements of Ralahine, or else be but another social purgatory for her poor – a purgatory where the pangs of the sufferers will be heightened by remembering the delusive promises of political reformers.

In the most crime-ridden county in Ireland this partial experiment in Socialism abolished crime; where the fiercest fight for religious domination had been fought it brought the mildest tolerance; where drunkenness had fed fuel to the darkest passions it established sobriety and gentleness; where poverty and destitution had engendered brutality, midnight marauding, and a contempt for all social bonds, it enthroned security, peace and reverence for justice, and it did this solely by virtue of the influence of the new social conception attendant upon the institution of common property bringing a common interest to all. Where such changes came in the bud, what might we not expect from the flower? If a partial experiment in Socialism, with all the drawbacks of an experiment, will achieve such magnificent results what could we not rightfully look for were all Ireland, all the world, so organised on the basis of common property, and exploitation and mastership forever abolished?

The downfall of the Association came as a result of the iniquitous land laws of Great Britain refusing to recognise the right of such a community to hold a lease or to act as tenants. The landlord, Mr. Vandeleur, lost his fortune in a gambling transaction in Dublin, and fled in disgrace, unable to pay his debts. The persons who took over the estate under bankruptcy proceedings refused to recognise the community, insisted upon treating its members as common labourers on the estate, seized upon the buildings and grounds and broke up the Association.

So Ralahine ended. But in the rejuvenated Ireland of the future the achievement of those simple peasants will be dwelt upon with admiration as a great and important landmark in the march of the human race towards its complete social emancipation. Ralahine was an Irish point of interrogation erected amidst the wildernesses of capitalist thought and feudal practice, challenging both in vain for an answer. Other smaller communities were also established in Ireland during the same period. A Lord Wallscourt established a somewhat similar community on his estate in County Galway; *The Quarterly Review* of November, 1819, states that there was then a small community existent nine miles outside Dublin, which held thirty acres, supported a priest and a school of 300 children, had erected buildings, made and sold jaunting cars, and comprised butchers, carpenters and wheelwrights; the Quakers of Dublin established a Co-operative Woollen Factory, which flourished until it was destroyed by litigation set on foot by dissatisfied members who had been won over to the side of rival capitalists, and a communal home was established and long maintained in Dublin by members of the same religious sect, but without any other motive than that of helping forward the march of social amelioration.[94] We understand that the extensive store of Messrs. Ganly & Sons on Usher's Quay in Dublin was the home of this community, who lived, worked and enjoyed themselves in the spacious halls, and slept in the smaller rooms of what is now the property of a capitalist auctioneer.

Chapter XII: A Chapter of Horrors: Daniel O'Connell and the Working Class

> ''Tis civilisation, so ye say, and cannot be changed for the weakness of men,
> Take heed, take heed, 'tis a dangerous way to drive the wild wolf to the end of his den.
> There are times, as Paris in '93, when the commonest men play terrible parts,
> Take heed of your progress, its feet are shod with the souls it slew, with its own pollutions,
> Submission is good, but the order of God may flame the torch of the revolutions.'
> John Boyle O'Reilly[95]

For both Ireland and Great Britain the period between the winning of Catholic Emancipation (1829) and the year 1850 was marked by great misery and destitution amongst the producing classes, accompanied by abortive attempts at revolution in both countries, and the concession of some few unimportant political and social reforms. In Ireland the first move against the forces of privilege was the abolition of the Tithes, or, more correctly speaking, the abolition of the harsh and brutal features

---

[94] Joseph Henry Blake, 3rd Baron Wallscourt (1797–1849), Irish aristocrat and early socialist, moved by the example of Ralahine.
[95] John Boyle O'Reilly (1844–1890), Irish poet and journalist. Transported to Australia for his membership of the Irish Republican Brotherhood.

attendant upon the collection of the tithes. The clergy of the Episcopalian Church, the Church by law established in Ireland, were legally entitled to levy upon the people of each district, irrespective of religion, a certain tax for the upkeep of that Church and its ministers. The fact that this was in conformity with the practice of the Catholic Church in countries where it was dominant did not, of course, make this any more palatable to the Catholic peasantry of Ireland, who continually saw a part of their crops seized upon and sold to maintain a clergy whose ministrations they never attended, and whose religion they detested. Eventually their discontent at the injustice grew so acute as to flare forth in open rebellion, and accordingly all over Ireland the tenants began to resist the collection of tithes by every means in their power.

The Episcopalian clergymen called on the aid of the law, and, escorted by police and military, seized the produce of the poor tenants and carried it off to be sold at auction; the peasantry, on the other hand, collected at dead of night and carried off the crops and cattle from farms upon which the distraint was to be made, and, when that was impossible, they strove by acts of violence to terrorise auctioneers and buyers from consummating the sale. Many a bright young life was extinguished on the gallows, or rotted away in prison cells, as a result of this attempt to sustain a hated religion by contributions exacted at the point of the bayonet, until eventually the struggle assumed all the aspect of a civil war. At several places when the military were returning from raiding the farm of some poor peasant, the country people gathered, erected barricades, and opposed their passage by force. Significantly enough of the temper and qualities of the people in those engagements, they generally succeeded in rescuing their crops and cattle from the police and military, and in demonstrating that Ireland still possessed all the material requisite for armed rebellion.

In one conflict at Newtownbarry, twelve peasants were shot and twenty fatally wounded; in another at Carrigshock eleven policemen were killed and seventeen wounded; and at a great fight at Rathcormack, twelve peasants were killed in a fight with a large body of military and armed police. Eye-witnesses declared that the poor farmers and labourers engaged, stood the charge and volleys of the soldiers as firmly as if they had been seasoned troops, a fact that impressed the Government more than a million speeches could have done. The gravity of the crisis was enhanced by the contrast between the small sum often involved, and the bloodshed necessary to recover it. Thus, at Rathcormack, twelve peasants were massacred in an attempt to save the effects of a poor widow from being sold to pay a sum of forty shillings due as tithes.

The ultimate effect of all this resistance was the passage of a *Tithes Commutation Act* by which the collection of tithes was abolished, and the substitution in its place of a 'Tithe Rent Charge' by means of which the sums necessary for the support of the Episcopalian clergy were included in the rent and paid as part of that tribute to the landed aristocracy.[96] In other words, the economic drain remained, but it was deprived of all the more odious and galling features of its collection. The secret Ribbon and Whiteboy Societies were the most effective weapons of the peasantry in this fight, and to their activities the victory is largely to be attributed. The politicians gave neither help nor countenance to the fight, and save for the advocacy of one small Dublin newspaper, conducted by a small but brilliant band of young Protestant writers, no journal in all Ireland championed their cause. For the Catholic clergy it is enough to say that while this tithe war was being waged, they were almost universally silent about that 'grievous sin of secret conspiracy' upon which they are usually so eloquent. We would not dare to say that they recognised that, as the secret societies were doing their work against a rival priesthood, it was better to be sparing in their denunciations for the time being; perhaps that is not the explanation, but at all events it is noteworthy that as soon as the tithe war was won, all the old stock invectives against every kind of extra-constitutional action were immediately renewed.

Contemporaneously with this tithe-war had grown up the agitation for repeal of the Legislative Union led by Daniel O'Connell, and supported by the large body of the middle classes, and by practically all the Catholic clergy. At the outset of this agitation the Irish working class, partly because they accepted O'Connell's explanation of the decay of Irish trade as due to the Union, and partly because they did not believe he was sincere in his professions of loyalty to the English monarchy, nor in his desire to limit his aims to repeal, enthusiastically endorsed and assisted his agitation. He, on his part, incorporated the trades bodies in his association with rights equal to that of regularly enrolled members, a proceeding which evoked considerable dissent from many quarters. Thus the *Irish Monthly Magazine* (Dublin), a rabidly O'Connellite journal, in its issue of September, 1832, complains that the National Union (of Repealers) is in danger because 'there is a contemporary union composed of the tradesmen and operative classes, the members of which

---

[96] Tithe commutation was legislated for England and Wales in 1836, and for Ireland in 1838. But the tithe burden was not fully lifted until the passage of the Irish Church Act of 1869, which disestablished the Church of Ireland.

are qualified to vote at its sittings, and who are in every respect put upon a perfect equality with the members of the National Union'. And in its December number of the same year it returns to the charge with the significant statement that 'In fact we apprehend great mischief and little good from the trades union as at present constituted.' The representative of the English King in Ireland, Lord Lieutenant Anglesey, apparently coincided in the opinion of this follower of O'Connell as to the danger of Irish trade unions in politics, for when the Dublin trade bodies projected a mammoth demonstration in favour of Repeal, he immediately proclaimed it, and ordered the military to suppress it, if necessary, by armed force.[97] But as O'Connell grew in strength in the country, and attracted to himself more and more of the capitalist and professional classes in Ireland, and as he became more necessary to the schemes of the Whig politicians in England, and thought these latter more necessary to his success, he ceased to play for the favour of organised labour, and gradually developed into the most bitter and unscrupulous enemy of trade unionism Ireland has yet produced, signalising the trades of Dublin always out for his most venomous attack.

In 1835 O'Connell took his seat on the Ministerial side of the House of Commons as a supporter of the Whig Government. At that time the labouring population of England were the most exploited, degraded, and almost dehumanised of all the peoples of Europe. The tale of their condition reveals such inhumanity on the part of the masters, such woeful degradation on the side of the toilers, that were it not attested by the sober record of witnesses before various Parliamentary Commissions the record would be entirely unbelievable. Women worked down in coal mines, almost naked, for a pitiful wage, often giving birth to children when surprised by the pains of parturition amidst the darkness and gloom of their places of employment; little boys and girls were employed drawing heavy hutches (wagons) of coal along the pit-floors by means of a strap around their bodies and passing through between their little legs; in cotton factories little tots of eight, seven, and even six years of age of both sexes were kept attending machinery, being hired like slaves from workhouses for that purpose, and worked twelve, fourteen, and even sixteen hours per day, living, sleeping, and working under conditions which caused them to die off as with a plague; in pottery works, bakeshops, clothing factories and workrooms the overwork and unhealthy conditions of employment led to such suffering and degradation and

---

[97] Henry Paget, 1st Marquis of Anglesey (1768–1854), British soldier and politician, Lord Lieutenant of Ireland 1828–1829 and 1830–1833.

shortening of life that the very existence of the working-class was endangered. In the agricultural districts the sufferings of the poor were so terrible that the English agricultural labourer – the most stolidly patient, unimaginative person on the face of the earth – broke out into riots, machine-breaking, and hay-rick burning. As in Ireland, Captain Rock or Captain Moonlight had been supposed to be the presiding genius of the nocturnal revolts of the peasantry, so in England, Captain Swing, an equally mythical personage, took the blame or the credit.[98] In a booklet circulated amongst the English agricultural labourers, Captain Swing is made to say: 'I am not the author of these burnings. These fires are caused by farmers having been turned out of their lands to make room for foxes, peasants confined two years in prison for picking up a dead partridge, and parsons taking a poor man's only cow for the tithe of his cabbage garden.' So great was the distress, so brutal the laws, and so hopelessly desperate the labourers, that in the Special Assize held at Winchester in December, 1830, no less than three hundred prisoners were put upon trial, a great number of whom were sentenced to death. Of the number so condemned, six were actually hanged, twenty transported for life, and the rest for smaller periods. We are told in the *English Via Dolorosa*, of William Heath, that 'a child of fourteen had sentence of death recorded against him; and two brothers, one twenty, the other nineteen, were ruthlessly hanged on Penenden Heath, whither they were escorted by a regiment of Scots Greys'.[99] As to whom was responsible for all this suffering, contemporary witnesses leave no doubt: The London *Times*, most conservative of all capitalist papers, in its issue of December 27, 1830, declared: – 'We do affirm that the actions of this pitiable class of men (the labourers) are a commentary on the treatment experienced by them at the hands of the upper and middling classes. The present population must be provided for in body and spirit on more liberal and Christian principles, or the whole mass of labourers will start into legions of *banditti* – *banditti* less criminal than

---

[98] Captain Rock, Captain Moonlight and Captain Swing are all names used for mythical avenging figures of agrarian resistance and rebellion in Ireland and England during the eighteenth and early nineteenth centuries. The Irish Whiteboy movement issued proclamations or delivered threatening letters to landlords in the name of 'Captain Moonlight', and their nineteenth-century descendants used the name 'Captain Rock' to the same purpose. 'Captain Swing' appeared to similar ends in England in the 1830s, particularly during the Swing Riots in southern England, which were protests over the mechanisation of threshing.

[99] Richard Heath, *The English Via Dolorosa; or, Glimpses of the History of the Agricultural Labourer* (1884).

those who have made them so; those who by a just but fearful retribution will soon become their victims.'[100] And in 1833 a Parliamentary Commission reported that 'The condition of the agricultural labourers was brutal and wretched; their children during the day were struggling with the pigs for food, and at night were huddled down on damp straw under a roof of rotten thatch.'[101]

In the large towns the same state of rebellion prevailed, the military were continually on duty, and so many people were killed that the coroners ceased to hold inquests. Such was the state of England – misery and revolt beneath, and sanguinary repression coupled with merciless greed above – at the time when O'Connell, taking his seat in Parliament, threw all his force on the side of capitalist privilege and against social reform.

In 1838 five cotton-spinners in Glasgow, in Scotland, were sentenced to seven years' transportation for acts they had committed in connection with trade union combination to better the miserable condition of their class. As the punishment was universally felt to be excessive, even in the brutal spirit of the times, Mr. Walkley, Member of Parliament for Finsbury, on the 13th of February of that year, brought forward a motion in the House of Commons for a 'Select Committee to enquire into the constitution, practices, and effects of the Association of Cotton Operatives of Glasgow'.[102] O'Connell opposed the motion, and used the opportunity to attack the Irish trade-unions. He said: –

> 'There was no tyranny equal to that which was exercised by the trade-unionists in Dublin over their fellow labourers. One rule of the workmen prescribed a minimum rate of wages *so that the best workman received no more than the worst*. Another part of their system was directed towards depriving the masters of all freedom in their power of selecting workmen, the names of the workmen being inscribed in a book, and the employer compelled to take the first on the list.'

He said that at Bandon a large factory had been closed, through the efforts of the men to get higher wages, ditto at Belfast, and 'it was calculated that wages to the amount of £500,000 per year were lost to Dublin by trade-unions. The combination of tailors in that city, for instance, had raised the price of clothes to such a pitch that it was

---

[100] 'Banditti', from the Italian *bandito*, were bandits or robbers.
[101] In the 1820s and 1830s, Parliament appointed several Select Committees on Agriculture, and also on Agricultural Distress – Connolly is referring to a report issued by one of these Committees.
[102] Thomas Wakley (1795–1862), English doctor and Member of Parliament. Founder of the famous medical journal *The Lancet* in 1823.

worth a person's while to go to Glasgow and wait a couple of days for a suit, the difference in the price paying the expense of the trip.' He also ascribed the disappearance of the shipbuilding trades from Dublin to the evil effects of trade unions.

Because of O'Connell's speech his friends, the Whig Government, appointed a committee, not to enquire into the Glasgow cases, but to investigate the acts of the Irish, and especially of the Dublin, trade unions. The Special Committee sat and collected two volumes of evidence, O'Connell producing a number of witnesses to bear testimony against the Irish trade unionists, but the report of the committee was never presented to the House of Commons. In June of the same year, 1838, O'Connell had another opportunity to vent his animus against the working class, and serve the interest of English and Irish capitalism, and was not slow to take advantage of it. In the year 1833, mainly owing to the efforts of the organised factory operatives, and some high-spirited philanthropists, a law had been enacted forbidding the employment of *children under nine years of age* in factories except silk-mills, and forbidding those under thirteen from working more than forty-eight hours per week, or nine hours per day. The ages mentioned will convey to the reader some idea of how infantile flesh and blood had been sacrificed to sate the greed of the propertied class. Yet this eminently moderate enactment was fiercely hated by the godly capitalists of England, and by every unscrupulous device they could contrive they strove to circumvent it. So constant and effective was their evasion of its merciful provisions that on the 23rd of June the famous friend of the factory operatives, Lord Ashley, in the House of Commons, moved as an amendment to the Order of the Day the second reading of a *Bill to more effectually regulate Factory Works*, its purpose being to prevent or punish any further infringement of the Act of 1833.[103] O'Connell opposed the motion, and attempted to justify the infringement of the law by the employers by stating that 'they (Parliament) had legislated against the nature of things, and against the right of industry'. 'Let them not', he said, 'be guilty of the childish folly of regulating the labour of adults, and go about parading before the world *their ridiculous humanity*, which would end by convert-

---

[103] Anthony Ashley-Cooper, 7th Earl of Shaftesbury (1801–1885), English politician, reformer and philanthropist. Through the nineteenth century, as British industry expanded enormously, a long series of Acts of Parliament were passed (often amidst great controversy, as Connolly explains) which sought to ameliorate working conditions, which were often brutal and dangerous. Connolly here refers to the 1833 Labour of Children in Factories Act, which regulated the ages and working hours of children in factories.

ing their manufacturers into beggars'. The phrase about regulating the labour of adults was borrowed from the defence set up by the capitalists that preventing the employment of children also interfered with the labour of adults – freeborn Englishmen! O'Connell was not above using this clap-trap, as he on a previous occasion had not been above making the lying pretence that the enforcement of a *minimum* wage prevented the payment of *high* wages to any specially skilled artisan.

On this question of the attitude to be taken up towards the claims of labour, O'Connell differed radically with one of his most capable lieutenants, Fergus O'Connor.[104] The latter, being returned to Parliament as a Repealer, was struck by the miserable condition of the real people of England in whose interests Ireland was supposed to be governed, and as the result of his investigation into its cause, he arrived at the conclusion that the basis of the oppression of Ireland was economic, that labour in England was oppressed by the same class and by the operation of the same causes as had impoverished and ruined Ireland, and that the solution of the problem in both countries required the union of the democracies in one common battle against their oppressors. He earnestly strove to impress this view upon O'Connell, only to find, that in the latter class-feeling was much stronger than desire for Irish National freedom, and that he, O'Connell, felt himself to be much more akin to the propertied class of England than to the working class of Ireland. This was proven by his actions in the cases above cited. This divergence of opinion between O'Connell and O'Connor closed Ireland to the latter and gave him to the Chartists as one of their most fearless and trusted leaders.

When he died, more than 50,000 toilers marched in the funeral procession which bore his remains to his last resting-place. He was one of the first of that long list of Irish fighters in Great Britain whose unselfish sacrifices have gone to make a record for an 'English' Labour movement. That the propertied and oppressing classes were well aware of the value of O'Connell's services against the democracy, and were believed to be grateful for the same was attested by the action of Richard Lalor Shiel [*sic*] when, defending him during the famous State trials, he claimed the consideration of the Court for O'Connell, because he had stood between the people of Ireland and the people of England, and so 'prevented a junction which would be formidable enough to overturn any administration that could be formed'.[105] But, as zealous as O'Connell

---

[104] Fergus Edward O'Connor (1794–1855), Irish politician and a leader of the British Chartist working-class movement for social reform.

[105] Richard Lalor Sheil (1794–1851), Irish politician, orator and playwright.

and the middle class repealers were to prevent any international action of the democracies, the Irish Working Class were as enthusiastic in their desire to consummate it. Irish Chartist Associations sprang up all over the island, and we are informed by a writer in the *United Irishman* of John Mitchel, 1848, that in Dublin they had grown so strong and so hostile to O'Connellism that at one time negotiations were in progress for a public debate between the Liberator and a representative of the Dublin trades.[106] But upon the arrest and imprisonment of O'Connell, he continues, the Working Class were persuaded to abandon their separate organisations for the sake of presenting a common front to the Government, a step they afterwards regretted. To this letter John Mitchel, as editor, appended a note reminding his readers of the anti-labour record of O'Connell, and adducing it as a further reason for repudiating his leadership. Yet it is curious that in his *History of Ireland* Mitchel omits all reference to this disgraceful side of O'Connell's career, as do indeed all the other Irish 'Historians'.[107] If silence gives consent, then all our history writing scribes have consented to, and hence approved of, this suppression of the facts of history in order to assist in perpetuating the blindness and the subjection of labour.

Chapter XIII: Our Irish Girondins Sacrifice the Irish Peasantry upon the Altar of Private Property

'There is a class of Revolutionists named Girondins whose fate in history is remarkable enough. Men who rebel, and urge the lower classes to rebel, ought to have other than formulas to go upon. Men who discern in the misery of the toiling, complaining millions, not misery but only a raw material which can be wrought upon and traded in for one's own poor hide-bound theories and egoisms, to whom millions of living fellow-creatures with beating hearts in their bosoms – beating, suffering, hoping – are 'masses', mere explosive masses, for blowing down Bastilles with, for voting at hustings for 'us', such men are of the questionable species.'
– **Thomas Carlyle**[108]

---

[106] Chartism was an English working-class reform movement, particularly strong in the industrialised parts of England and in the 1830s and 1840s. It took its name from the People's Charter of 1838, which set out its demands. These included universal male suffrage, secret ballots, annual elections, and an end to a property qualification for Members of Parliament. John Mitchel published the *United Irishman* in 1848. It ran to only 16 issues, before it was suppressed.

[107] Mitchel published his *History of Ireland, from the Treaty of Limerick to the Present Time*, in 1864.

[108] The Girondins were a political grouping within the National Legislative Assembly

The outbreak of the famine, which commenced on a small scale in 1845, and increased in area and intensity until 1849, brought to a head the class antagonism in Ireland, of which the rupture with the trades was one manifestation, and again revealed the question of property as the test by which the public conduct is regulated, even when those men assume the garb of revolution.[109] Needless to say, this is not the interpretation of the history of that awful period we are given by the orthodox Irish or English writers upon the subject. Irish Nationalists of all stripes and English critics of every variety agree, with wonderful unanimity, in ascribing a split in the Repeal Association which led to the formation by the seceders of the body known as the Irish Confederation to the academic question of whether force might or might not be employed to achieve a political end.[110] The majority of the Repeal Association, we are told, subscribed to the principle enunciated by O'Connell that 'the greatest sublunary blessings were not worth the shedding of a single drop of human blood', and John Mitchel, Father Meehan, Gavan Duffy, Thomas Francis Meagher, Devin Reilly, William Smith O'Brien, Fintan Lalor, and others repudiated that doctrine, and on this point of purely theoretical divergence the secession from O'Connell took place.[111] It is difficult to believe that any large number of Irishmen ever held such a doctrine seriously; it is quite certain that the Irish Catholic priesthood, O'Connell's chief lieutenants, did not hold nor counsel such a doctrine during the Tithe War. O'Connell himself had declared that he would willingly join in helping England in 'bringing down the American eagle in its highest pride of flight', which surely would have involved war, and in the House of Commons on one occasion, in reply to Lord Lyndhurst,

---

of France, during the Revolution, in the years 1791–1795. Some of them were Jacobins. They resisted the radicalism of the 'Mountain', a faction within the Jacobin Club, and this led to their fall and mass execution, precipitating the Reign of Terror. Thomas Carlyle (1795–1881), Scottish philosopher, essayist and historian. *The French Revolution: A History* (1837) is a classic study, and was the inspiration for Charles Dickens's novel *A Tale of Two Cities*.

[109] The Great Irish Famine (1845–1852) was the defining historical event of nineteenth-century Ireland. It was caused by the destruction of the potato crop, on which large numbers of the population was dependent for food, by blight. Approximately 1 million people died in these years, and another 1 million emigrated.

[110] The Repeal Association was the political organisation set up by O'Connell in 1830 to campaign for the repeal of the Act of Union of 1800. It collapsed with O'Connell's death in 1847. The Irish Confederation was formed by a split in the Repeal Association, and provided the structure for the Young Ireland movement.

[111] Father Charles Meehan (1812–1890), Charles Gavan Duffy (1816–1903), Thomas Francis Meagher (1823–1867), Thomas Devin Reilly (1823–1854), James Fintan Lalor (1807–1849), along with Mitchel, were all involved in the Young Ireland movement.

who had characterised the Irish as 'aliens in blood, in language, and in religion', Richard Lalor Shiel [sic], a champion of O'Connellism, had delivered a magnificent oration vaunting the prowess of Irish soldiers in the English army. In passing we note that Shiel considered the above phrase of Lord Lyndhurst an insult; modern Irish Nationalists triumphantly assert the idea, embodied in that phrase, as the real basis of Irish nationalism.[112]

Nor yet were the seceders, the Young Irelanders as they were called, in favour of physical force, save as a subject for flights in poetry and oratory. In reality the secession took place on a false issue; the majority on either side being disinclined to admit, even if they recognised, the real issue dividing them. That issue was the old and ever-present one of the Democratic principle in human society versus the Aristocratic. The Young Irelanders, young and enthusiastic, felt the force of the Democratic principle then agitating European society, indeed the very name of Young Ireland was an adaptation of the names used by the Italian revolutionist Mazzini for the revolutionary associations, Young Italy, Young Switzerland, Young France, and Young Germany, he founded after the year 1831.[113] And as the progress of the revolutionary movement on the Continent, (accompanied as it was by the popularisation of Socialistic ideas among the revolutionary masses) synchronised with the falling apart of the social system in Ireland owing to the famine, the leaders of the Young Ireland party responded to and moved along with the revolutionary current of events without ever being able to comprehend the depth and force of the stream upon whose surface they were embarked. The truth of this is apparent to all who study their action when at last the long talked of day-for-revolution had arrived. By that time, 1848, Ireland was in the throes of the greatest famine in her history.

A few words explanatory of that famine may not be amiss to some of our readers. The staple food of the Irish peasantry was the potato; all other agricultural produce, grains and cattle, was sold to pay the landlord's rent. The ordinary value of the potato crop was yearly approximately twenty million pounds in English money; in 1848, in

---

[112] John Singleton Copely, 1st Baron Lyndhurst (1772–1863), English lawyer and politician. Served as Lord Chancellor for three terms.

[113] Young Ireland was a political and cultural movement in mid-nineteenth century Ireland. Its newspaper was *The Nation*, founded by Thomas Davis, John Blake Dillon and Charles Gavan Duffy. *The Nation* was instrumental in forming and shaping Irish mass nationalist culture in English. The movement collapsed after its failed rebellion of 1848.

the midst of the famine the value of agricultural produce in Ireland was £44,958,120. In that year the entire potato crop was a failure, and to that fact the famine is placidly attributed, yet those figures amply prove that there was food enough in the country to feed double the population, were the laws of capitalist society set aside, and human rights elevated to their proper position. It is a common saying amongst Irish Nationalists that 'Providence sent the potato blight; but England made the famine.' The statement is true, and only needs amending by adding that 'England made the famine by a rigid application of the economic principles that lie at the base of capitalist society.' No man who accepts capitalist society and the laws thereof can logically find fault with the statesmen of England for their acts in that awful period. They stood for the rights of property and free competition, and philosophically accepted their consequences upon Ireland; the leaders of the Irish people also stood for the rights of property, and refused to abandon them even when they saw the consequences in the slaughter by famine of over a million of the Irish toilers. The first failure of the potato crop took place in 1845, and between September and December of that year 515 deaths from hunger were registered, although 3,250,000 quarters of wheat and numberless cattle had been exported. From that time until 1850 the famine spread, and the exports of food continued. Thus in 1848 it was estimated that 300,000 persons died of hunger and 1,826,132 quarters of wheat and barley were exported. Typhus fever, which always follows on the heels of hunger, struck down as many as perished directly of famine, until at last it became impossible in many districts to get sufficient labourers with strength enough to dig separate graves for the dying. Recourse was had to famine pits, into which the bodies were thrown promiscuously; whole families died in their miserable cabins, and lay and rotted there, and travellers in remote parts of the country often stumbled upon villages in which the whole population had died of hunger. In 1847, 'black '47', 250,000 died of fever; 21,770 of starvation. Owing to the efforts of emigration agents and remittances sent from relatives abroad in the same year, 89,783 persons embarked for Canada. They were flying from hunger, but they could not fly from the fever that follows in the wake of hunger, and 6,100 died and were thrown overboard on the voyage, 4,100 died on their arrival in Canada, 5,200 in hospitals, and 1,900 in interior towns.

Great Britain was nearer than America, and many who could not escape to America rushed to the inhospitable shores of Britain; but pressure was brought to bear upon the steamship companies, and they raised the rates upon all passengers by steerage to an almost prohibitive price.

In this flight to England occurred one of the most fearful tragedies of all history, a tragedy which, in our opinion, surpasses that of the Black Hole of Calcutta in its accumulation of fearful and gruesome horrors. On December 2, 1848, a steamer left Sligo with 200 steerage passengers on board bound for Liverpool. On that bleak north-western coast such a passage is at all times rough, and storms are both sudden and fierce. Such a storm came on during the night, and as the unusual number of passengers crowded the deck the crew unceremoniously and brutally drove them below decks, and battened down the hatches to prevent their re-emergence. In the best of weather the steerage of such a coasting vessel is, even when empty of human freight, foul, suffocating and unbearable; the imagination fails to realise what it must have been on that awful night when 200 poor wretches were driven into its depths. To add to the horror, when some of the more desperate beat upon the hatches and demanded release, the mate, in a paroxysm of rage, ordered a tarpaulin to be thrown across the opening to stifle their cries. It did stifle the cries, it also excluded the air and the light, and there in that inferno those 200 human beings fought, struggled and gasped for air while the elements warred outside and the frail tub of a ship was tossed upon the surface of the waters. At last, when some one stronger than the rest managed to break through and reach the deck, he confronted the ship's officers with the news that their brutality had made them murderers, that grim death was reaping his harvest amongst the passengers. It was too true. Out of the 200 passengers battened down below decks, 72, more than a third of the entire number, had expired, suffocated for want of air or mangled to death in the blind struggle of despair in the darkness. Such is the tale of that voyage of the ship *Londonderry*, surely the most horrible tale of the sea in the annals of any white people!

Amidst such conditions the Irish Confederation had been preaching the moral righteousness of rebellion, and discoursing learnedly in English to a starving people, the most of whom knew only Irish, about the historical examples of Holland, Belgium, Poland, and the Tyrol. A few men, notably John Mitchel, James Fintan Lalor, and Thomas Devin Reilly, to their credit be it said, openly advocated, as the first duty of the people, the refusal to pay rents, the retention of their crops to feed their own families, and the breaking-up of bridges and tearing-up of railroad lines, to prevent the removal of food from the country. Had such advice been followed by the Young Irelanders as a body it would, as events showed, have been enthusiastically adopted by the people at large, in which event no force in the power of England could have saved landlordism or the British Empire in Ireland. As explained by Fintan

Lalor, the keenest intellect in Ireland in his day, it meant the avoidance of all pitched battles with the English army, and drawing it into a struggle along lines and on a plan of campaign where its discipline, training, and methods would be a hindrance rather than a help, and where no mobilisation, battalion-drilling nor technical knowledge of military science was required of the insurgent masses. In short, it involved a social and a national revolution, each resting upon the other. But the men who advocated this were in a hopeless minority, and the chiefs of the Young Irelanders were as rabidly solicitous about the rights of the landlord as were the chiefs of the English Government. While the people perished, the Young Irelanders talked, and their talk was very beautiful, thoroughly grammatical, nicely polished, and the proper amount of passion introduced always at the proper psychological moment. But still the people perished. Eventually the Government seized upon the really dangerous man – the man who had hatred of injustice deeply enough rooted to wish to destroy it at all costs, the man who had faith enough in the masses to trust a revolutionary outbreak to their native impulses, and who possessed the faculty of combining thought with action, John Mitchel. With his arrest the people looked for immediate revolution, so did the Government, so did Mitchel himself. All were disappointed. John Mitchel was carried off to penal servitude in Van Diemen's Land (Tasmania) after scornfully refusing to sign a manifesto presented to him in his cell by Thomas Francis Meagher and others, counselling the people *not* to attempt to rescue him. The working class of Dublin and most of the towns were clamouring for their leaders to give the word for a rising; in many places in the country the peasantry were acting spontaneously. Eventually news reached Dublin in July, 1848, that warrants were issued for the arrest of the chiefs of the Young Ireland party. They determined to appeal to the country. But everything had to be done in a 'respectable' manner; English army on one side, provided with guns, bands, and banners; Irish army on the other side, also provided with guns, bands and banners, 'serried ranks with glittering steel', no mere proletarian insurrection, and no interference with the rights of property. When C.G. Duffy was arrested on Saturday, 9th of July, in Dublin, the Dublin workers surrounded the military escort on the way to the prison at Newgate, stopped the carriage, pressed up to Duffy and offered to begin the insurrection then and there. 'Do you wish to be rescued?' said one of the leaders. 'Certainly not', said Duffy. And the puzzled toilers fell back and allowed the future Australian Premier to go to prison. In Cashel, Tipperary, Michael Doheny was arrested. The people stormed the jail and rescued him. He insisted upon giving himself up again and applied for bail. In Waterford Meagher was arrested. As he was being taken through the city, guarded by troops, the people erected a barricade in the way across a narrow bridge over the River Suir, and when the carriage reached the bridge some cut the traces of the horses and brought the cavalcade to a standstill. Meagher ordered them to remove the barricade; they begged him to give the word for insurrection and they would begin then and there. The important city was in their hands, but Meagher persisted in going with the soldiers, and the poor working-class rebels of Waterford let him go, crying out as they did so, 'You will regret it, you will regret it, and it is your own fault.' Meagher afterwards proved himself a fearless soldier of a regular army, but as an insurgent he lacked the necessary initiative.

But the crowning absurdity of all was the leadership of William Smith O'Brien. He wandered through the country telling the starving peasantry to get ready, but refusing to allow them to feed themselves at the expense of the landlords who had so long plundered, starved, and evicted them; he would not allow his followers to seize upon the carts of grain passing along the roads where the people were dying of want of food; at Mullinahone he refused to allow his followers to fell trees to build a barricade across the road until they had asked permission of the landlords who owned the trees; when the people of Killenaule had a body of dragoons entrapped between two barricades he released the dragoons from their dangerous situation upon their leader assuring him that he had no warrant for his (O'Brien's) arrest; in another place he surprised a party of soldiers in the Town Hall with their arms taken apart for cleaning purposes, and instead of confiscating the arms, he told the soldiers that their arms were as safe as they would be in Dublin Castle.

When we remember the state of Ireland then, with her population perishing of famine, all the above recital reads like a page of comic opera. Unfortunately it is not; it is a page from the blackest period of Ireland's history. Reading it, we can understand why Smith O'Brien has a monument in Dublin, although Fintan Lalor's name and writings have been boycotted for more than fifty years. W.A. O'Connor, B.A., in his *History of the Irish People*, sums up Smith O'Brien's career thus: – 'The man had broken up a peaceful organisation in the cause of war, promised war to a people in desperate strait, went into the country to wage war, then considered it guilt to do any act of war.'[114] It must, of course, be conceded that Smith O'Brien was a man of high moral probity, but it is equally necessary to affirm that he was a landlord, vehemently

---

[114] William Anderson O'Connor, *History of the Irish People* (1883).

solicitous for the rights of his class, and allowing his solicitude for those rights to stand between the millions of the Irish race and their hopes of life and freedom. It ought, however, also be remembered, in extenuation of his conduct in that awful crisis, that he had inherited vast estates as the result of the social, national, and religious apostacy of his forefathers, and in view of such an ancestry, it is more wonderful that he had dreamed of rebellion than that he had repudiated revolution.

Had Socialist principles been applied to Ireland in those days not one person need have died of hunger, and not one cent of charity need have been subscribed to leave a smirch upon the Irish name. But all except a few men had elevated landlord property and capitalist political economy to a fetish to be worshipped, and upon the altar of that fetish Ireland perished. At the lowest computation 1,225,000 persons died of absolute hunger; all of these were sacrificed upon the altar of capitalist thought.

Early in the course of the famine the English Premier, Lord John Russell, declared that nothing must be done to interfere with private enterprise or the regular course of trade, and this was the settled policy of the Government from first to last.[115] A Treasury *Minute* of August 31, 1846, provided that 'depots for the sale of food were to be established at Longford, Banagher, Limerick, Galway, Waterford, and Sligo, and subordinate depots at other places on the western coast', but the rules provided that such depots were not to be opened where food could be obtained from private dealers, and, when opened, food was to be sold at prices which would permit of private dealers competing. In all the Acts establishing relief works, it was stipulated that all the labour must be entirely unproductive, so as not to prevent capitalists making a profit either then or in the future. Private dealers made fortunes ranging from £40,000 to £80,000. In 1845 a Commissariat Relief Department was organised to bring in Indian Corn for sale in Ireland, but *none was to be sold until all private stores were sold out*: the State of Massachusetts hired an American ship-of-war, the *Jamestown*, loaded it with grain, and sent it to Ireland; the Government placed the cargo in storage, claiming that putting it on the market would disturb trade. A *Poor Relief Bill* in 1847 made provision for the employment of labour on public works, but stipulated that none should be employed who retained more than a quarter of an acre of land; this induced tens of thousands to surrender

---

[115] John Russell, 1st Earl Russell (1792–1878), English Whig and Liberal politician, Prime Minister during the Famine. His government adhered to what was called 'laissez-faire' economics, a form of economic liberalism which sought to avoid interference in the supposedly self-regulating market.

their farms for the sake of a bite to eat, and saved the landlords all the trouble and expense of eviction. When this had been accomplished to a sufficient extent 734,000 persons were discharged, and as they had given up their farms to get employment on the works they were now as helpless as men on a raft in mid-ocean. Mr. Mulhall, in his *Fifty Years of National Progress*, estimates the number of persons evicted between 1838 and 1888 as 3,668,000; the greater number of these saw their homes destroyed during the years under consideration, and this *Poor Relief Bill*, nick-named an 'Eviction-Made-Easy-Act', was one main weapon for their undoing.[116] In 1846, England, hitherto a Protectionist country, adopted Free Trade, ostensibly in order to permit corn to come freely and cheaply to the starving Irish. In reality, as Ireland was a corn and grain exporting country, the measure brought Continental agricultural produce to England into competition with that of Ireland, and hence, by lowering agricultural prices, still further intensified the misery of the Irish producing classes. The real meaning of the measure was that England, being a manufacturing nation, desired to cheapen food in order that its wage-slaves might remain content with low wages, and indeed one of the most immediate results of free trade in England was a wholesale reduction of the wages of the manufacturing proletariat.

The English capitalist class, with that hypocrisy that everywhere characterises the class in its public acts, used the misery of the Irish as a means to conquer the opposition of the English landlord class to free trade in grains, but in this, as in every other measure of the famine years, they acted consistently upon the lines of capitalist political economy. Within the limits of that social system and its theories their acts are unassailable and unimpeachable; it is only when we reject that system, and the intellectual and social fetters it imposes, that we really acquire the right to denounce the English administration of Ireland during the famine as a colossal crime against the human race. The non-socialist Irish man or woman who fumes against that administration is in the illogical position of denouncing an effect of whose cause he is a supporter. That cause was the system of capitalist property. With the exception of those few men we have before named, the Young Ireland leaders of 1848 failed to rise to the grandeur of the opportunity offered them to choose between human rights and property rights as a basis of nationality, and the measure of their failure was the measure of their country's disaster.

---

[116] Michael George Mulhall, *Fifty Years of National Progress 1837–1887* (1887).

Chapter XIV: Socialistic Teaching of the Young Irelanders: The Thinkers and the Workers

'What do ye at our door,
Ye guard our master's granaries from the thin hands of the poor.'
Lady Wilde (Speranza)[117]

'God of Justice, I cried, send Thy spirit down
On those lords so cruel and proud.
Soften their hearts and relax their frown,
Or else, I cried aloud,
Vouchsafe strength to the peasant's hand
To drive them at length from out the land'.
Thomas Davis

We have pointed out that the Young Ireland chiefs who had so fervently declaimed about the revolution were utterly incapable of accepting it when at last it presented itself to them; indeed Doheny uses that very word in describing the scenes at Cashel. 'It was the revolution', he said, 'if we had accepted it'. We might with perfect justice apply to these brilliant but unfortunate men the words of another writer, Lissagaray, in describing a similar class of leaders in France, and say 'having all their life sung the glories of the Revolution, when it rose up before them they ran away appalled, like the Arab fisher at the apparition of the genie'.[118] To the average historian who treats of the relations between Ireland and England as of a struggle between two nations, without any understanding of the economic conditions, or of the great world movements which caught both countries in their grasp, the hesitancy and vacillation of the Young Ireland chiefs in the crisis of their country's fate constitutes an insoluble problem and has too often been used to point a sneer at Irishmen when the writer was English; or to justify a sickening apology when the writer was Irish. Neither action is at all warranted. The simple fact is that the Irish workers in town and country were ready and willing to revolt, and that the English Government of the time was saved from serious danger only by the fact that Smith O'Brien and those who patterned after him, dreaded to trust the nation to the passion

---

[117] Jane Francesca Agnes, Lady Wilde (1821–1896), Irish poet under the pen-name 'Speranza'. A nationalist, she was a collector of fairy tales and folklore and a contributor to the Irish Literary Revival. Mother of the Irish poet, dramatist and wit Oscar Wilde.

[118] Prosper-Olivier Lissagaray (1838–1901), French writer and revolutionary socialist. Wrote an early history of the Paris Commune, and was a lover of Marx's daughter, Eleanor.

of the so-called lower classes. Had rebellion broken out at the time in Ireland, the English Chartists, who had been arming and preparing for a similar purpose would, as indeed Mitchel pointed out continually in his paper, have seized the occasion to take the field also. Many regiments of the English army were also honey-combed with revolt, and had repeatedly shown their spirit by publicly cheering for the Irish and Chartist cause. An English leader of the Chartists, John Frost, was sentenced to a heavy term of transportation for his seditious utterances at this time, and another great English champion of the working class, Ernest Jones, in commenting upon the case, declared defiantly in a public meeting that 'the time would come when John Mitchel and John Frost would be brought back, and Lord John Russell sent to take their place, and the Green Flag would fly in triumph over Downing Street and Dublin Castle', Downing Street was the residence of the English Prime Minister. For uttering this sentiment, Ernest Jones was arrested and sentenced to twelve months' imprisonment.[119]

In their attitude towards all manifestation of working-class revolt in England the Young Irelanders were sorely divided. In his paper *The United Irishman* John Mitchel hailed it exultantly as an aid to Ireland, and as a presage of the victory of real democracy, setting aside a large portion of his space in every issue to chronicle the progress of the cause of the people in England. His attitude in this matter was one of the most potent causes of his enduring popularity amongst the masses. On the other hand, the section of Young Irelanders who had made Smith O'Brien their idol for no other discoverable reason than the fact that he was rich and most respectable, strove by every means in their power to disassociate the cause of Ireland from the cause of democracy. A wordy war between Mitchel and his critics ensued, each side appealing to the precedent of 1798, with the result that Mitchel was easily able to prove that the revolutionists of that period – notably Wolfe Tone – had not only allied the cause of Ireland with the cause of democracy in general, but had vehemently insisted upon the necessity of a social revolution in Ireland at the expense of the landed aristocracy. Copying Fintan Lalor, Mitchel made the principles involved in those ideas the slogans of his revolutionary campaign. He insisted correctly upon a social insurrection as the only possible basis for a national revolution, that the same insurrectionary upheaval that destroyed and ended the social subjection of the producing classes would end the hateful foreign tyranny reared

---

[119] John Frost (1784–1877), Welsh Chartist leader. Ernest Jones (1819–1869), English poet, novelist and Chartist.

upon it. Two passages from his writings are especially useful as bearing out and attesting his position on those points – points that are still the fiercest subjects of dispute in Ireland. In his *Letter to the Farmers of Ireland*, March 4, 1848, he says, 'But I am told it is vain to speak thus to you; that the peace policy of O'Connell is dearer to you than life and honour – that many of your clergy, too, exhort you to die rather than violate what the English call "law" – and that you are resolved to take their bidding. Then die – die in your patience and perseverance, but be well assured of this – that the priest who bids you perish patiently amidst your own golden harvest preaches the gospel of England, insults manhood and common sense, bears false witness against religion, and blasphemes the Providence of God.'

When the Republican Government, which came into power in Paris after the revolution of February, 1848, recognizing that it owed its existence to the armed working men, and that those workers were demanding some security for their own class as a recompense for their bloody toil, enacted a law guaranteeing 'the right to work' to all, and pledging the credit of the nation to secure that right, Mitchel joyfully hailed that law as an indication that the absurd theories of what he rightfully styled the 'English system', or capitalism, had no longer a hold upon the minds of the French people. We quote a portion of that article. Our readers will note that the Free Trade referred to is Free Trade in Labour as against State Protection of the rights of the workers:

> 'Dynasties and thrones are not half so important as workshops, farms and factories. Rather we may say that dynasties and thrones, and even provisional governments, are good for anything exactly in proportion as they secure fair play, justice, and freedom to those who labour.
>
> 'It is here that France is really ahead of all the world. The great Third Revolution has overthrown the enlightened pedantic political economy (what we know in Ireland as the English political economy, or the Famine Political Economy), and has established once and for all the true and old principles of protection to labour, and the right and duty of combination among workmen by a decree of the Provisional Government dated February 25th:
>
> "It engages to guarantee work to all citizens. It recognises the right of workmen to combine for the purpose of enjoying the lawful proceeds of their labour."
>
> 'The French Republicans do not, like ignorant and barbarous English Whigs, recognise a right to pauper relief and make it a premium upon idleness. They know that man has a charter to eat bread in the sweat of his brow and not otherwise, and they acknowledge that highest and most sacred mission of government to take care that bread may be had for the

earning. For this reason they expressly, and in set terms, renounce "competition" and "free trade" *in the sense in which an English Whig uses these words*, and deliberately adopt combination and protection – that the nation should combine to protect by laws its own national industry, and that individuals should combine with other individuals to protect by trades associations the several branches of national industry.

'The free trade and competition – in other words the English system – is pretty well understood now; its obvious purpose and effect are to make the rich richer and the poor poorer, to make capital the absolute ruler of the world, and labour a blind and helpless slave. By free trade the manufacturers of Manchester are enabled to clothe India, China, and South America, and the artizans of Manchester can hardly keep themselves covered from the cold. By dint of free trade Belfast grows more linen cloth than it ever did before; but the men who weave it have hardly a shirt to their backs. Free trade fills with corn the stores of speculating capitalists, but leaves those who have sown and reaped the corn without a meal. Free trade unpeoples villages and peoples poorhouses consolidates farms and gluts the graveyards with famished corpses.

'There is to be no more of this free trade in France. Men can no longer "do what they like with their own" there.

'February, 1848, came, and the pretext of the reform banquet. Again Paris had her three days' agony, and was delivered of her third and fairest born revolution.

'There could be no mistake this time; the rubbish of thrones and dynasties is swept out for ever, and the people sit sovereign in the land. One of their first and greatest acts is the enactment of a commission to inquire into the whole of the great labour question, and to all the documents issued by this commission appear signed the names of Louis Blanc and the insurgent of Lyons, Albert Ouvrier (workman). He is not ashamed of his title, though now a great officer of the State. He is a working man, and is proud of it "in any bond, bill, quittance, or obligation", Ouvrier.

'Sixty-six years ago the farmers of France had their revolution. Eighteen years ago the "respectable" middle classes had theirs, and have made a good penny in it since, but upon this third and last all the world may see the stamp and impress of the man who made it – Albert Ouvrier, his mark. We have all three revolutions to accomplish, and the sooner we set about it the better. Only let us hope all the work may be done in one. Let not the lessons of history be utterly useless.

'The detestable system of "free trade" and "fair competition" which is described by Louis Blanc as "that specious system of leaving unrestricted all pecuniary dealings between man and man, which leaves the poor man at the mercy of the rich, and promises to cupidity, that waits its time, an easy victory over hunger that cannot wait", the system that seeks to make Mammon and not God or justice rule this world – in one word, the English or famine system – must be abolished utterly; in farms or workshops, in town and country, abolished utterly; and to do this were worth three revolutions, or three times three.'

So wrote Mitchel when, burning with a holy hatred of tyranny, he poured the vitriol of his scorn upon all the pedants who strutted around him, pedants who were as scrupulous in polishing a phrase for a lecture as a sword for a parade – and incapable of advancing beyond either.

His joy was, we now know, somewhat premature, as the government which passed the law was itself a capitalistic government, and as soon as it found itself strong enough, and had won over the army, repealed its own law, and suppressed, with the most frightful bloodshed, the June insurrection of the workmen striving to enforce its fulfilment. It is the latter insurrection which Mitchel denounces in his *Jail Journal* when, led astray by the garbled reports of English newspapers, he anathematises the very men whom he had in this article, when fuller sources of information were available, courageously and justly praised. But another revolutionist, Devin Reilly, in *The Irish Felon*, more correctly appraised the position of the June insurgents, and also appreciated the fact that Ireland for its redemption required something more far-reaching, something sounding deeper springs of human action, something more akin to the teachings that inspired the heroic workers of France than was to be found in the 'personal probity', or 'high principles', or 'aristocratic descent', or 'eminent respectability' of a few leaders.[120]

When Mitchel was arrested and his paper suppressed, two other papers sprang up to take the post of danger thus left vacant. One, *The Irish Tribune*, represented the element which stood for the 'moral right of insurrection', and the other, *The Irish Felon*, embodied the ideas of those who insisted that the English conquest of Ireland was two-fold, social, or economic, and political, and that therefore the revolution must also have these two aspects. These latter were at all times in the fullest sympathy with the movements of the working-class democracy at home and abroad. John Martin edited *The Irish Felon*, James Fintan Lalor and Devin Reilly were its chief writers. Reilly, who hailed originally from Monaghan, had long been a close observer of, and sympathiser with, the movements of the working class, and all schemes of social redemption. As a writer on *The Nation* newspaper he had contributed a series of articles on the great French Socialist, Louis Blanc, in a review of his

---

[120] *The Irish Felon* was a newspaper, associated with the Young Ireland movement, set up by John Martin and James Fintan Lalor in 1848, following the suppression of Mitchel's *United Irishman*.

great work *Dix Ans* (Ten Years), in which, while dissenting from the 'State Socialistic' schemes of social regeneration favoured by Blanc, he yet showed the keenest appreciation of the gravity and universality of the social question, as well as grasping the innate heroism and sublimity of the working-class movement.[121] This attitude he preserved to the last of his days. When in exile in America, after the insurrection, he was chosen by the printers of Boston to edit a paper, the *Protective Union*, they had founded on co-operative principles to advocate the rights of labour, and was thus one of the first pioneers of labour journalism in the United States – a proud and fitting position for a true Irish revolutionist. As writer in *The American Review* he wrote a series of articles on the European situation, of which Horace Greeley said that, if collected and published as a book, they would create a revolution in Europe.[122] Commenting upon the uprising in France in June he says in *The Irish Felon*:

> 'We are not Communists – we abhor communism for the same reason we abhor poor-law systems, and systems founded on the absolute sovereignty of wealth. Communism destroys the independence and dignity of labour, makes the workingman a State pauper and takes his manhood from him. But, communism or no communism, these 70,000 workmen had a clear right to existence – they had the best right to existence of any men in France, and if they could have asserted their right by force of arms they would have been fully justified. *The social system in which a man willing to work is compelled to starve, is a blasphemy, an anarchy, and no system.* For the present these victims of monarchic rule, disowned by the republic, are conquered; 10,000 are slain, 20,000 perhaps doomed to the Marquesas. *But for all that the rights of labour are not conquered, and will not and cannot be conquered. Again and again the labourer will rise up against the idler – the workingmen will meet this bourgeoisie, and grapple and war with them till their equality is established, not in word, but in fact.*'

This was the spirit of the men grouped around *The Irish Felon*, its editor alone excepted. Students of Socialism will recognise that many who are earnest workers for Socialism to-day would, like Devin Reilly, have 'abhorred' the crude Communism of 1848. The fact that he insisted

---

[121] Louis Jean Joseph Charles Blanc (1811–1882), French historian and socialist politician. His *Histoire de Dix Ans, 1830–1840* (1841) was a critique of the July Monarchy.

[122] Connolly may be mistaken here, confusing the *United States Magazine and Democratic Review* with the *American Review*, or with the *Democratic Review*. Horace Greeley (1811–1872), American journalist, congressman and Presidential candidate. Edited the *New York Tribune* 1841–1872.

upon the unqualified right of the working class to work out its own salvation, by force of arms if necessary, is what entitles Devin Reilly to a high place of honour in the estimation of the militant proletariat of Ireland. The opening passage in an *Address of the Medical Students of Dublin to All Irish Students of Science and Art*, adopted at a meeting held in Northumberland Buildings, Eden Quay, on April 4, 1848, and signed by John Savage as Chairman and Richard Dalton Williams as Secretary, shows also that amongst the educated young men of that generation there was a general recognition of the fact that the struggle of Ireland against her oppressors was naturally linked with, and ought to be taken in conjunction with, the world-wide movement of the democracy.[123] It says 'a war is waging at this hour all over Europe between Intelligence and Labour on the one side and Despotism and Force on the other', a sentiment which Joseph Brennan versified in a poem on *Divine Right*, in which the excellence of the sentiment must be held to atone for the poverty of the poetry. One verse says: –

> The only right acknowledged
> By the people living now,
> Is the right to obtain honour
> By the sweat of brain and brow.
> The Right Divine of Labour
> To be first of earthly things,
> That the Thinker and the Worker
> Are manhood's only kings.

But the palm of honour for the clearest exposition of the doctrine of revolution, social and political, must be given to James Fintan Lalor, of Tenakill, Queen's County. Lalor, unfortunately, suffered from a slight physical disability, which incapacitated him from attaining to any leadership other than intellectual, a fact that, in such a time and amidst such a people, was fatal to his immediate influence. Yet in his writings, as we study them to-day, we find principles of action and of society which have within them not only the best plan of campaign suited for the needs of a country seeking its freedom through insurrection against a dominant nation, but also held the seeds of the more perfect social peace of the future. All his writings at this period are so illuminating that we find it difficult to select from the mass any particular passages which more deserve reproduction than others. But as an indication of the line

---

[123] John Savage (1828–1888), Irish poet and journalist. A member of both the Young Ireland movement and the Fenians. Richard D'Alton Williams (1822–1862), Irish doctor and poet of the Young Ireland movement.

of argument pursued by this peerless thinker, and as a welcome contrast to the paralysing respect, nay, reverence, for landlordism evidenced by Smith O'Brien and his worshippers, perhaps the following passages will serve. In an article entitled *The Faith of a Felon*, published July 8, 1848, he tells how he had striven to convert the Irish Confederation to his views and failed, and says:

> 'They wanted an alliance with the landowners. They chose to consider them as Irishmen, and imagined they could induce them to hoist the green flag. They wished to preserve an aristocracy. They desired, not a democratic, but merely a national, revolution. Had the Confederation, in the May or June of '47, thrown heart and mind and means into the movement, I pointed out they would have made it successful, and settled at once and forever all questions between us and England. The opinions I then stated and which I yet stand firm to, are these:
>
> '1. That in order to save their own lives, the occupying tenants of the soil of Ireland ought, next autumn, to refuse all rent and arrears of rent then due, beyond and except the value of the overplus of harvest-produce remaining in their hands, after having deducted and reserved a due and full provision for their own subsistence during the next ensuing twelve months.
>
> '2. That they ought to refuse and resist being made beggars, landless and homeless, under the English law of ejection.
>
> '3. That they ought further, *on principle*, to refuse *all rent* to the present usurping proprietors, until the people, the *true proprietors* (or lords paramount, in legal parlance) have, in national congress or convention, decided what rents they are to pay, and to whom they are to pay them.
>
> '4. And that the people, on grounds of policy and economy, ought to decide (as a general rule admitting of reservations) that these rents shall be paid to *themselves*, the people, for public purposes, and for behoof and benefit of them, the entire general people.
>
> 'It has been said to me that such a war, on the principles I propose, would be looked on with detestation by Europe. I assert the contrary; I say such a war would propagate itself throughout Europe. Mark the words of this prophecy – the principle I propound goes to the foundations of Europe, and sooner or later will cause Europe to outrise. *Mankind will yet be masters of the earth*. The right of the people to make the laws – this produced the first great modern earthquake, whose latent shocks, even now, are heaving in the heart of the world. The right of the people to own the land – this will produce the next. Train your hands, and your sons' hands, gentlemen of the earth, for you and they will yet have to use them.'[124]

---

[124] *The Irish Felon*, 1848. The Socialist Party of Ireland later published a collection of Lalor's writings *The Rights of Ireland and the Faith of a Felon* (n.d.) with an introduction by Connolly.

The paragraph is significant, as demonstrating that Fintan Lalor, like all the really dangerous revolutionists of Ireland, advocated his principles as part of the creed of the democracy of the world, and not merely as applicable only to the incidents of the struggle of Ireland against England. But this latter is the interpretation which the middle-class politicians and historians of Ireland have endeavoured to give his teachings after the failure of their attempt, continued for half a century, to ignore or suppress all reference to his contribution to Irish revolutionary literature. The working-class democracy of Ireland will, it is to be hoped, be, for their part, as assertive of the universality of Lalor's sympathies as their bourgeois compatriots are in denying it. That working class would be uselessly acquiescing in the smirching of its own record, were it to permit emasculation of the message of this Irish apostle of revolutionary Socialism. And, in emphasising the catholicity of his sympathies as well as the keenness of his insight into the social structure, that Irish working class will do well to confront the apostate patriotism of the politicians and anti-Socialists of Ireland with the following brilliant passage from the work already quoted, and thus show how Lalor answered the plea of those who begged him to moderate or modify his position, to preach it as a necessity of Ireland's then desperate condition, and not as a universal principle.

> 'I attest and urge the plea of utter and desperate necessity to fortify her (Ireland's) claim, but not to found it. *I rest it on no temporary and passing conditions, but on principles that are permanent, and imperishable, and universal – available to all times and to all countries as well as to our own* – I pierce through the upper stratum of occasional and shifting circumstances to bottom and base on the rock below. I put the question in its eternal form – the form in which, how often so ever suppressed for a season, it can never be finally subdued, but will remain and return, outliving and outlasting the cowardice and corruption of generations. I view it as ages will view it – *not through the mists of a famine, but by the living lights of the firmament.*'

By such lights the teachings of Fintan Lalor are being viewed to-day, with the result that, as he recedes from us in time, his grandeur as a thinker is more and more recognised; his form rises clearer and more distinct to our view, as the forms of the petty agitators and phrase-mongering rebels who seemed to dominate the scene at that historic period sink into their proper place, as unconscious factors in the British Imperial plan of conquest by famine. Cursed by the fatal gift of eloquence, our Irish Girondins of the Confederation enthralled the

Irish people and intoxicated themselves out of the possibility of serious thinking; drunken with words they failed to realise that the ideas originating with Fintan Lalor, and in part adopted and expounded with such dramatic power by Mitchel, were a more serious menace to the hated power of England than any that the dream of a union of classes could ever materialise on Irish soil; the bones of the famine victims, whitening on every Irish hill and valley, or tossing on every wave of the Atlantic, were the price Ireland paid for the eloquence of its rebels, and their scornful rejection of the Socialistic teachings of its thinkers.

Chapter XV: Some More Irish Pioneers of the Socialist Movement

> *'Either the Sermon on the Mount can rule this world or it cannot. The Devil has a right to rule if we let him, but he has no right to call his rule Christian Civilisation.'*
> – John Boyle O'Reilly

Looking backward to that eventful period (after '48) we can now see that all hopes of a revolutionary movement had perished for that generation, had been strangled in the love embraces of our Girondins; but that fact naturally was not so apparent to the men of the time. Hence it is not to be wondered at that journalistic activity on the part of the revolutionists did not cease with the suppression of *The United Irishman*, *The Irish Tribune*, or *The Irish Felon*. A small fugitive publication entitled the *Irish National Guard*, published apparently by a body of courageous Dublin workingmen of advanced opinions, also led a chequered existence championing the cause of revolution, and in January, 1849, another paper, *The Irishman*, was set on foot by Bernard Fullam, who had been business manager of *The Nation*. Fullam also started a new organisation, the Democratic Association, which is described as 'an association with aims almost entirely socialistic and revolutionary'. This association also spread amongst the Irish workers in Great Britain, and had the cordial support and endorsement of Fergus O'Connor, who saw in it the realisation of his long-hoped for dream of a common programme uniting the democracies of Ireland and Great Britain. But the era of revolution was past for that generation in both countries, and it was too late for the working-class revolutionists to repair the harm the middle-class doctrinaires had done. The paper died in May, 1850, after an existence of seventeen months. Among its contributors was Thomas Clarke Luby, afterwards one of the chief writers on the staff of

The Irish People, organ of the Fenian Brotherhood, a fact that explains much of the advanced doctrine advocated by that journal.[125] Another of the staff of *The Irishman* in those days was Joseph Brennan, whom we have already quoted as writing in *The Irish Tribune*. Brennan finally emigrated to America and contributed largely to the pages of the New Orleans *Delta*, many of his poems in that journal showing the effects of his early association with the currents of social-revolutionary thought in Ireland.[126]

Before leaving this period a few words should be said of the impress left upon the labour movement of Great Britain by the working-class Irish exiles. An English writer, H.S. Foxwell, has said that 'Socialist propagandism has been mainly carried on by men of Celtic or Semitic blood', and, however true that may be, as a general statement, it is at least certain that to the men of Celtic blood the English-speaking countries are indebted for the greater part of the early propaganda of the Socialist conception of society. We have already referred to Fergus O'Connor; another Irishman who carved his name deep on the early structures of the labour and socialist movement in England as an author and Chartist leader was James Bronterre O'Brien.[127] Among his best known works are: – *The Rise, Progress and Phases of Human Slavery: How it Came into the World, and How it May be Made to Go Out of it*, published in 1830; *Address to the Oppressed and Mystified People of Great Britain*, 1851; *European Letters*; and the pages of the *National Reformer*, which he founded in 1837. At first an advocate of physical force, he in his later days gave himself almost exclusively to the development of a system of land banks, in which he believed he had found a way to circumvent the political and military power of the capitalist class. Bronterre O'Brien is stated to have been the first to coin in English the distinctive title of 'social democrat', as an appellation for the adherents of the new order.

An earlier Irish apostle of the Socialist movement of the working

---

[125] Thomas Clarke Luby (1822–1901), Irish revolutionary and writer, and a founder of the Irish Republican Brotherhood.

[126] Connolly here discusses several newspapers of a socialist or proto-socialist character, which tackled the issue of uniting rural and urban radicalisms, a problem Connolly himself would later face. The description of the Democratic Association as 'almost entirely socialistic and revolutionary' is a quotation from Richard Pigott, *Recollections of an Irish National Journalist* (1883).

[127] James Bronterre O'Brien (1805–1864), Irish writer and militant Chartist leader, editor of *Poor Man's Guardian* 1831–1835, and a contributor to many other radical newspapers.

class, John Doherty, is much less known to the present generation than O'Brien, yet his methods bore more of the marks of constructive revolutionary statesmanship, and his message was equally clear.[128] He appears to have been an almost dominant figure in the labour movement of England and Ireland between the years 1830 and 1840, spent little time in the development of Socialist theories, but devoted all his energies to organising the working-class and teaching it to act on its own initiative. He was General Secretary of the Federation of Spinning Societies, which aimed to unite all the textile industries in one great national industrial union and was widespread throughout Great Britain and Ireland; he founded a National Association for the Protection of Labour, which directed its efforts towards building up a union of the working class, effective alike for economic and political ends, and reached to 100,000 members, the Belfast trades applying in a body for affiliation; he founded and edited a paper, *The Voice of the People*, in 1831, which, although sevenpence per copy, attained to a circulation of 30,000, and is described as 'giving great attention to Radical politics, and the progress of revolution on the Continent'. In his *History of Trades Unionism*, Sidney Webb quotes Francis Place – the best informed man in the labour movement in the England of his day – as declaring that, during the English Reform Bill crisis in 1832, Doherty, instead of being led astray, as many labour leaders were, to rally to the side of the middle-class reformers, was 'advising the working class to use the occasion for a Social Revolution'.[129] This was indeed the keynote of Doherty's message: whatever was to be done was to be done by the working class. He is summed up as of 'wide information, great natural shrewdness, and far-reaching aims'. He was born in Larne in 1799.

Another Doherty, Hugh, attained to some prominence in Socialistic circles in England, and we find him in 1841 in London editing a Socialist paper, *The Phalanx*, which devoted itself to the propagation of the views of the French Socialist, Fourier.[130] It had little influence on the labour movement owing to its extremely doctrinaire attitude, but appears to have had circulation and correspondents in the United States. It was one of the first journals to be set up by a type-setting machine, and one of

---

[128] John Doherty (1798–1854), Irish trade unionist and reformer. Ambitious for and in the union movement, his major initiatives – the General Union of Cotton Spinners and the National Association for the Protection of Labour – were short-lived.

[129] Sidney James Webb, 1st Baron Passfield (1859–1947), English socialist and economist. A co-founder of the London School of Economics, he was also an early member of the Fabian Society. Published *The History of Trade Unionism* in 1894.

[130] Hugh Doherty (d. 1891), Irish socialist and journalist.

its numbers contains a minute description of the machine, which forms curious reading to-day.

In general, the effect upon the English labour movement of the great influx of Irish workers, seems to us to have been beneficial. It is true that their competition for employment had at first a seriously evil effect upon wages, but, on the other hand, a study of the fugitive literature of the movement of that time shows that the working-class Irish exiles were present and active in the ranks of militant labour in numbers out of all proportion to the ratio they bore to the population at large. And always they were the advanced, the least compromising, the most irreconcilable element in the movement. Of course the Socialist sectarians and philosophers did not love the Irish – Charles Kingsley, that curious combination of Prelate, Socialist, Chauvinist and Virulent Bigot, can scarcely remain within the bounds of decent language when he brings an Irishman into the thread of his narrative – but the aversion was born out of their fear of the Irish workers' impatience of compromise and eagerness for action.[131] And hence, the very qualities which endeared the Irish worker to the earnest rebel against capitalist iniquity, estranged him from the affections of those whose social position enabled them to become the historians of his movements.

Chapter XVI: The Working Class: The Inheritors of the Irish Ideals of the Past – The Repository of the Hopes of the Future

'Is a Christian to starve, to submit, to bow down
As at some high consecrated behest,
Hugging close the old maxims, that "Weakness is strength",
And "Whatsoever is is best"?
O, texts of debasement! O, creed of deep shame!
O, Gospel of infamy treble.
Who strikes when he's struck, and takes when he starves,
In the eyes of the Lord is no rebel.'
J.F. O'Donnell[132]

This book does not aspire to be a history of labour in Ireland; it is rather a record of labour in Irish History. For that reason the plan of

---

[131] Charles Kingsley (1819–1875), English priest of the Church of England, Christian socialist, university professor, historian and novelist. Author of the historical novel *Westward Ho!* (1855) and the children's novel *The Water Babies* (1863), Kingsley was anti-Catholic and expressed racist attitudes regarding the Irish.

[132] John Francis O'Donnell (1837–1874), Irish poet, novelist and journalist. Wrote for *The Nation* and *The Irish People*.

the book has precluded any attempt to deal in detail with the growth, development, or decay of industry in Ireland, except as it affected our general argument. That argument called for an explanation of the position of labour in the great epochs of our modern history, and with the attitude of Irish leaders towards the hopes, aspirations, and necessities of those who live by labour. Occasionally, as when analysing the 'prosperity' of Grattan's Parliament, and the decay of Irish trade following the Legislative Union of 1800, we have been constrained to examine the fundamental causes which make for the progress, industrially or commercially, of some nations and the retrogression of others. For this apparent digression no apology is made, and none is called for; it was impossible to present our readers with a clear idea of the historical position of labour at any given moment, without explaining the economic and political causes which contributed to make possible or necessary its attitude. For the same reason it has been necessary sometimes to retrace our footsteps over some period already covered, in order to draw attention to a phase of the subject, the introduction of which in the previous narrative would have marred the view of the question then under examination. Thus the origin of trade unionism in Ireland has not been dealt with, although in the course of our study we have shown that the Irish trades were well organised. Nor are we now prepared to enter upon that subject. Perhaps at some more propitious moment we will be enabled to examine the materials bearing upon the matter, and trace the growth of the institution in Ireland. Sufficient for the present to state that Trades Guilds existed in Ireland as upon the Continent and England, during Roman Catholic, pre-Reformation days; that after the Reformation those Trade Guilds became exclusively Protestant, and even anti-Catholic, within the English Pale; that they continued to refuse admission to Catholics even after the passage of the Catholic Emancipation Act, and that these old Trade Guilds were formally abolished by law in 1840. But the Catholic and Protestant workmen who were excluded from guild membership (Episcopalians only being eligible) did nevertheless organise themselves, and it was their trade unions which dominated the labour world to the wrath of the capitalists and landlords, and the chagrin of the Governments. One remarkable and instructive feature of their organisation in town and country was the circumstance that every attempt at political rebellion in Ireland was always preceded by a remarkable development of unrest, discontent, and class consciousness amongst their members, demonstrating clearly that, to the mind of the thoughtful Irish worker political and social subjection were very nearly related. In the *Dublin Chronicle,* January 28, 1792, there is a record of a great strike of the journeymen tailors of Dublin, in the course of which, it is stated, armed tailors went to the workrooms of Messrs. Miller, Ross Lane; Leet, Merchant's Quay; Walsh, Castle Street; and Ward, Cope Street, attacked certain scabs who were working there, cut off the hands of two, and threw others in the river. In another and later issue of the same journal there is a record of how a few coal porters (dock labourers) were seized by His Majesty's press-gang with the intention of compelling them to serve in the navy, and how the organised quay labourers, on hearing of it, summoned their members, and marching upon the guard-house where the men were detained, attacked it, defeated the guard and released their comrades. In the same paper, January 3, 1793, there is a letter from a gentleman resident at Carrickmacross, Co. Monaghan, describing how an armed party of Defenders paraded through that town on its way to Ardee, how the army was brought out to attack them and a number were killed. On January 24, 1793, another correspondent tells how a battle took place between Bailieborough and Kingscourt, Co. Cavan, 'between those deluded persons styling themselves Defenders and a part of the army', when eighteen labourers were killed, five badly wounded, and thirty taken prisoners 'and lodged in Cavan gaol'. There is also on July 23, 1793, the following account of a battle at Limerick: –

> 'Last night we hear that an express arrived from Limerick with the following intelligence – that on Saturday night a mob of 7 or 8,000 attacked that city and attempted to burn it; that the army, militia and citizens were obliged to join to repel these daring offenders, and to bring the artillery into the streets, and that after a severe and obstinate resistance the insurgents were dispersed with a loss of 140 killed and several wounded.'

Similar battles between the peasantry and the soldiery, aided by the local landlords, occurred in the county Wexford.

In the Reports of the Secret Committee of the House of Lords, 1793, speaking of the Defenders (who, as we have stated before, were the organised labourers striving to better their condition by the only means open to them), it says 'they first appeared in the county Louth', 'soon spread through the counties of Meath, Cavan, Monaghan and parts adjacent', and 'their measures appear to have been concerted and conducted with the utmost secrecy and a degree of regularity and system not usual to people in such mean condition, and as if directed by men of a superior rank'.

All this, be it noted, was on the eve of the revolutionary struggle of 1798, and shows how the class struggle of the Irish workers formed the preparatory school for the insurrectionary effort.

The long-drawn-out struggle of the fight against tithes and the militant spirit of the Irish trades and Ribbonmen we have already spoken of, as providing the revolutionary material for 1848, which Smith O'Brien and his followers were unfit to use. For the next revolutionary period, that known as the Fenian Conspiracy, the same coincidence of militant class feeling and revolutionary nationalism is deeply marked. Indeed it is no wonder that the real nationalists of Ireland, the Separatists, have always been men of broad human sympathies and intense democracy, for it has ever been in the heart of the working class at home that they found their most loyal support, and in the working class abroad their most resolute defenders.

The Fenian Brotherhood was established in 1857, according to the statement of John O'Mahony, one of its two chiefs, James Stephens being the other.[133] Of O'Mahony, John O'Leary says, in his *Recollections of Fenians and Fenianism*, that he was an advanced democrat of Socialistic opinions, and W.A. O'Connor, in his *History of the Irish People*, declares that both O'Mahony and Stephens had entered into the secret societies of France, O'Mahony 'from mere sympathy'.[134] A further confirmation of this view of the character of the men responsible for the Fenian Society is found in a passage in a journal established in the interests of Fenianism, and published in London after the suppression of the organ of the Brotherhood, *The Irish People*, in Dublin, in 1865. This journal, *The Flag of Ireland*, quoting from the Paris correspondent of *The Irishman*, says on October 3, 1868: –

'It took its rise in the Latin Quarter of this city when John O'Mahony, Michael Doheny, and James Stephens were here in exile after '48.

'This was the triumvirate from whose plotting brains the idea of Fenianism sprung. O'Mahony, deep in lore of Ireland and loving her traditions, found its name for the new society; Doheny, with his dogged, acute and vigorous character, stamped it with much of the force that helped it into life, but to Stephens is due the direction it took in line of sympathy with the movements of the Revolution on the Continent. He saw that the Irish question was no longer a question of religion; his common sense was too large to permit him to consider it a question of race even; he felt it was

---

[133] John Francis O'Mahony (1816–1877), American scholar of Irish culture, and founding member of the Fenian Brotherhood, the arm of the Irish Republican Brotherhood (IRB) in America. James Stephens (1825–1901), founder-member of the IRB.

[134] John O'Leary (1830–1907), Irish revolutionary and leading member of the IRB. Imprisoned for his activities, later a friend to W. B. Yeats, who immortalised him in his poem *September 1913*: 'Romantic Ireland's dead and gone/It's with O'Leary in the grave'. Published *Recollections of Fenians and Fenianism* in 1896.

the old struggle which agitated France at the end of last century, transferred to new ground; the opposing forces were the same, with this difference, that in Ireland the people had not the consolation in all cases of saluting their tyrants as their countrymen.'

The circumstances that the general chosen by Stephens to be the Commander-in-Chief of the Irish Republican army was no less a character than General Cluseret, afterwards Commander-in-chief of the Federals during the Commune of Paris, says more for the principles of the men who were the brains of the Fenian movement than any testimony of subordinates.[135]

Coincident with the inception of Fenianism, 1857, commenced in Ireland a determined labour agitation which culminated in a vigorous movement amongst the baker journeymen against night labour and in favour of a reduction of the working hours. Great meetings were held all over the country during the years 1858–60, in which the rights of labour were most vehemently asserted and the tyranny of the Irish employers exposed and denounced. In Wexford, Kilkenny, Clonmel and Waterford night-work was abolished and day labour established. The movement was considered so serious that a Parliamentary Committee sat to investigate it; from its report, as quoted by Karl Marx in his great work on *Capital*, we take the following excerpts: –

'In Limerick, where the grievances of the journeymen are demonstrated to be excessive, the movement had been defeated by the opposition of the master bakers, the miller bakers being the greatest opponents. The example of Limerick led to a retrogression in Ennis and Tipperary. In Cork, *where the strongest possible demonstration of feeling took place*, the masters by exercising their power of turning men out of employment, have defeated the movement. In *Dublin the master bakers have offered the most determined opposition* to the movement, and, by discountenancing as much as possible the journeymen promoting it, have succeeded in leading the men into acquiescence in Sunday work and night work, contrary to the convictions of the men.

'The Committee believe that the hours of labour are limited by natural laws which cannot be violated with impunity. That for master bakers to induce their workmen by the fear of losing employment, to violate their religious convictions and their better feelings, to disobey the laws of the land, and to disregard public opinion, is calculated to provoke ill-feeling between workmen and masters – and affords an example dangerous to religion,

---

[135] Gustave Paul Cluseret (1823–1900), French soldier and socialist politician. Served with the Union Army during the American Civil War, took part in the Fenian rising in Ireland in 1867, and later participated in the Paris Commune.

morality *and social order*. The Committee believe that any constant work beyond twelve hours a day encroaches on the domestic and private life of the working man, and leads to disastrous moral results, interfering with each man's home, and the discharge of his family duties as son, brother, husband, or father. That work beyond twelve hours has a tendency to undermine the health of the working man, and so leads to premature old age and death, to the great injury of families of working men, thus deprived of the care and support of the head of the family when most required.'

The reader will observe that the cities where this movement was strongest, where the workers had made the strongest fight and class-feeling was highest, were the places where Fenianism developed the most; it is a matter of historical record that Dublin, Cork, Wexford, Clonmel, Kilkenny, Waterford and Ennis and their respective counties were the most responsive to the message of Fenianism. Richard Pigott, who, before he succumbed to the influence of the gold offered by the London *Times*, had a long and useful career as responsible figurehead for advanced journals in Ireland, and who in that capacity acquired a thorough knowledge of the men and movements for whom he was sponsor, gives in his *Recollections of an Irish Journalist*, this testimony as to the *personnel* of Fenianism, a testimony, it will be observed, fully bearing out our analysis of the relation between the revolutionary movement and the working class: –

'It is notorious that Fenianism was regarded with unconcealed aversion, not to say deadly hatred, not merely by the landlords and the ruling class, but by the Catholic clergy, the middle-class Catholics, and the great majority of the farming classes. *It was in fact only amongst the youngest and most intelligent of the labouring class, of the young men of the large towns and cities engaged in the humbler walks of mercantile life, of the artisan and working classes, that it found favour.*'

Karl Marx quotes from *Report of the Poor Law Inspectors on the Wages of Agricultural Labourers in Dublin, 1870*, to show that between the years 1849 and 1869, while wages in Ireland had risen fifty or sixty per cent, the prices of all necessaries had more than doubled.[136] He gives the following extract from the official accounts of an Irish workhouse: –

Year ended	Provisions and Necessaries	Clothing	Total
29th Sept., 1849	1s. 3¼d.	3d.	1s. 6¼d.
29th Sept., 1869	2s. 7¼d.	6d.	3s. 1¼d.

---

[136] *Report of the Poor Law Inspectors on the Wages of Agricultural Labourers in Ireland* (1870).

These facts demonstrate, that in the period during which the Fenian movement obtained its hold upon the Irish masses in the cities, the workers were engaged in fierce struggles with their employers, and the price of all necessaries of life had increased twofold – two causes sufficient to produce revolutionary ferment, even in a country without the historical justification for revolution possessed by Ireland. Great Britain was also in the throes of a fierce agitation as a result of the terrible suffering of the working class resultant from the industrial crisis of 1866–7. *The Morning Star*, London paper, stated that in six districts of London 15,000 workmen were in a state of destitution with their families; *Reynolds' Newspaper*, on January 20, 1867, quoted from a large poster, which it says was placarded all over London, the words 'Fat Oxen, Starving Men – the fat oxen from their palaces of glass, have gone to feed the rich in their luxurious abode, while the starving poor are left to rot and die in their wretched dens', and commented that 'this reminds one of the secret revolutionary associations which prepared the French people for the events of 1789. At this moment, while English workmen with their wives and children are dying of cold and hunger, there are millions of English gold – the produce of English labour – being invested in Russian, Spanish, Italian and other foreign enterprises.'[137] And the London *Standard* of April 5, 1866, stated: 'A frightful spectacle was to be seen yesterday in one part of the metropolis. Although the unemployed thousands of the East End did not parade with their black flags *en masse* the human torrent was imposing enough. Let us remember what these people suffer. They are dying of hunger. That is the simple and terrible fact. There are 40,000 of them. In our presence, in one quarter of this wonderful metropolis, are packed – next door to the most enormous accumulation of wealth the world ever saw – cheek by jowl with this are 40,000 helpless, starving people. These thousands are now breaking in upon the other quarters.'[138]

This state of hunger and revolt in Great Britain offers an explanation of the curious phenomenon mentioned by A.M. Sullivan in *New Ireland*, that the Home Rule or constitutional journals held their own easily in Ireland itself against *The Irish People*, but in Great Britain the Fenian journal simply swept the field clear of its Irish competitors.[139] The Irish

[137] The *Morning Star* was a radical Liberal newspaper founded by Richard Cobden and John Bright in 1856. *Reynold's Weekly Newspaper* was a liberal Sunday newspaper founded in 1850 and edited by George Reynolds, a former Chartist.
[138] The London *Standard* was founded in 1827 by Stanley Lees Giffard, an Irish barrister and journalist.
[139] Alexander Martin Sullivan (1830–1884), Irish politician, lawyer and journalist, supporter of Young Ireland and one-time editor of *The Nation*. Published *New Ireland*:

working-class exiles in Great Britain saw that the nationalist aspirations of their race pointed to the same conclusion, called for the same action, as the material interests of their class – viz., the complete overthrow of the capitalist government and the national and social tyranny upon which it rested. Any thoughtful reader of the poems of J.F. O'Donnell – such, for instance, as *An Artisan's Garret*, depicting in words that burn, the state of mind of an unemployed Fenian artisan of Dublin, beside the bedside of his wife dying of hunger – or the sweetly pleading poetry of J.K. Casey (Leo), cannot wonder at the warm reception journals containing such teaching met in Great Britain amidst the men and women of Irish race and of a subject class.[140]

Just as '98 was an Irish expression of the tendencies embodied in the first French Revolution, as '48 throbbed in sympathy with the democratic and social upheavals on the Continent of Europe and England, so Fenianism was a responsive throb in the Irish heart to those pulsations in the heart of the European working class which elsewhere produced the International Working Men's Association.[141] Branches of that Association flourished in Dublin and Cork until after the Paris Commune, and it is an interesting study to trace the analogy between the course of development of the Socialist movement of Europe after the Commune and that of the Irish revolutionary cause after the failure of '67. In both cases we witness the abandonment of insurrectionism and the initiation of a struggle in which the revolting class, while aiming at revolution, consistently refuse the arbitrament of an armed struggle. When the revolutionary nationalists threw in their lot with the Irish Land League, and made the land struggle the basis of their warfare, they were not only placing themselves in touch once more with those inexhaustible quarries of material interests from which all the great Irish statesmen from St. Laurence O'Toole to Wolfe Tone drew the stones upon which they built their edifice of a militant patriotic Irish organisation, but they were also, consciously or unconsciously, placing themselves in accord with the principles which underlie and inspire the modern movement of labour. This fact was recognised at the time by

---

Political Sketches and Personal Reminiscences of Thirty Years of Irish Public Life in 1877.

[140] John Keegan 'Leo' Casey (1846–1870), Irish poet, novelist and revolutionary, contributor to *The Nation* and participant in the Fenian Rising of 1867.

[141] The International Working Men's Association, also known as the First International (1864–1876), was an international organisation which brought together a wide variety of leftist and radical political groups in the wake of the failed revolutions of 1848. Marx and Engels were leading members.

most dispassionate onlookers.¹⁴² Thus, in a rather amusing book published in France in 1887, under the title of *Chez Paddy*, Englished as *Paddy at Home*, the author, a French aristocrat, Baron E. de Mandat-Grancey giving an account of a tour in Ireland in 1886, in the course of which he made the acquaintance of many of the Land League leaders, as well as visited at the mansions of a number of the landlords, makes this comment: –

> 'For in fact, however they may try to dissimulate it, the Irish claims, if they do not yet amount to Communism as their avowed object – and they may still retain a few illusions upon that point – still it is quite certain that the methods employed by the Land League would not be disowned by the most advanced Communists.'¹⁴³

It was a recognition of this fact which induced *The Irish World*, the chief advocate of the Land League in America, to carry the sub-title of *American Industrial Liberator*, and to be the mouthpiece of the nascent labour movement of those days, as it was also a recognition of this fact which prompted the Irish middle-class leaders to abandon the land fight, and to lend their energies to an attempt to focus the whole interest of Ireland upon a Parliamentary struggle as soon as ever a temporary set back gave them an opportunity to counsel a change of tactics.¹⁴⁴

They feared to call into existence a spirit of inquiry into the rights of property which would not halt at a negation of the sacredness of fortunes founded upon rent, but might also challenge the rightfulness of fortunes drawn from profit and interest. They instinctively realised that such an inquiry would reveal that there was no fundamental difference between such fortunes: that they were made, not from land in the one case nor workshops in the other, but from the social subjection of the non-possessing class, compelled to toil as tenants on the land or as employees in workshop or factory.

For the same reason the Land League (which was founded in 1879 at Irishtown, Co. Mayo, at a meeting held to denounce the exactions of a certain priest in his capacity as a rackrenting landlord) had had at the outset to make headway in Ireland against the opposition of all the

---

¹⁴² The Irish National Land League, an organisation dedicated to the betterment of poor tenant farmers, was founded in 1879. Charles Stewart Parnell, later leader of the Irish Parliamentary Party, and Michael Davitt were among its chief leaders.

¹⁴³ Edmond de Mandat-Grancey (1842–1911), French aristocrat and writer. Published *Chez Paddy* in 1887.

¹⁴⁴ The *Irish World and American Industrial Liberator* began publication in New York in 1870.

official Home Rule Press, and in Great Britain amongst the Irish exiles to depend entirely upon the championship of poor labourers and English and Scottish Socialists. In fact those latter were, for years, the principal exponents and interpreters of Land League principles to the British masses, and they performed their task unflinchingly at a time when the 'respectable' moneyed men of the Irish communities in Great Britain cowered in dread of the displeasure of their wealthy British neighbours.

Afterwards, when the rising tide of victorious revolt in Ireland compelled the Liberal Party to give a half-hearted acquiescence to the demands of the Irish peasantry, and the Home Rule-Liberal alliance was consummated, the Irish business men in Great Britain came to the front and succeeded in worming themselves into all the places of trust and leadership in the Irish organisations. One of the first and most bitter fruits of that alliance was the use of the Irish vote against the candidates of the Socialist and Labour Parties. Despite the horrified and energetic protests of such men as Michael Davitt, the solid phalanx of Irish voters was again and again hurled against the men who had fought and endured suffering, ostracism and abuse for Ireland, at a time when the Liberal Government was packing Irish jails with unconvicted Irish men and women. In so manoeuvring to wean the Irish masses in Great Britain away from their old friends, the Socialist and Labour Clubs, and to throw them into the arms of their old enemies the Liberal capitalists, the Irish bourgeois politicians were very astutely following their class interests, even while they cloaked their action under the name of patriotism. Obviously a union of Irish patriotism and Socialist activity, if furthered and endorsed by Irish organisations in Great Britain, could not long be kept out of, or if introduced could not well be fought in, Ireland. Hence their frantic and illogical endeavour to twist and distort the significance of Irish history, and to put the question of property, its ownership and development, out of order in all discussions on Irish nationality.

But that question so dreaded rises again; it will not lie down, and cannot be suppressed. The partial success of the Land League has effected a change in Ireland, the portent of which but few realise. Stated briefly, it means that the recent Land Acts, acting contemporaneously with the development of trans-Atlantic traffic, are converting Ireland from a country governed according to the conception of feudalism into a country shaping itself after capitalistic laws of trade.[145] To-day the com-

---

[145] Between 1870 and 1909, the British government introduced five Land Acts in a process of land reform, which permitted Irish tenant farmers eventually to buy out their holdings, and thereby led to the fall of the Anglo-Irish landlord class.

petition of the trust-owned farms of the United States and the Argentine Republic is a more deadly enemy to the Irish agriculturist than the lingering remnants of landlordism or the bureaucratic officialism of the British Empire. Capitalism is now the enemy, it reaches across the ocean; and, after the Irish agriculturist has gathered his harvest and brought it to market, he finds that a competitor living three thousand miles away under a friendly flag has undersold and beggared him. The merely political heresy under which middle class *doctrinaires* have for nearly 250 years cloaked the Irish fight for freedom has thus run its course. The fight made by the Irish septs against the English pale and all it stood for; the struggle of the peasants and labourers of the 18th and 19th centuries; the great social struggle of all the ages will again arise and re-shape itself to suit the new conditions. The war which the Land League fought, and then abandoned, before it was either lost or won, will be taken up by the Irish toilers on a broader field with sharper weapons, and a more comprehensive knowledge of all the essentials of permanent victory. As the Irish septs of the past were accounted Irish or English according as they rejected or accepted the native or foreign social order, as they measured their oppression or freedom by their loss or recovery of the collective ownership of their lands, so the Irish toilers henceforward will base their fight for freedom, not upon the winning or losing the right to talk in an Irish Parliament, but upon their progress towards the mastery of those factories, workshops and farms upon which a people's bread and liberties depend.

As we have again and again pointed out, the Irish question is a social question, the whole age-long fight of the Irish people against their oppressors resolves itself, in the last analysis into a fight for the mastery of the means of life, the sources of production, in Ireland. Who would own and control the land? The people or the invaders; and if the invaders, which set of them – the most recent swarm of land-thieves, or the sons of the thieves of a former generation? These were the bottom questions of Irish politics, and all other questions were valued or deprecated in the proportion to which they contributed to serve the interests of some of the factions who had already taken their stand in this fight around property interests. Without this key to the meaning of events, this clue to unravel the actions of 'great men', Irish history is but a welter of unrelated facts, a hopeless chaos of sporadic outbreaks, treacheries, intrigues, massacres, murders, and purposeless warfare. With this key all things become understandable and traceable to their primary origin; without this key the lost opportunities of Ireland seem such as to bring a blush to the cheek of the Irish worker; with this key Irish history is a lamp to his feet in the stormy paths of to-day. Yet plain as this is to us to-day, it is undeniable that for two hundred years at least all Irish political movements ignored this fact, and were conducted by men who did not look below the political surface. These men, to arouse the passions of the people, invoked the memory of social wrongs, such as evictions and famines, but for these wrongs proposed only political remedies, such as changes in taxation or transference of the seat of Government (class rule) from one country to another. Hence they accomplished nothing, because the political remedies proposed were unrelated to the social subjection at the root of the matter. The revolutionists of the past were wiser, the Irish Socialists are wiser to-day. In their movement the North and the South will again clasp hands, again will it be demonstrated, as in '98, that the pressure of a common exploitation can make enthusiastic rebels out of a Protestant working class, earnest champions of civil and religious liberty out of Catholics, and out of both a united Social democracy.

Chapter 4

Empire and Revolution

The South African War I

Workers' Republic (19 August 1899)

Connolly's opinions and writings about the South African War (sometimes called the Boer War) seem anomalous and even reprehensible to us now – his support for white European colonists (who would later institutionalise racial supremacism in the form of the apartheid regime in South Africa in 1948) seems to run counter to his avowed anti-imperialism and support for the oppressed, and his internationalism generally. But we must see these attitudes in their context (while retaining our repugnance of them): many shades of Irish political opinion supported the Boers in their struggle with the British Empire, and the idea that native African peoples might have some kind of political agency – that they might at some point in the future wrest control of their political destinies – was rarely articulated.

At the time of going to press it seems probable that in a few weeks at most the British Government will have declared war against the South African Republic.[1] Ostensibly in pursuance of a chivalrous desire to obtain political concessions in their adopted country for British citizens anxious to renounce their citizenship, but in reality for the purpose of enabling an unscrupulous gang of capitalists to get into their hands

---

[1] The war referred to here is the Second Boer War, often called simply 'the Boer War', since the First Boer War (1880–1881) is much less known. The Second Boer War was fought between 1899 and 1902, between Britain (including Ireland) and the South African Republic (the Transvaal Republic) and the Orange Free State. It ended with defeat for the Boer forces and the annexation of the republics. Irish nationalists often sympathised with the Boers, the Dutch colonists who had arrived in Southern Africa in the seventeenth century.

the immense riches of the diamond fields. Such a war will undoubtedly take rank as one of the most iniquitous wars of the century. Waged by a mighty empire against a nation entirely incapable of replying in any effective manner, by a government of financiers upon a nation of farmers, by a nation of filibusterers upon a nation of workers, by a capitalist ring, who will never see a shot fired during the war, upon a people defending their homes and liberties – such is the war upon which the people of England are criminally or stupidly, and criminally even if stupidly, allowing their government to enter. No better corroboration of the truth of the socialist maxim that the modern state is but a committee of rich men administering public affairs in the interest of the upper class, has been afforded of late years, than is furnished by this spectacle of a gang of South African speculators setting in motion the whole machinery of the British Empire in furtherance of their own private ends. There is no pretence that the war will benefit the English people, yet it is calmly assumed the people will pay for the war, and, if necessary, fight in it.

It must be admitted that the English people are at present doing their utmost to justify the low estimate in which their rulers hold them; a people who for centuries have never heard a shot fired in anger upon their shores, yet who encourage their government in its campaign of robbery and murder against an unoffending nation; a people, who, secure in their own homes, permit their rulers to carry devastation and death into the homes of another people, assuredly deserve little respect no matter how loudly they may boast of their liberty-loving spirit.

For the Irish worker the war will contain some valuable lessons. In the first place it will serve to furnish a commentary upon the hopes of those in our ranks who are so fond of dilating upon the 'peaceful' realisation of the aims of socialism. We do not like to theorise upon the function of force as a midwife to progress – that, as we have ere now pointed out, is a matter to be settled by the enemies of progress – but we cannot afford to remain blind to the signs of the time. If, then, we see a small section of the possessing class prepared to launch two nations into war, to shed oceans of blood and spend millions of treasure, in order to maintain intact a *small portion* of their privileges, how can we expect the entire propertied class to abstain from using the same weapons, and to submit peacefully when called upon to *yield up for ever all their privileges*? Let the working-class democracy of Ireland note that lesson, and, whilst working peacefully while they may, keep constantly before their minds the truth that the capitalist class is a beast of prey, and cannot be moralised, converted, or conciliated but must be extirpated.

One other lesson is, that Ireland is apparently a negligible factor in the calculations of the Imperial Government. In certain 'advanced' circles we hear much about the important position of Ireland in international politics. The exact value of such talk may be gauged by the fact that troops are being taken from Ireland to be sent to the Transvaal. The British Government has no fears on the score of Ireland; the Home Rule Party, and their good friends the Constabulary, may be trusted to keep this country quiet. But if the working class of Ireland were only united and understood their power sufficiently well, and had shaken off their backs the Home Rule-Unionist twin brethren – keeping us apart that their class may rob us – they would see in this complication a chance for making a long step forward towards better conditions of life – and, seeing it, act upon it in a manner that would ensure the absence from the Transvaal of a considerable portion of the British army. The class-conscious workers who chafe under our present impotence, and long to remove it, will find the path pointed out to them in the ranks of the Irish Socialist Republican Party.

Imperialism and Socialism

Workers' Republic (4 November 1899)

At Connolly's time, as we note in the Introduction, 'imperialism' was thought of – even on the Marxist left – as the system of alliances and rivalries between the European 'great powers', and not as the systems by which those powers exerted control over territories across the globe. The very division of socialist opinion Connolly refers to here shows how complex this matter was. The crux of the argument below is Connolly's seemingly contradictory position which seems both to welcome the colonisation of 'semi-civilised' parts of the world, in order to bring them into the capitalist system, and to argue that such expansion be denied to the British Empire in order to precipitate its crisis. Hence his assertion of the contradiction between British imperialism and British socialism.

As Socialists – and therefore anxious to at all times throw the full weight of whatever influence we possess upon the side of the forces making most directly for Socialism – we have often been somewhat disturbed in our mind by observing in the writings and speeches of some of our foreign comrades a tendency to discriminate in favour of Great Britain in all the international complications in which that country may be involved over questions of territorial annexation, spheres of influence, etc., in barbarous or semi-civilised portions of the globe. We are, we repeat, disturbed in our mind upon the subject because we ourselves do not at all sympathise with this pro-British policy, but, on the contrary, would welcome the humiliation of the British arms in any one of the conflicts in which it is at present engaged, or with which it has been lately menaced. This we freely avow, but the question then arises: Is this hostility to the British Empire due to the fact of our national and racial subjection by that power, and does it exist in spite of our Socialism, or is it consistent with the doctrines we hold as adherents of the Marxist propaganda, and believers in the Marxist economics.

This is the question we propose briefly to discuss in our article this week. We are led to the discussion of this topic by observing that the English Socialists are apparently divided over the question of the war on the Transvaal; one section of the Social Democratic Federation going strongly for the Boers and against the war; another also declaring against the war, but equally denouncing the Boers; and, finally, one Socialist leader, Mr. Blatchford, editor of the *Clarion* and author of *Merrie England*, coming out bluntly for the war and toasting the health of the queen, and the 'Success of the British arms'.[2] On the other hand all the journals of the party on the continent of Europe and in America, as far as we are aware, come out in this instance whole-heartedly on the side of the Transvaal and against what the organ of our Austrian comrades fittingly terms England's act of 'blood-thirsty piracy'.

We ask then is there no common ground upon which Socialists can agree to treat all matters of international politics – a common standpoint from which all questions of race or nationality shall be carefully excluded, and every question dealt with from the position of its effect upon the industrial development required to bring the Socialist movement to a head? Nominally all Socialists hold to the international solidarity of Labour, and the identity of the interests of the workers the world over, and during the Franco-German and Spanish-American wars the Socialists of those countries demonstrated that the belief was no mere abstract theory, but a living, concrete fact. But our English friend, Mr. Blatchford, deliberately throws the doctrine to the winds, and declares that 'when England is at war he is English and regards all

---

[2] Officially, the Social Democratic Federation took an anti-war stance in regard to the Boer War. However, elements of the party leadership made public statements in favour of Britain's offensive against the Boers, with the leader Henry Hyndman stating in 1901 that campaigning against the war was 'a waste of time and money'. This dispute crystallised wider conflicts in the party. Robert Blatchford (1851–1943), English socialist and journalist; launched *The Clarion* in 1891; *Merrie England*, a collection of Clarion articles on socialism, was published in 1893.

those who have taken up arms against England as enemies to be fought and beaten'. This is unqualifiedly chauvinist, and as a brutal endorsement of every act of brigandage and murder in which the capitalists of England may involve their country it throws a curious sidelight on the mental make-up of this man – who very nearly shed tears of pity over the wrongs and 'Christ-like appearance' of the Anarchists expelled from the International Socialist Congress in London.[3] Our esteemed comrade, H.M. Hyndman of the Social Democratic Federation, also in an article contributed to the Berlin *Vorwaerts* and reprinted in *Justice* took the position that England ought not to have given way to Russia at Port Arthur, but ought to have fought her and asserted English supremacy in the Far East. His reason for so contending being the greater freedom enjoyed under British than under Russian rule.

Mr. Blatchford's chauvinist pronouncement can be ignored as simply a personal predilection, and therefore binding no one, but the opinions of our comrades in the Social Democratic Federation of England hardly stand upon the same footing, but require severer consideration.

That we may not be accused of criticising the attitude of others without stating our own, we hereby place on record our position on all questions of international policy.

Scientific revolutionary Socialism teaches us that Socialism can only be realised when Capitalism has reached its zenith of development; that consequently the advance of nations industrially undeveloped into the capitalistic stage of industry is a thing highly to be desired, since such advance will breed a revolutionary proletariat in such countries and force forward here the political freedom necessary for the speedy success of the Socialist movement; and finally, that as colonial expansion and the conquest of new markets are necessary for the prolongation of the life of capitalism, the prevention of colonial expansion and the loss of markets to countries capitalistically developed, such as England, precipitates economic crises there, and so gives an impulse to revolutionary thought and helps to shorten the period required to develop backward countries and thus prepare the economic conditions needed for our triumph.

That is our position. Arguing from such premises we hold that as England is the most capitalistically developed country in Europe, every fresh conquest of territory by her armies, every sphere of influence acquired in the interests of her commercialists, is a span added to the life of capitalist

---

[3] At the 1896 meeting in London of the Second International, anarchists were expelled due to their opposition to parliamentary democracy. The International, made up of national parties, supported parliamentary politics.

society; and that every market lost, every sphere of influence captured by the non-capitalist enemies of England, shortens the life of capitalism by aiding the development of reactionary countries, and hurling back upon itself the socially conservative industrial population of England.

Comrade Hyndman claims that we should oppose Russia because her people are ruled despotically, and favour England because her people are politically free. But that is the reasoning of a political Radical, not the dispassionate analysis of contemporary history we have a right to expect from an economist and a Socialist of Hyndman's reputation. Our comrade quite forgets to apply that materialist philosophy of history which he himself has done so much to popularise in its Marxian form, viz., that the economic system of any given society is the basis of all else in that society – its political superstructure included. If he did so apply it, he would realise that the political freedom of England is born of her capitalism. Her capitalist class required a wage slave class possessing such freedom or mobility of movement as would make them available at short notice wherever the exigencies of capitalism demanded. To gain such absolute freedom of migration a political movement had to be inaugurated placing the capitalist class in a position to break the bonds of serfdom for the labourer. This once achieved the capitalistic concentration of the workers in great centres of population gave to the proletariat the sense of numbers and opportunities of organisation required to complete the work of political enfranchisement. Thus the economic necessities of capitalism always and everywhere beget a measure of political freedom for its slaves.

Russia is not yet a capitalist country, therefore her people bow beneath the yoke of an autocrat. This is only saying that her capitalist class is not strong enough yet to force upon the government laws establishing the conditions most helpful to capitalist development. But every forward move of Russia in the direction of colonial expansion strengthens that capitalist class in Russia and in so doing breeds there the revolutionary working class. On the other hand, if the wishes of comrade Hyndman were to be realised Russian capitalism would be checked in its growth, and the discontent in that country, lacking capitalistic conditions, would resolve itself into a purely agrarian movement. The revolutionary proletariat would remain unborn.

Drive the Russian out of Poland! By all means! Prevent his extension towards Europe! certainly; but favour his extension and his acquisition of new markets in Asia (at the expense of England if need be) if you would see capitalism hurry onward to its death.

It may be urged that our Irish nationality plays a large part in forming this conception of international politics here set forth. We do not plead guilty, but even if it were so the objection would be puerile. As Socialists we base our political policy on the class struggle of the workers, because we know that the self-interest of the workers lies our way. That the self-interest may sometimes be base does not affect the correctness of our position. In like manner the mere fact that the inherited (and often unreasoning) anti-British sentiment of a chauvinist Irish patriot impels him to the same conclusion as we arrived at as the result of our economic studies does not cause us to shrink from proclaiming our position, but rather leads us to rejoice that our propaganda is thus made all the easier by this none too common identity of aim established as a consequence of what we esteem the strong and irreconcilable hostility between English Imperialism and Socialism.

Resolution of Sympathy with the Boer Republics

Workers' Republic (30 June 1900)

Again, Irish secessionists (nationalist and socialist) supported the Boers. We can learn from this that even the most radical movements have weaknesses and blind spots in their vision and ideology.

**Resolution Drafted by James Connolly and Adopted at a Public Meeting to Express Sympathy with the Boer Republics,
Held in Foster Place, Dublin on August 27th, 1899**

WHEREAS the government of this country is maintained upon the bayonets of an occupying army against the will of the people;
WHEREAS there were in India, Egypt and other portions of the British Empire other and much larger populations also kept down in forced subjection;
WHEREAS a country that thus keeps down subject populations by the use of the hangman, the bullet or the sword, has no right to preach to another about its duties towards its population; THEREFORE BE IT RESOLVED that this meeting denounces the interference of the British capitalist government in the internal affairs of the Transvaal Republic as an act of criminal aggression, wishes long life to the Republic, and trusts that our fellow-countrymen will, if need be, take up arms in defence of their adopted country.

This meeting was held by the Irish Socialist Republican Party, and was their first public meeting held in Ireland to express sympathy with the Boers.

A GREAT OPPORTUNITY

The British Army is getting its hands full in South Africa. The defeated, demoralised, disheartened, subjugated, routed, dispersed, conquered, disarmed and humiliated Boers are still toppling over British battalions, capturing British convoys, cutting British lines of communication, and keeping Lord Roberts and all his generals in a state of almighty panic and unrest, and not a single soldier can be spared from South Africa for a long time to come.[4]

The Boxers in China have developed a sudden aptitude for war, are prowling around on the hunt for foreign devils, and with a smile that is child-like and bland are offering to box all Europe, with Japan and America thrown in as appetisers.[5] Great Britain is in want of soldiers there also.

Now it only wants a native rising in India, and then would come our Irish opportunity.[6]

With war in Africa, war in China, war in India, we of the unconquered Celtic race would rise up in our millions from Malin Head to Cape Clear, from Dublin to Galway, and – and well, pass 'strong' resolutions, and then go home and pray that somebody else may beat the Sasanach.

The Boers are invulnerable on kopjes, the Boxers are death on missionaries, but we are irresistible on 'resolutions'.

The Coming Revolt in India I: Its Political and Social Causes

The Harp (January 1908)

It is unclear whether Connolly read Marx's famous journalism on India. Reading Connolly on India, we are inclined to notice his interest in Indian native politics, where he does not actually see any native African politics in his writings about South Africa. At least one reason for this is that where southern Africa at the turn of the twentieth century was made up of a complex of *settler* colonies, India was a vast *administrative* colony, i.e.

---

[4] Field Marshal Frederick Roberts, 1st Earl Roberts (1832–1914), British general who served in India, Abyssinia and Afghanistan, before his victory in the Second Boer War.

[5] The Boxer Rebellion was a nationalist and anti-imperialist rebellion in China which occurred at the end of the Qing Dynasty, between 1899 and 1901. It was started by the *Yihetuan* (the 'Militia United in Righteousness'), but was defeated by intervention by the great powers.

[6] Since the Great Indian Rebellion of 1857, anti-British nationalism developed rapidly in India.

England had never transferred a significant population (of farmers and workers) to the South Asian subcontinent, and it is estimated that the British government of India was composed of less than 100,000 civil servants. Accordingly, Indian nationalist and anti-imperialist agitation was visible to him in a way that that of black Africans was not.

I

> 'The educated classes of India may find fault with their exclusion from full political rights . . . But it was by force that India was won, and it is for force India must be governed' – London *Times*, Feb. 1, 1886.

The appearance at the International Socialist Congress at Stuttgart of an Indian delegate, voicing the aspirations of the people of India for freedom, and the news items continually appearing in the capitalist press of sporadic acts of revolt in that country – harbingers of the greater revolt now fermenting throughout that vast empire – justify us in placing before our readers the following brief résumé of conditions in that country in order that it might be more possible for them to intelligently follow events as they develop.[7]

British rule in India, like British rule in Ireland, is a political and social system established and maintained by the conquerors in the interest of the conquered. So runs the legend. But there are not wanting men and women who, strangely enough, maintain that British rule, whether in India or Ireland, is one of the heaviest curses ever inflicted upon an unfortunate people; that its fruits are famine, oppression and pestilence, and that it has but one animating principle wherever found, viz., to extract the utmost possible tribute from the labor of its unfortunate subjects. With that aspect of British rule peculiar to Ireland we are all in a position to be thoroughly acquainted, but there are, unfortunately, many reasons why a like acquaintance with the history and facts of British rule in India is impossible of attainment to the vast majority of our fellow countrymen. Therefore the writer, having had for some time exceptional opportunities of learning the real position of affairs in that country, feels he is doing a service to the cause of freedom and humanity in laying before the readers of the *Harp* a short sketch of the predisposing causes which had led up to the devastating famine which at present holds and the incipient rebellion which threatens the Indian

---

[7] The International Socialist Congress held at Stuttgart in Germany in 1907 was the seventh congress of the Second International. It was attended by 900 delegates and was concerned particularly with matters of colonialism, women's rights, and militarism.

Peninsula.⁸ The first point to note is that the reader must in discussing Indian affairs at once rid himself of all the extravagant ideas about the 'wealth of India' with which the reading public have been familiarized through the writings of ignorant English romancers, avaricious English adventurers or unscrupulous English statesmen. India is, in reality, one of the poorest, if not the poorest, of all the countries in the world. Her immense population live from generation to generation in a state of such chronic misery that death from actual hunger excites no comment whatever except when, as in the present famine, their numbers swell so that it is feared even the patient Hindoo may refuse to bear it longer. Thus when we read that the tribute extracted from India by the imperial government in payment of home charges, pensions to retired officials, remittances, contributions to imperial expenditure, etc., reaches an annual total of from 20 to 27 million pounds sterling, the sum, though large in itself, does not at first appear so exorbitant when levied on a population of two hundred million people. It is only when we are aware of the average daily income of the people upon whose labor this tax is levied that we begin to understand how it is that the 'inestimable benefits of British rule' have been so potent a factor in working out the destruction of this people that the failure of a single harvest is enough to bring upon them all the horrors of famine.

The wages of the agricultural laborers of India – where 70 per cent of the population derive their sole subsistence directly from the cultivation of the soil – are not such as to induce any very extravagant mode of living or to fire the imagination of a glutton. In Bihar, the northwest provinces, the greater portion of the Deccan and Oudh, the average remuneration of the laborer is certainly not more than one anna, six pie, or one and one-half pence (three cents) per day. In some portions of East Bengal the wage sometimes rises to three pence (six cents), or four pence (eight cents) per day – an almost princely remuneration. It should also be remembered that the entire native population is excluded from all share in the government of their country, except in the most menial positions, and that on the other hand the Indian Civil Service is entirely manned by Englishmen, whose salaries are the highest in the world for such services.⁹ Thus the poorest people under the sun are taxed to support

---

⁸ Severe famines struck various regions of India in the years shortly before Connolly's writing: in 1896–1897, an estimated 5 million people died in the British territories of the Bombay Deccan, Madras and Bengal, and in 1905–1906, a quarter of a million people died in the Bombay area due to famine and famine-related disease.

⁹ The Indian Civil Service, known in the nineteenth century as the Imperial Civil Service, was the elite of the British civil government in India between 1858 and 1947.

the wealthiest (and most insolent) official class. It might be interesting, in order to bring the matter more vividly before the reader, to give a few instances of the disparity of means between official England in India and the unfortunate people upon whom it is quartered. The late Professor Fawcett, in an article upon a proposed loan to India, called attention to a few items illustrating the extravagant expenditure of Anglo-Indians when the cost of such extravagance can be saddled upon the Indian people.[10] Two of these items, viz., £1,200 for outfit and passage of a member of the Governor-General's Council, and £2,450 for outfit and passage of the Bishops of Calcutta and Bombay, convey their own lesson so well that no words of mine could possibly add point to their eloquence. Ten million pounds have been spent by the imperial government in erecting for their military garrisons regimental quarters so luxuriously equipped that one Anglo-Indian writer, General Strachey, enthusiastically declared 'our soldiers' barracks are now beyond comparison the finest in the world', whilst Florence Nightingale, a thoroughly impartial witness, wrote: 'We do not care for the people of India; the saddest sight in the East, nay, probably in the world, is the peasant of our Indian empire.'[11] 'We suppose', says a young Indian writer, 'it is inseparable from an alien rule that the living of an English soldier should be of primary importance'. And again, 'ten million pounds wrung from the hard earnings of semi-starved dwellers in mud hovels for the rearing of "palatial" barracks. Surely we should pause before we congratulate ourselves on this.' We are constantly informed by all Anglo-Indian writers that the English in India have been mighty instruments of Divine Providence for winning the land from anarchy and oppression, bringing it within the area of civilization and order; and, finally, of introducing its people to all the inestimable benefits of modern civilization.

We Irish are, of course, well enough acquainted with the ways of English officialdom to be able to discount to a certain extent the brightly colored reports of progress emanating from such sources, and they constitute the sole medium by which Indian news is allowed to filter through to the reading public. But it would, nevertheless, be a mistake to suppose that the present writer denies that progress has been made in India under British rule. The only question is, in what degree is that progress due

---

[10] Henry Fawcett (1833–1884), English economist and professor at Cambridge. In 1880, he published *Indian Finances*, a study of taxation in India.

[11] Lieutenant-General Sir Richard Strachey (1817–1908), English soldier and administrator in India. Florence Nightingale (1820–1910), English social reformer and manager of nursing for the British Army during the Crimean War.

to British rule, and in what degree is it that progress which, under any circumstances, would have been made by an intellectual people with a continuity of literary and philosophic activity stretching back for two thousand years and more? We are told that the English rulers of India were the first to abolish the hideous custom of suttee, by which the Hindoo widow was forced to sacrifice herself on the funeral pyre of her deceased husband.[12]

But an educated Hindoo, Ram Mohun Roy, greatly venerated by his countrymen, had begun a crusade against the custom ten years before the edict was first formulated in 1829.[13] It is more than probable that the exertions of this Indian patriot would eventually have been successful even without English intervention, which at the most perhaps, hastened the desired consummation.

The vast irrigation works established throughout India are also often alluded to as specimens of the advance of civilization in the East, largely resultant from the paternal efforts of the English government on behalf of its Indian subjects.

Here again the reader is apt to draw erroneous conclusions and picture to himself the government of England laboriously instructing the ignorant Indian natives in the functions and uses, theory and practice of irrigation works. But the remorseless hand of history rudely shatters all belief in the fidelity to truth of any such picture. So far from such irrigation works being the product of English enterprise or genius they are, as a matter of fact, only feeble and halting imitations of the magnificent works and public enterprise of the former Mohammedan rulers whom the English have supplanted. Dr. Spry, writing in 1837, on *Modern India*, declared:

> 'It is in the territory of the independent native chiefs and princes that great and useful works are found and maintained.
>
> In our territories the canals, bridges and reservoirs, wells, groves, etc., the works of our predecessors from revenues expressly appropriated to such undertakings, are going fast to decay.'[14]

---

[12] 'Suttee' or *sati* was a practice which evolved in south Asia between the fifth and ninth centuries CE. It was banned by the East India Company in 1829, banned in the princely states in the decades thereafter, and comprehensively outlawed in a royal edict by Queen Victoria in 1861.

[13] Raja Ram Mohun Roy (1772–1833), Indian reformer and prominent figure in the Bengali Renaissance of the eighteenth and early nineteenth centuries.

[14] Henry Harpur Spry (1804–1842), army surgeon and author; published *Modern India* in 1837.

It is noteworthy also that while the former rulers of India neither expected nor accepted any return for the money they voluntarily expended in their irrigation and other public works, the English government could only be induced to embark on such enterprises by the hopes of reaping enormous profits therefrom – hopes which have never been realized. Lord Lawrence in a letter to Lord Cranborne stated that the general opinion held that these works would yield an average profit of 25, 50 or even 100 per cent. To the no small chagrin of the ruling classes of India these high expectations were doomed to disappointment, the full measure of which is revealed in the words of Lord Salisbury, valuable as a no doubt unwilling tribute to British official incompetence and to the superior engineering genius of their predecessors.[15]

> 'The irrigation works that have been carried out', he said, 'if they had for their basis the former works of native rulers, have in many instances been a financial success. But ... when we have begun the projects of irrigation for ourselves we have not, I believe, in any instance the desired result of a clean balance sheet.'

Will the reader please contrast this confession of bungling incompetence, allied to a greed to pay dividends, with the conduct of Runjeet Singh, the 'Lion of the Punjab', whom the English have always vilified as a barbarian and a tyrant, but of whom Marshman tells us that 'he always advanced money free of interest to his peasantry for the purposes of irrigation'.[16] That he was no exception to the rule is amply borne out by the following significant statement in Arnold's *Dalhousie*: 'The Musselman rulers were bold engineers in this respect; not only did they cover India with fine roads, shaded with trees in places which are now tiger walks, but they remembered the Arabic proverb that "water is the earth's wealth". The irrigation works were so benevolently attended to that the fees for wells and artificial reservoirs were always deducted from the produce of every village before the government claim was paid'.* In almost every detail of Indian administration the same tale remains to be told.

---

[15] John Mair Lawrence, 1st Baron Lawrence (1811–1879), Viceroy of India 1864–1869; Robert Gascoyne-Cecil, 3rd Marquis of Salisbury (1830–1903), English Conservative politician and three-time Prime Minister; also known as Viscount Cranborne.

[16] Maharaja Ranji Singh (1780–1839), founder of the Sikh Empire, forged from various Sikh polities and lasting from 1799 to 1849.

* Sir Edwin Arnold, *The Marquis of Dalhousie's Administration of British India* (Saunders, Otley & Co., London, 1862).

The Coming Revolt in India II: Its Political and Social Causes

The Harp (February 1908)

II

India is regarded by its alien rulers as a huge human cattle farm to be worked solely in the interest of the dominant class of another nation. Whatever is done for the development of its vast internal resources is done not for the benefit of the Indian people but primarily with a view to the dividends which the investing classes of England may draw from such development. The salt tax, a tax upon a first necessary of life, is ten times higher today than it was ever known to be under the Mussulman rulers of India.[17] More than one humane English Governor has confessed his reluctance to increase this tax upon the helpless peasantry, yet it is to-day as high as 1,000 or 1,200 per cent. As in Ireland during the famine years, the Government rated famine-stricken districts for the relief of their own poor, and so crushed into pauperism those who had managed to survive the loss of their potato crop; so in India, whenever the Government extends financial help to a famine-stricken population it seeks to recoup itself for the outlay by an increase in the salt tax. In other words, it gives relief with one hand and with the other increases the taxes upon the food of a famishing people. In the great famine of thirty years ago in Southern India, when it was estimated that no less than six millions of people had perished of hunger, the salt tax was increased by forty-five per cent. The benevolent rulers of India have also, in order to secure this source of income to their exchequer, prohibited under severe penalties all native manufacture of salt, and when the helpless people, unable to buy salt to season their food, endeavoured to scrape a condiment from the deposits left by the receding ocean upon the rocks and pebbles of the sea-shore, they were prosecuted for defrauding the revenue. This devotion of the rulers of India to the letter of the law in this respect stands out in marked contrast to their action in another, viz., in squandering in useless frontier expeditions the Famine Relief Fund, which, as its name indicates, was intended for emergencies like the present.

---

[17] Salt has been taxed in India since ancient times. The British East India Company greatly raised salt taxes as it established its control of Indian provinces in the seventeenth and eighteenth centuries. When the British Crown took over administration of India in 1858, salt taxes were not abolished; this only came when Jawarhalal Nehru led the Interim Government in 1946.

During the nineteenth century India lost no less than sixteen million (16,000,000) people by starvation. All this time she has enjoyed the ameliorative influence of civilization on the British Imperial pattern, and in the full felicity borne of that enjoyment her children have died off like rotten sheep, while the hack-apologists of the English governing classes have vied with each other in unctuous laudations of 'our civilizing mission', and our 'benign rule'.

Yet, in spite of all their anxiety to suppress the truth about India, the official class in whose interests this systematic distortion of facts is practised cannot entirely exclude even from their own organs in the press the awful record of the results of their rule. Here for instance is an extract from the *Indian Pioneer*, an organ of Anglo-Indian officialdom, of 7th February, 1880, which tells its own tale:

> The hired laborer is always on the verge of starvation. Out of the 109,000,000 in British India, laborers are estimated at 30,000,000. Last year after the heavy rainfall there was frightful mortality from fever, according to the recent sanitary report an increase of 900,000 on the average rate of mortality. There would appear to be a good deal of truth in the opinion of one officer, who reported that *the disease is aggravated by want of food, which at all times prevails amongst the lowest classes.*[18]

Yet that great Home Ruler, Mr. Alfred Webb, not so long ago informed the readers of the *Freeman's Journal* that 'the Indians know their duty to their Sovereign *and are loyal*'. To what?[19]

But, at least, we may be told, India has profited intellectually by her subjection; is not education fostered by the Imperial Government? Yes; it spends on education in India one-fiftieth part of its net revenue there, whereas in England and Scotland alone it spends under the same heading about one twenty-fourth part of the revenue of the United Kingdom. Again, as Irish Nationalists remember that it was the wholesome fear engendered in the English governing classes by the Fenian conspiracy, which led to the disestablishment of the Irish Church, so thoughtful Indians are not likely to forget that the year which saw the establishment of the universities of Bombay, Calcutta and Madras had also seen the smoke and fire of the Indian mutiny.[20]

---

[18] The *Pioneer*, an English-language newspaper, was founded in Allahabad in 1865 by George Allen, an English tea-grower, and remains in publication.

[19] The *Freeman's Journal* was the leading Irish newspaper of Connolly's day, founded in 1763.

[20] Connolly alludes here to the fact that in the same year – 1857 – that the Court of Directors of the East India Company recommended the foundation of universities in Bombay, Calcutta and Madras, the great Indian Rebellion took place.

But has not religion benefited by the British Conquest of India? Well, for every Christian Church in India maintained by the free contributions of Christian people at home the Government establishes brothels for the use of its soldiers, the one frequently in sight of the other. For every Christian made the example of the British garrison from Tommy Atkins upward has made an hundred drunkards. Am I exaggerating? Listen to the words of this Englishman, Mr. Alfred S. Dyer, writing some years ago from Allahabad to the *Christian Commonwealth*:

> If the people of Great Britain, and especially the Christians of Great Britain, do not interfere to stop the mad career of the handful of sin-supporting politicians who are at present in power in India, there can be no doubt that that career will be stopped by other means ...
>
> As I stood amid the scenes of the mutiny at Cawnpore, and then at Lucknow, and then at Delhi, I realized how easily national judgment can follow national sin, as effect follows cause. I realized it afresh as a few weeks since at Peshawur, the border city of India and Afghanistan, I looked towards the entrance of the Khyber Pass, of disastrous memory, and remembered the tale of the first British Afghan campaign. History uses the convenient word 'emeute' to cover the character of the incident which led to the fatal ending of that unjustifiable enterprise. The truth seems to be that the indignation of the Afghans at the treatment of their women, principally by officers, led to the rising which turned the tide against the licentious English, and led to the retreat to Jellalabad, in which the whole army perished with the exception of one man.
>
> Another so-called 'emeute' similar to that may occur among the hardy race in northernmost India at any time. Licensed sin is in full blast at Peshawur and other cities and places near. At Peshawur, from the door of their compound, the women can see the men, for whose lust they are licensed, paraded for 'divine service'. The people talk about these things. The impurity of the officers, as well as the rank and file, is thrown up in the faces of the missionaries, as two at Peshawur themselves told me.
>
> Religion, in fact, in India, as everywhere else, loses by being identified with the forces of a tyrannical government.[21]

The earlier English East India Company, when it totally prohibited the teaching of Christianity to the natives under its control, did not do as much to prevent its adoption by the Indians as the present governors do when they ostentatiously parade their Sunday religion before a people who have witnessed the immorality of their week-day lives. Even the ordinary administration of law in India in the most peaceful

---

[21] The *Christian Commonwealth* was a Christian newspaper founded in London in 1881.

times is saturated with a barbarism unknown elsewhere, and only partly approximated to by the expiring Russian despotism in its present fight against freedom. For instance: According to Sir Henry Cotton, M.P., K.C.S.I., floggings in India are publicly inflicted upon adult male and female offenders, and for petty theft and the like. The last year for which figures are available, 1902, no fewer than 25,186 judicial floggings were inflicted. These are carried out in public. 'The triangles', he writes, 'are an unpleasant feature outside every Court in India. I have known floggings so severe that the victims have died in the triangles to which they were tied.'[22]

England, in short, has only one use for India. She sees there a spot revealed by an All-wise Providence for the specific purpose of providing comfortable positions and fat salaries and pensions to the younger sons and poor relations of the English moneyed classes. Therefore, as any efforts to entrust the government of India to the children of the soil would necessarily displace those sinecurists from their snug berths and salaries, all suggestions pointing in that direction must be branded as rank heresy, if not political incendiarism. In Java, under the rule of the Dutch, the natives share in the government of their country. In the words of Sir David Wedderburn, 'the Asiatic races are subordinated to their own recognized chiefs, and these are responsible to the Government for the maintenance of order'.[23] Thus the most important official positions are open to the natives. In the independent native States of India, before the Conquest, all posts, according to the Anglo-Indian writer, Marshman, were open to universal competition.[24] What, then is the net result of British rule in India? 'The main evil of our rule', said Sir T. Munro, Governor of Madras in 1819, 'is the degraded state in which we hold the native', and as a corollary to this statement one of our contemporary writers, Sir James Caird, informs us from personal investigation that 'in the native States the people are more prosperous than under our rule, and they have not been driven into the evil hands of the sowcars (money-lenders) as our ryots (peasants) have been'.[25] A few months ago famine in all its horrors was once more devastating the country, and once more the native States were exempt from the calamity.

---

[22] Sir Henry John Cotton (1845–1915), English civil servant in India, and later Liberal Member of Parliament. He was sympathetic to Indian nationalism.

[23] Sir David Wedderburn (1835–1882), English Liberal Member of Parliament of republican tendencies.

[24] John Clarke Marshman (1794–1877), English journalist and historian of India.

[25] Sir Thomas Munro (1761–1827), Scottish soldier and colonial official. Sir James Caird (1864–1954), Scottish shipowner and East India merchant.

The English Government officials for months denied the accuracy of the reports which, despite their vigilance, filtered through to Europe, and then, when the awful truth could no longer be concealed, they, like Pilate of old, called heaven and earth to witness they were guiltless of the blood of this people. And once more they called upon the charitable to contribute to the relief of the destitute, whilst they prepared, horse, foot and artillery, to insure that not one penny of the tribute, the exaction of which has created the destitution, shall be withheld from the British Exchequer, or devoted to the people they have ruined. The people in India require justice, but justice is exactly what they must not expect. Justice is prosaic, dull and unsentimental, and cannot be advertised in Mansion House Funds, or prated about by royal and aristocratic dignities. Charity, however, though utterly useless for the purpose of staying the ravages of famine among a population of thirty-six millions perishing beneath it, yet fulfils the purpose of those who desire to hear their own trumpet blowing and see their names advertised side by side with the elite of society and in company with royalty. Above all, it does not interfere with the ceaseless flow of Indian tribute into the coffers of their conquerors. Therefore, justice India must not expect, but charity (D.V.) she will have. 'Look well at the background of this fine picture, and lo, the reeking shanks and yellow chapless skulls of Skibbereen, and the ghosts of starved Hindoos in dusky millions.'

Our Duty in this Crisis

Irish Worker (8 August 1914)

The *Irish Worker* was the newspaper of the Irish Transport and General Workers' Union, founded by James Larkin in 1909. The union was inspired by syndicalism, and was at the heart of the Dublin Lock-Out of 1913.

What should be the attitude to the working-class democracy of Ireland in face of the present crisis?[26] I wish to emphasise the fact that the question is addressed to the 'working-class democracy' because I believe that it would be worse than foolish – it would be a crime against all our hopes and aspirations – to take counsel in this matter from any other source.

Mr. John E. Redmond has just earned the plaudits of all the bitterest enemies of Ireland and slanderers of the Irish race by declaring, in the

---

[26] The 'crisis' to which Connolly refers was the onset of the First World War.

name of Ireland that the British Government can now safely withdraw all its garrisons from Ireland, and that the Irish slaves will guarantee to protect the Irish estate of England until their masters come back to take possession – a statement that announces to all the world that Ireland has at last accepted as permanent this status of a British province.[27] Surely no inspiration can be sought from that source.

The advanced Nationalists have neither a policy nor a leader. During the Russian Revolution such of their Press as existed in and out of Ireland, as well as their spokesmen, orators and writers vied with each other in laudation of Russia and vilification of all the Russian enemies of Czardom. It was freely asserted that Russia was the natural enemy of England; that the heroic revolutionalists were in the pay of the English Government and that every true Irish patriot ought to pray for the success of the armies of the Czar. Now, as I, amongst other Irish Socialists, predicted all along, when the exigencies of diplomacy makes it suitable, the Russian bear and the English lion are hunting together and every victory for the Czar's Cossacks is a victory for the paymasters of those King's Own Scottish Borderers who, but the other day, murdered the people of Dublin in cold blood.[28] Surely the childish intellects that conceived of the pro-Russian campaign of nine years ago cannot give us light and leading in any campaign for freedom from the British allies of Russia today? It is well to remember also that in this connection since 1909 the enthusiasm for the Russians was replaced in the same quarter by as blatant a propaganda in favour of the German War Lord. But since the guns did begin to speak in reality this propaganda had died out in whispers, whilst without a protest, the manhood of Ireland was pledged to armed warfare against the very power our advanced Nationalist friends have wasted so much good ink in acclaiming.

Of late, sections of the advanced Nationalist press have lent themselves to a desperate effort to misrepresent the position of the Carsonites, and to claim for them the admiration of Irish Nationalists on the grounds that these Carsonites were fearless Irishmen who had refused to take dictation from England.[29] A more devilishly mischievous and lying doctrine was never preached in Ireland. The Carsonite position is indeed

---

[27] John Redmond (1856–1918), Irish politician, barrister and Home Rule Member of Parliament; leader of the Irish Parliamentary Party 1900–1918.

[28] Cossacks, an ethnic grouping living in various parts of Russia and the Ukraine, often served in Russian armies, particularly as cavalry. The King's Own Scottish Borderers was an infantry regiment of the British Army, first raised in 1689.

[29] Followers of Edward Carson, leader of Ulster Unionism and a prominent anti-Home Rule campaigner.

plain – so plain that nothing but sheer perversity of purpose can misunderstand it, or cloak it with a resemblance to Irish patriotism. The Carsonites say that their fathers were planted in this country to assist in keeping the natives down in subjection that this country might be held for England. That this was God's will because the Catholic Irish were not fit for the responsibilities and powers of free men and that they are not fit for the exercise of these responsibilities and powers till this day. Therefore, say the Carsonites, we have kept our side of the bargain; we have refused to admit the Catholics to power and responsibility; we have manned the government of this country for England, we propose to continue to do so, and rather than admit that these Catholics – these 'mickies and teagues' – are our equals, we will fight, in the hope that our fighting will cause the English people to revolt against their government and re-establish us in our historic position as an English colony in Ireland, superior to, and unhampered by, the political institutions of the Irish natives.

How this can be represented as the case of Irishmen refusing to take dictation from England passeth all comprehension. It is rather the case of a community in Poland, after 250 years colonisation, still refusing to adopt the title of natives, and obstinately clinging to the position and privileges of a dominant colony.[30] Their programme is summed up in the expression which forms the dominant note of all their speeches, sermons and literature:

> 'We are loyal British subjects. We hold this country for England. England cannot desert us.'

What light or leading then can Ireland get from the hysterical patriots who so egregiously misrepresent this fierce contempt for Ireland as something that ought to win the esteem of Irishmen?

What ought to be the attitude of the working-class democracy of Ireland in face of the present crisis?

In the first place, then, we ought to clear our minds of all the political cant which would tell us that we have either 'natural enemies' or 'natural allies' in any of the powers now warring. When it is said that we ought to unite to protect our shores against the 'foreign enemy' I confess to be unable to follow that line of reasoning, as I know of no foreign enemy of this country except the British Government and know that it is not the British Government that is meant.

---

[30] Poland has contained communities of ethnic Germans since the Middle Ages, often afforded particular rights.

In the second place we ought to seriously consider that the evil effects of this war upon Ireland will be simply incalculable, that it will cause untold suffering and misery amongst the people, and that as this misery and suffering have been brought upon us because of our enforced partisanship with a nation whose government never consulted us in the matter, we are therefore perfectly at liberty morally to make any bargain we may see fit, or that may present itself in the course of events.

Should a German army land in Ireland tomorrow we should be perfectly justified in joining it if by doing so we could rid this country once and for all from its connection with the Brigand Empire that drags us unwillingly into this war.

Should the working class of Europe, rather than slaughter each other for the benefit of kings and financiers, proceed tomorrow to erect barricades all over Europe, to break up bridges and destroy the transport service that war might be abolished, we should be perfectly justified in following such a glorious example and contributing our aid to the final dethronement of the vulture classes that rule and rob the world.

But pending either of these consummations it is our manifest duty to take all possible action to save the poor from the horrors this war has in store.

Let it be remembered that there is no natural scarcity of food in Ireland. Ireland is an agricultural country, and can normally feed all her people under any sane system of things. But prices are going up in England and hence there will be an immense demand for Irish produce. To meet that demand all nerves will be strained on this side, the food that ought to feed the people of Ireland will be sent out of Ireland in greater quantities than ever and famine prices will come in Ireland to be immediately followed by famine itself. Ireland will starve, or rather the townspeople of Ireland will starve, that the British army and navy and jingoes may be fed. Remember, the Irish farmer like all other farmers will benefit by the high prices of the war, but these high prices will mean starvation to the labourers in the towns. But without these labourers the farmers' produce cannot leave Ireland without the help of a garrison that England cannot now spare. We must consider at once whether it will not be our duty to refuse to allow agricultural produce to leave Ireland until provision is made for the Irish working class.

Let us not shrink from the consequences. This may mean more than a transport strike, it may mean armed battling in the streets to keep in this country the food for our people. But whatever it may mean it must not be shrunk from. It is the immediately feasible policy of the working-class democracy, the answer to all the weaklings who in this crisis of our country's history stand helpless and bewildered crying for guidance, when they are not hastening to betray her.

Starting thus, Ireland may yet set the torch to a European conflagration that will not burn out until the last throne and the last capitalist bond and debenture will be shrivelled on the funeral pyre of the last war lord.

A Continental Revolution

Forward (15 August 1914)

Forward was the newspaper of the Independent Labour Party (ILP), in Britain. This journal was Connolly's main outlet for his writings between 1910 and 1914. Its editorial policy was eclectic to the point of incoherence, but it allowed Connolly to assert his anti-war position – one held by many members of the ILP.

The outbreak of war on the continent of Europe makes it impossible this week to write to *Forward* upon any other question. I have no doubt that to most of my readers Ireland has ere now ceased to be, in colloquial phraseology, the most important place on the map, and that their thoughts are turning gravely to a consideration of the position of the European socialist movement in the face of this crisis.

Judging by developments up to the time of writing, such considerations must fall far short of affording satisfying reflections to the socialist thinker. For, what is the position of the socialist movement in Europe to-day? Summed up briefly it is as follows:

For a generation at least the socialist movement in all the countries now involved has progressed by leaps and bounds, and more satisfactory still, by steady and continuous increase and development.

The number of votes recorded for socialist candidates has increased at a phenomenally rapid rate, the number of socialist representatives in all legislative chambers has become more and more of a disturbing factor in the calculations of governments. Newspapers, magazines, pamphlets and literature of all kinds teaching socialist ideas have been and are daily distributed by the million amongst the masses; every army and navy in Europe has seen a constantly increasing proportion of socialists amongst its soldiers and sailors, and the industrial organisations of the working class have more and more perfected their grasp over the economic machinery of society, and more and more moved responsive to the socialist conception of their duties. Along with this, hatred of militarism has spread through every rank of society, making everywhere its recruits, and raising an aversion to war even amongst those who in other things accepted the capitalist order of things. Anti-militarist societies and anti-militarist campaigns of socialist societies and parties, and anti-militarist resolutions of socialist and international trade union conferences have become part of the order of the day and are no longer phenomena to be wondered at. The whole working-class movement stands committed to war upon war – stands so committed at the very height of its strength and influence.

And now, like the proverbial bolt from the blue, war is upon us, and war between the most important, because the most socialist, nations of the earth. And we are helpless!

What then becomes of all our resolutions; all our protests of fraternisation; all our threats of general strikes; all our carefully-built machinery of internationalism; all our hopes for the future? Were they all as sound and fury, signifying nothing? When the German artilleryman, a socialist serving in the German army of invasion, sends a shell into the ranks of the French army, blowing off their heads, tearing out their bowels, and mangling the limbs of dozens of socialist comrades in that force, will the fact that he, before leaving for the front 'demonstrated' against the war be of any value to the widows and orphans made by the shell he sent upon its mission of murder? Or, when the French rifleman pours his murderous rifle fire into the ranks of the German line of attack, will he be able to derive any comfort from the probability that his bullets are murdering or maiming comrades who last year joined in thundering 'hochs' and cheers of greeting to the eloquent Jaurès, when in Berlin he pleaded for international solidarity?[31] When the socialist pressed into the army of the Austrian Kaiser, sticks a long, cruel bayonet-knife into the stomach of the socialist conscript in the army of the Russian Czar, and gives it a twist so that when pulled out it will pull the entrails out along with it, will the terrible act lose any of its fiendish cruelty by the fact of their common theoretical adhesion to an anti-war propaganda in times of peace? When the socialist soldier from the Baltic provinces of Russia is sent forward into Prussian Poland to bombard towns and villages until a red trail of blood and fire covers the homes of the unwilling Polish subjects of Prussia, as he gazes upon the corpses of those he has slaughtered and the homes he has destroyed, will he in his turn be

---

[31] Auguste Marie Joseph Jean Jaurès (1859–1914), French socialist, leader of the French Socialist Party. An anti-militarist, he was assassinated on 31 July 1914, as he was preparing to attend a meeting of the Second International to agitate against war.

comforted by the thought that the Czar whom he serves sent other soldiers a few years ago to carry the same devastation and murder into his own home by the Baltic Sea?

But why go on? Is it not as clear as the fact of life itself that no insurrection of the working class; no general strike; no general uprising of the forces of Labour in Europe, could possibly carry with it, or entail a greater slaughter of socialists, than will their participation as soldiers in the campaigns of the armies of their respective countries? Every shell which explodes in the midst of a German battalion will slaughter some socialists; every Austrian cavalry charge will leave the gashed and hacked bodies of Serbian or Russian socialists squirming and twisting in agony upon the ground; every Russian, Austrian, or German ship sent to the bottom or blown sky-high will mean sorrow and mourning in the homes of some socialist comrades of ours. If these men must die, would it not be better to die in their own country fighting for freedom for their class, and for the abolition of war, than to go forth to strange countries and die slaughtering and slaughtered by their brothers that tyrants and profiteers might live?

Civilisation is being destroyed before our eyes; the results of generations of propaganda and patient heroic plodding and self-sacrifice are being blown into annihilation from a hundred cannon mouths; thousands of comrades with whose souls we have lived in fraternal communion are about to be done to death; they whose one hope it was to be spared to cooperate in building the perfect society of the future are being driven to fratricidal slaughter in shambles where that hope will be buried under a sea of blood.

I am not writing in captious criticism of my continental comrades. We know too little about what is happening on the continent, and events have moved too quickly for any of us to be in a position to criticise at all. But believing as I do that any action would be justified which would put a stop to this colossal crime now being perpetrated, I feel compelled to express the hope that ere long we may read of the paralysing of the internal transport service on the continent, even should the act of paralysing necessitate the erection of socialist barricades and acts of rioting by socialist soldiers and sailors, as happened in Russia in 1905.[32] Even an unsuccessful attempt at social revolution by force of arms, following

---

[32] Starting in January 1905, a wave of strikes, unrest, military mutinies and other forms of protest spread across Tsarist Russia, including the famous mutiny in Odessa aboard the warship *Potemkin*. The revolution, a precursor to the Bolshevik Revolution of 1917, brought in such reforms as the Russian *Duma* (parliament) and the Constitution of 1906.

the paralysis of the economic life of militarism, would be less disastrous to the socialist cause than the act of socialists allowing themselves to be used in the slaughter of their brothers in the cause.

A great continental uprising of the working class would stop the war; a universal protest at public meetings will not save a single life from being wantonly slaughtered.

I make no war upon patriotism; never have done. But against the patriotism of capitalism – the patriotism which makes the interest of the capitalist class the supreme test of duty and right – I place the patriotism of the working class, the patriotism which judges every public act by its effect upon the fortunes of those who toil. That which is good for the working class I esteem patriotic, but that party or movement is the most perfect embodiment of patriotism which most successfully works for the conquest by the working class of the control of the destinies of the land wherein they labour.

To me, therefore, the socialist of another country is a fellow-patriot, as the capitalist of my own country is a natural enemy. I regard each nation as the possessor of a definite contribution to the common stock of civilisation, and I regard the capitalist class of each nation as being the logical and natural enemy of the national culture which constitutes that definite contribution.

Therefore, the stronger I am in my affection for national tradition, literature, language, and sympathies, the more firmly rooted I am in my opposition to that capitalist class which in its soulless lust for power and gold would bray the nations as in a mortar.

Reasoning from such premises, therefore, this war appears to me as the most fearful crime of the centuries. In it the working class are to be sacrificed that a small clique of rulers and armament makers may sate their lust for power and their greed for wealth. Nations are to be obliterated, progress stopped, and international hatreds erected into deities to be worshipped.

In Praise of the Empire

Workers' Republic (9 October 1915)

Connolly here emulates Swift's *Modest Proposal*, to which he had referred in *Labour in Irish History*, in a blackly ironic endorsement of empire.

We want to say a few words in praise of the Empire. Now, do not get startled, or shocked, nor yet think that we are only sarcastic. We are not abandoning our principles, nor forgetting our wrongs, nor giving up as hopeless the fight for our rights, nor yet exercising the slave's last privilege – that of sneering at his masters.

We do not love the Empire; we hate it with an unqualified hatred, but, nevertheless, we admire it. Why should we not!

Consider well what this Empire is doing today, and then see if you can withhold your admiration.

At the present moment this Empire has dominions spread all over the seven seas. Everywhere it holds down races and nations, that it might use them as its slaves, that it might use their territories as sources of rent and interest for its aristocratic rulers, that it might prevent their development as self-supporting entities and compel them to remain dependent customers of English produce, that it might be able to strangle every race or nation that would enter the field as a competitor against British capitalism or assert its independence of the British capitalist.

To do this it stifles the ancient culture of India, strangles in its birth the new-born liberty of Egypt, smothers in the blood of ten thousand women and children the republics of South Africa, betrays into the hands of Russian despotism the trusting nationalists of Persia, connives at the partition of China, and plans the partition of Ireland.[33]

North, south, east and west it has set its foot upon the neck of peoples, plundering and murdering, and mocking as it outraged. In the name of a superior civilisation it has crushed the development of native genius, and in the name of superior capitalist development it has destroyed the native industries of a sixth of the human race.

In the name of liberty it hangs and imprisons patriots, and whilst calling High Heaven to witness its horror of militarism it sends the shadow of its swords between countless millions and their hopes of freedom.

Despite all this, despite the fact that every day the winds of the earth are laden with the curses which its unwilling subjects in countless millions pray upon its flag, yet that flag flies triumphantly over every one of its possessions, even whilst its soldiers are reeling discomfited and beaten before the trenches of Turk and German.

The British Empire never fought a white European foe single-handed,

---

[33] Connolly refers here to British and French moves to buttress the power of the Khedive Tewfic of Egypt against rising popular and nationalist sentiment in the 1880s; to the Boer Wars; to Britain's signing of the Anglo-Russian Entente of 1907 which increased Russian influence over Persia (Iran) and ended Persian autonomy; and to the 'Open Door' policy of the West vis-à-vis China, which encouraged Western powers to maintain separate 'spheres of influence' in China.

never dared yet to confront an equal unaided, yet it has laid upon its subjects everywhere from Ireland to India and from India to Africa, the witchcraft of belief in its luck, so that even whilst they see it beaten to its knees they are possessed with the conviction that it will pull through in some fashion. The Devil's children have their father's luck!

Without that belief, without that conviction of the slaves that their master must remain in possession of his mastership, the British Empire would today be everywhere lit up with the fires of mutiny and insurrection.

In the labour movement we have long ago learned that it is the worker who is convinced of the power of the capitalist, who believes that 'the big fellows are sure to win', it is he who really keeps labour in subjection, defeats strikes and destroys Trade Unions. The problem before the labour movement is always to find out how this hopeless feeling can be destroyed, and confidence implanted in the bosom where despair usually reigns.

The moment the worker no longer believes in the all-conquering strength of the employer is the moment when the way opens out to the emancipation of our class.

The master class realise this, and hence all their agencies bend their energies towards drugging, stupefying and poisoning the minds of the workers – sowing distrust and fear amongst them.

The ruling class of the British Empire also know it, and hence they also utilise every agency to spread amongst the subject races a belief in the luck of England, in the strength of England, in the omnipotence of England. That belief is worth more to the British Empire than ten army corps; when it goes, when it is lost, there will be an uprising of resurgent nationalities – and a crash of falling Empires.

Should we not therefore admire the Empire that in face of danger can yet fascinate and enthral the minds of its slaves and keep them in mental as well as physical subjection?

A War for Civilization

Workers' Republic (30 October 1915)

In a striking, and properly dialectical, manner Connolly here eviscerates the idea that the First World War was fought for 'civilisation' or was fought by 'civilised' nations. In doing so, he anticipates Walter Benjamin's famous formulation that 'there is no document of civilisation which is not at the same time a document of barbarism'.

We are hearing and reading a lot just now about a war for civilization. In some vague, ill-defined manner we are led to believe that the great empires of Europe have suddenly been seized with a chivalrous desire to right the wrongs of mankind, and have sallied forth to war, giving their noblest blood and greatest measures to the task of furthering the cause of civilization.

It seems unreal, but it may be possible. Great emotions sometimes master the most cold and calculating individuals, pushing them on to do that which in their colder moments they would have sneered at. In like manner great emotions sometimes master whole communities of men and women, and nations have gone mad, as in the Crusades, over matters that did not enter into any scheme of selfish calculation.

But in such cases the great emotions manifested themselves in at least an appropriate manner. Their actions under the influence of great emotions had a relation to the cause or the ideal for which they were ostensibly warring.

In the case of the war for civilization, however, we look in vain for any action which in itself bears the mark of civilization. As we count civilization it means the ascendancy of industry and the arts of industry over the reign of violence and pillage. Civilization means the conquest by ordered law and peaceful discussion of the forces of evil, it means the exaltation of those whose strength is only in the righteousness of their cause over those whose power is gained by a ruthless seizing of domination founded on force.

Civilization necessarily connotes the gradual supplanting of the reign of chance and muddling by the forces of order and careful provision for the future; it means the levelling up of classes, and the initiation of the people into a knowledge and enjoyment of all that tends to soften the natural hardships of life and to make that life refined and beautiful.

But the war for civilization has done none of those things – aspires to do none of these things. It is primarily a war upon a nation whose chief crime is that it refuses to accept a position of dependence, but insists instead upon organizing its forces so that its people can co-operate with nature in making their lives independent of chance, and independent of the goodwill of others.

The war for civilization is a war upon a nation which insists upon organizing its intellect so as to produce the highest and best in science, in art, in music, in industry; and insists moreover upon so co-ordinating and linking up all these that the final result shall be a perfectly educated nation of men and women.

In the past civilization has been a heritage enjoyed by a few upon a basis of the brutalization of the vast multitude; that nation aims at a civilization of the whole resting upon the whole, and only made possible by the educated co-operation of an educated whole.

The war for civilization is waged by a nation like Russia, which has the greatest proportion of illiterates of any European power, and which strives sedulously to prevent education where it is possible, and to poison it where prohibition is impossible.

The war for civilization is waged by a nation like Britain which holds in thrall a sixth of the human race, and holds as a cardinal doctrine of its faith that none of its subject races may, under penalty of imprisonment and death, dream of ruling their own territories. A nation which believes that all races are subject to purchase, and which brands as perfidy the act of any nation which, like Bulgaria, chooses to carry its wares and its arms to any other than a British market.

This war for civilization in the name of neutrality and small nationalities invades Persia and Greece, and in the name of the interests of commerce seizes the cargo of neutral ships, and flaunts its defiance of neutral flags.

In the name of freedom from militarism it establishes military rule in Ireland, battling for progress it abolishes trial by jury, and waging war for enlightened rule it tramples the freedom of the press under the heel of a military despot.

Is it any wonder then that that particular war for civilization arouses no enthusiasm in the ranks of the toiling masses of the Irish nation?

But there is another war for civilization in which these masses are interested. That war is being waged by the forces of organized labour.

Civilization cannot be built upon slaves; civilization cannot be secured if the producers are sinking into misery; civilization is lost if they whose labour makes it possible share so little of its fruits that its fall can leave them no worse than its security.

The workers are at the bottom of civilized society. That civilization may endure they ought to push upward from their poverty and misery until they emerge into the full sunlight of freedom. When the fruits of civilization, created by all, are enjoyed in common by all, then civilization is secure. Not till then.

Since this European war started the workers as a whole have been sinking. It is not merely that they have lost in comfort – have lost a certain standard of food and clothing by reason of the increase of prices – but they have lost in a great measure, in Britain at least, all those hard won rights of combination and freedom of action, the possession of which was the foundation upon which they hoped to build the greater freedom of the future.

From being citizens with rights the workers were being driven and betrayed into the position of slaves with duties. Some of them may have been well-paid slaves, but slavery is not measured by the amount of oats in the feeding trough to which the slave is tied. It is measured by his loss of control of the conditions under which he labours.

We here in Ireland, particularly those who follow the example of the Irish Transport and General Workers Union, have been battling to preserve those rights which others have surrendered; we have fought to keep up our standards of life, to force up our wages, to better our conditions.[34]

To that extent we have been truly engaged in a war for civilization. Every victory we have gained has gone to increase the security of life amongst our class, has gone to put bread on the tables, coals in the fires, clothes on the backs of those to whom food and warmth and clothing are things of ever pressing moment.

Some of our class have fought in Flanders and the Dardanelles; the greatest achievement of them all combined will weigh but a feather in the balance for good compared with the achievements of those who stayed at home and fought to secure the rights of the working class against invasion.

The carnival of murder on the continent will be remembered as a nightmare in the future, will not have the slightest effect in deciding for good the fate of our homes, our wages, our hours, our conditions. But the victories of labour in Ireland will be as footholds, secure and firm, in the upward climb of our class to the fullness and enjoyment of all that labour creates, and organized society can provide.

Truly, labour alone in these days is fighting the real war for civilization.

---

[34] The Irish Transport and General Workers' Union (ITGWU) was founded by James Larkin in 1909.

Chapter 5

The Lock-Out, the First World War and the Rising

Mr. John E. Redmond, MP: His Strength and Weakness

Forward (11 March 1911)

Connolly offers here a powerful critique of the Home Rule leader and his bourgeois-nationalist constitutionalist politics, noting its relationship to the Unionism to which it was supposedly opposed, and its inability to attend to the poor.

In endeavouring to give readers in Great Britain some real conception of the realities of Irish political life, one finds the task of explanation made increasingly difficult by the spectacular nature of the campaign waged by the Redmondites on the one hand, and the reactionary, lying stupidities of the Irish Tories on the other. The fact that national political freedom is both desirable and necessary blinds many people to the truth that the advocates of such freedom on the political field may be most intensely conservative on the social or economic field and, indeed, may be purblind bigots in their opposition to all other movements making for human progress or enlightenment.

On the other hand there are not wanting, even among Socialists, many who seeing the socially reactionary character of much of the agitation for national freedom, became opposed to the principle because of the anti-Socialist character of some of its advocates.

The Socialist Party of Ireland avoids the dangers of either course. It recognises that national political freedom is an inevitable step towards the attainment of universal economic freedom, but it insists that the non-Socialist leaders of merely national movements should be regarded in their true light as champions of the old social order and not exalted into the position of popular heroes by any aid of

Socialist praise or glorification. A fact many of our British comrades are apt to forget.

We need not beslaver the United Irish League because we detest the Tories. We can detest them both. In fact they represent the same principle in different stages of social development. The Tories are the conservatives of Irish feudalism, the United Irish Leaguers are the conservatives of a belated Irish capitalism. It is our business to help the latter against the former only when we can do so without prejudice to our own integrity as a movement.

How difficult this becomes, at times, is best illustrated by the position of Mr. John E. Redmond, M.P., 'Leader of the Irish race', as his followers enthusiastically assure us.[1] Mr. Redmond has a record as a reactionist difficult to excel. Long before the Parnell split, he denounced the Irish agricultural labourers in a speech at Rathfarnham, near Dublin, for forming a trade union to protect their own interests. On the granting of Local Government in 1898, a measure that first enfranchised the Irish working class on local bodies, Mr. Redmond made a speech counselling the labourers to elect landlords to represent them – a speech truly characterised by Mr. Michael Davitt in the House of Commons as the 'speech of a half-emancipated slave'.[2] The labourers in town and country treated Mr. Redmond's advice with contempt and elected men of their own class all over Ireland. Compelled by the imperative necessity of maintaining in power a Home Rule government, Mr. Redmond votes for every measure of social reform the defeat of which would lead to the resignation of said government, but quietly acquiesces in every exemption of Ireland from progressive measures. Mr. Redmond believes that the Irish people are capable of governing their country, but opposed the proposal of Mr. T.W. Russell to allow the Irish people to control their own schools under the Local Government Act of 1898.[3] Mr. Redmond bewails the fact that lack of employment compels the Irish workers to emigrate at the rate of 30,000 per year, but opposed the attempt of the Labour party to compel the government to recognise its duty to provide work for them at home; Mr. Redmond believes that all public servants and representatives should be paid for their services to the State from the funds of the State, but is opposed to payment of

---

[1] John Redmond (1856–1918), Irish politician, leader of the United Irish League and the Irish Parliamentary Party at Westminster in the campaign for Home Rule.

[2] Michael Davitt (1846–1906), Irish republican and land reform campaigner, Member of Parliament and a founder of the Irish National Land League.

[3] Sir Thomas Russell (1841–1920), Irish politician and agrarian campaigner.

members being extended to Ireland; Mr. Redmond's heart bleeds for the poor of Ireland, but he would not vote for the Feeding of School Children's Act to be applied to Ireland, and Mr. Redmond is a friend of the Labour party in England (!), but his party fights to the death against every independent candidature of Labour throughout the purely Nationalist districts of Ireland.

If we are, as we are, capable of running our own country, how comes it we are not fit to be trusted with our own schools? And if the public control of schools by the Catholic Irish people would lead to atheism and to the persecution of the clergy, how has it not produced the same effect in Canada which Mr. Redmond is continually praising as an example for Ireland? Here is what a clergyman, the Rev. J.E. Burke, in a recent speech in the Assembly Hall, Belfast, said of the educational system of Canada – that country so beloved of Mr. T.P. O'Connor and Mr. Redmond:

> They had no church schools – nothing but state schools. While the priest and the parson were at liberty to visit the schools and give advice and encouragement, they had nothing to do in the management. The children of all nationalities and all creeds and classes attended these schools and grew up together in them, and he believed that the result of this was a better understanding amongst them in after life.

Mr. Redmond exalts Canada as a model for Irish Government, but opposes in Ireland all these domestic institutions which make free government a success in Canada.

If it was right, as it undoubtedly was, to demand aid for Irish farmers, why is it not equally right to demand state aid or local aid for starving Irish school children?

If, as Mr. Redmond claims, Ireland is overtaxed to the extent of over two millions per year, how will payment of Irish members of Parliament be a gift from the 'British' Treasury? Does one feel like the recipient of a 'gift' when you get back some of your own?

How then does Mr. Redmond and his party maintain their hold despite their essentially reactionary position? Simply because the Irish Unionists are still more reactionary. It is almost a choice between the devil and the deep sea.

Observe: In the debate in the House of Commons on the M'Cann case, Mr. Joseph Devlin, M.P., taunted the Orange bigots with the fact that none of their clergymen had been on the Anti-Sweating platform in the Ulster Hall, Belfast.[4] As a matter of fact, the same was true of the

---

[4] Joseph Devlin (1874–1931), Irish nationalist politician, journalist and Member of Parliament.

Catholic clergymen. None of them were on that platform either, but the stupid Orange reactionaries could not think of a better answer to Joe than to deny the fact of the sweating. The obvious retort was apparently beyond their capacities.

Another illustration: In the debate upon the issue of the writ for North Louth, an Orange member, Mr. William Moore, moved to suspend the issue of the writ for four months on the ground that 'Protestants' had been assaulted.[5] This motion was made despite the fact that the whole trend of the evidence had been to prove that every species of intimidation and bribery had been brought to bear upon Catholics who refused to bow to the dictates of the official Home Rule gang. That, in short, it was Catholics who needed to be protected and not Protestants.

A motion to suspend the issue of the writ pending a Parliamentary investigation into the workings of the organisations responsible for the wholesale terrorism exercised upon the electors of North Louth – irrespective of religion – would have opened the way for a capable man to give such an exposure of the workings of the Ancient Order of Hibernians (Board of Erin) and its relation to the United Irish League, as might have led to the extirpation of that pest in Ireland, but no one could expect such *statesmanship* from the Orange quarter.[6]

But just imagine what a real Irish democrat could have made of such a situation! Then he could have dealt with the pilgrimage of the MPs to America and Canada to beg from Irish exiles money towards the Irish cause, how our exiled brothers and sisters stinted themselves of, perhaps, even the necessaries of life in order to help to 'free Ireland and uplift poor Mother Erin', and how the money thus procured was used to debauch Irish men and women, to destroy political purity, to purchase bludgeons to smash in the heads of Irish men, and to terrorise the peaceful countryside?

A real representative of the Irish democracy might go on to show how Mr. Joseph Devlin's organisation, the A.O.H., supposed to be the Ancient Order of Hibernians, but by some believed to be the Ancient Order of Hooligans, has spread like an ulcer throughout Ireland, carrying social and religious terrorism with it into quarters hitherto noted for their broad-mindedness and discernment.

How it has organised the ignorant, the drunken and the rowdy, and

---

[5] Sir William Moore (1864–1944), Irish Unionist politician, judge and Member of Parliament.

[6] The Ancient Order of Hibernians is a Catholic fraternal organisation, originally set up in New York in 1836, but also with roots in agrarian radicalism in Ireland.

The Lock-Out, the First World War and the Rising

thrown the shield of religion around their excesses; how it has made it impossible to conduct a political contest in the South of Ireland except on the lines of civil war; and how, every man who dares to oppose the Redmondite party, or every man within that party who opposes the A.O.H., must be at all times prepared to take his life in his hands . . .

Every shade of political feeling in Ireland, outside of the official gang at the head of the United Irish League, agree that this organisation of Mr. Devlin's creation, and of whose work Mr. Redmond accepts the fruits, is the greatest curse yet introduced into the political and social life of Ireland. It is the organised ignorance of the community placing itself unreservedly at the disposal of the most insidious and inveterate enemies of enlightenment. In West Belfast it calls upon the Labour vote, upon the Socialists, to vote for 'Wee Joe Devlin', and in Queenstown it foments a riot in order to prevent a Socialist speaker delivering his message; it is a true reincarnation of mediaeval intolerance masquerading in the guise of Christian charity . . .[7]

Such is the problem, or rather some factors in the problem, in Ireland. Say, ye British Socialists, have your leaders any conception of this problem, or do they imagine that an Irish branch of a British Socialist organisation can grapple with this problem, or do anything with it save make a mess of it?

Or that it can be grappled with in any manner save from within the Irish nation by the workers of Ireland uniting in a party of their own to throw off the incubus of social slavery and religious intolerance? Such is the work the Socialist Party of Ireland sets out to accomplish. In that work the Socialists of Ireland know well that they can expect no help or countenance from the bigots of either Green or Orange persuasion, and while ever insisting upon the right of Ireland to control its own destinies, it allows precedence in its thoughts and plans to no interest but one, that of the working class. To the Redmonds and the Devlins, the Carsons and the Moores – it leaves the apostleship of religious bigotry; in our ranks there is no room for that type of politician of whom the poet writes that:–

> With all his conscience and with one eye askew,
> So false he partly took himself for true;
> Whose pious talk, when most his heart was dry,
> Made wet the crafty crow's-foot round his eye;
> Who never naming God except for gain,
> So never took that useful name in vain;

---

[7] Connolly refers here to an attack on his attempted talk in Queenstown (now Cobh).

> Made Him his cat's paw, and the Cross his tool,
> And Christ his bait to trap his dupe and fool;
> Nor deeds of gift, but gifts of grace, he forged,
> And, snakelike, slimed his victim ere he gorged.[8]

The Dublin Lock-Out: On the Eve

Irish Worker (30 August 1913)

Connolly here anticipates the tremendous battle which would be waged by Dublin workers (led by the ITGWU) and the employers in late 1913, a confrontation which some historians have argued was the climactic Irish labour struggle of the twentieth century.

Perhaps before this issue of *The Irish Worker* is in the hands of its readers the issues now at stake in Dublin will be brought to a final determination. All the capitalist newspapers of Friday last join in urging, or giving favourable publicity to the views of others urging the employers of Dublin to join in a general lock-out of the members of the Irish Transport and General Workers' Union. It is as well. Possibly some such act is necessary in order to make that portion of the working class which still halts undecided to understand clearly what it is that lies behind the tyrannical and brow-beating attitude of the proprietors of the Dublin tramway system.[9]

The fault of the Irish Transport and General Workers' Union! What is it? Let us tell it in plain language. Its fault is this, that it found the labourers of Ireland on their knees, and has striven to raise them to the erect position of manhood; it found them with all the vices of slavery in their souls, and it strove to eradicate these vices and replace them with some of the virtues of free men; it found them with no other weapons of defence than the arts of the liar, the lickspittle, and the toady, and it combined them and taught them to abhor those arts and rely proudly on the defensive power of combination; it, in short, found a class in whom seven centuries of social outlawry had added fresh degradations upon the burden it bore as the members of a nation suffering from the cumulative effects of seven centuries of national bondage, and out of this class,

---

[8] A quotation from Alfred Tennyson's *Sea-Dreams: An Idyll*.
[9] Dublin United Transport Company (DUTC) ran the city's tram system at this time. William Martin Murphy, leader of the business owners of the city during the Lock-Out, was a major shareholder in DUTC.

the degraded slaves of slaves more degraded still – for what degradation is more abysmal than that of those who prostitute their manhood on the altar of profit-mongering? – out of this class of slaves the labourers of Dublin, the Irish Transport and General Workers' Union has created an army of intelligent self-reliant men, abhorring the old arts of the toady, the lickspittle, and the crawler and trusting alone to the disciplined use of their power to labour or to withdraw their labour to assert and maintain their right as men. To put it in other words, but words as pregnant with truth and meaning: the Irish Transport and General Workers' Union found that before its advent the working class of Dublin had been taught by all the educational agencies of the country, by all the social influences of their masters, that this world was created for the special benefit of the various sections of the master class, that kings and lords and capitalists were of value; that even flunkeys, toadies, lickspittle and poodle dogs had an honoured place in the scheme of the universe, but that there was neither honour, credit, nor consideration to the man or woman who toils to maintain them all. Against all this the Irish Transport and General Workers' Union has taught that they who toil are the only ones that do matter, that all others are but beggars upon the bounty of those who work with hand or brain, and that this superiority of social value can at any time be realised, be translated into actual fact, by the combination of the labouring class. Preaching, organising, and fighting upon this basis, the Irish Transport and General Workers' Union has done what? If the value of a city is to be found in the development of self-respect and high conception of social responsibilities among a people, then the Irish Transport and General Workers' Union found Dublin the poorest city in these countries by reason of its lack of these qualities. And by imbuing the workers with them, it has made Dublin the richest city in Europe today, rich by all that counts for greatness in the history of nations. It is then upon this working class so enslaved, this working class so led and so enriched with moral purposes and high aims that the employers propose to make general war. Shall we shrink from it; cower before their onset? A thousand times no! Shall we crawl back into our slums, abase our hearts, bow our knees, and crawl once more to lick the hand that would smite us? Shall we, who have been carving out for our children a brighter future, a cleaner city, a freer life, consent to betray them instead into the grasp of the blood-suckers from whom we have dreamt of escaping? No, no, and yet again no! Let them declare their lock-out; it will only hasten the day when the working class will lock-out the capitalist class for good and all. If for taking the side of the Tram men we are threatened with suffering, why we have suffered before. But let them understand well that once they start that ball rolling no capitalist power on earth can prevent it continuing to roll, that every day will add to the impetus it will give to the working class purpose, to the thousands it will bring to the working-class ranks and every added suffering inflicted upon the workers will be a fresh obstacle in the way of moderation when the day of final settlement arrives.

Yes, indeed, if it is going to be a wedding, let it be a wedding; and if it is going to be a wake, let it be a wake: we are ready for either.

Glorious Dublin!

Forward (4 October 1913)

In this Scottish paper, Connolly lauds the courage and fighting spirit of the Dublin workers, whose struggle had produced complex echoes in the British labour and union movements.

To the readers of *Forward* possibly some sort of apology is due for the non-appearance of my notes for the past few weeks, but I am sure that they quite well understand that I was, so to speak, otherwise engaged. On the day I generally write my little screed, I was engaged on the 31st of August in learning how to walk around in a ring with about forty other unfortunates kept six paces apart, and yet slip in a word or two to the poor devil in front of or behind me without being noticed by the watchful prison warders.

The first question I asked was generally *'say, what are you in for?'* Then the rest of the conversation ran thus:

> *'For throwing stones at the police.'*
> *'Well, I hope you did throw them and hit.'*
> *'No, by God, that's the worst of it. I was pulled coming out of my own house.'*

'Pulled' is the Dublin word for arrested. It was somewhat mortifying to me to know that I was the only person apparently in prison who had really committed the crime for which I was arrested. It gave me a sort of feeling that I was lowering the moral tone of the prison by coming amongst such a crowd of blameless citizens.

But the concluding part of our colloquy was a little more encouraging. It usually finished in this way:

> *'Are you in the Irish Transport and General Workers' Union?'*
> *'Of course I am.'*

'Good. Well if they filled all the prisons in Ireland they can't beat us, my boy.'

'No, thank God, they can't; we'll fight all the better when we get out.'

And there you have the true spirit. Baton charges, prison cells, untimely death and acute starvation – all were faced without a murmur, and in face of them all, the brave Dublin workers never lost faith in their ultimate triumph, never doubted but that their organisation would emerge victorious from the struggle. This is the great fact that many of our critics amongst the British labour leaders seem to lose sight of. The Dublin fight is more than a trade union fight; it is a great class struggle, and recognised as such by all sides. We in Ireland feel that to doubt our victory would be to lose faith in the destiny of our class.

I heard of one case where a labourer was asked to sign the agreement forswearing the Irish Transport and General Workers' Union, and he told his employer, a small capitalist builder, that he refused to sign. The employer, knowing the man's circumstances, reminded him that he had a wife and six children who would be starving within a week. The reply of this humble labourer rose to the heights of sublimity. *'It is true, sir'*, he said, *'they will starve; but I would rather see them go out one by one in their coffins than that I should disgrace them by signing that'*. And with head erect he walked out to share hunger and privation with his loved ones. Hunger and privation – and honour.

Defeat, bah! How can such a people be defeated? His case is typical of thousands more. Take the case of the United Builders Labourers' Trade Union, for instance.[10] This was a rival union to the Irish Transport and General Workers' Union. Many sharp passages had occurred between them, and the employers counted confidently upon their cooperation in the struggle; Mr. William Martin Murphy especially praising them and exulting in their supposed acquiescence in his plans. Remember also that they were a dividing society, dividing their funds at the end of each year, and therefore without any strike funds. When the members of their union were asked to sign the agreement, promising never to join or help the Irish Transport and General Workers' Union, not one man consented – but all over Dublin their 2,500 members marched out 'to help the I.T.&G.W.U. boys'. Long ere these lines are written, they have experienced all the horrors of starvation, but with grim resolve they have tightened their belts and presented an unyielding front to the enemy.

---

[10] The United Builders Labourers' and General Workers of Dublin Trade Union was formed in Dublin in 1892.

It is a pleasure to me to recall that I was a member of their Union before I went to America, and that they twice ran me as their candidate for Dublin City Council before the Irish Transport and General Workers' Union was dreamed of.

What is true of that union is also true of most of the tradesmen. All are showing wonderful loyalty to their class. Coachbuilders, sawyers, engineers, bricklayers, each trade that is served by general labourers, walks out along with the Irish Transport and General Workers' Union boys; refuses to even promise to work with any one who signs the employers' agreement, and, cheering, lines up along with their class.

Or think of the heroic women and girls. Did they care to evade the issue, they might have remained at work, for the first part of the agreement asks them to merely repudiate the Irish Transport and General Workers' Union, and as women they are members of the Irish Women Workers' Union, not of the Irish Transport and General Workers' Union.[11] But the second part pledges them to refuse to 'help' the Irish Transport and General Workers' Union – and in every shop, factory and sweating hell-hole in Dublin, as the agreement is presented, they march out with pinched faces, threadbare clothes, and miserable footgear, but with high hopes, undaunted spirit, and glorious resolve shining out of their eyes. Happy the men who will secure such wives; thrice blessed the nation which has such girls as the future mothers of the race! Ah, comrades, it is good to have lived in Dublin in these days!

And then our friends write deprecatingly to the British press of the 'dislocation of trade' involved in sympathetic strikes, of the 'perpetual conflicts' in which they would involve great trade unions. To those arguments, if we can call them such, our answer is sufficient. It is this: If the capitalist class knew that any outrages upon a worker, any attack upon labour, would result in a prompt dislocation of trade, perhaps national in its extent; that the unions were prepared to spend their last copper if necessary rather than permit a brother or sister to be injured, then the knowledge would not only ensure a long cessation from industrial skirmishing such as the unions are harassed by today, it would not only ensure peace to the unions, but what is of vastly more importance, it would ensure to the individual worker a peace from slave-driving and harassing at his work such as the largest unions are apparently unable to guarantee under present methods.

Mark, when I say 'prepared to spend their last copper if necessary',

---

[11] The Irish Women Workers' Union was formed in 1911. Jim Larkin and Constance Markiewicz were prominent in its leadership.

I am not employing merely a rhetorical flourish, I am using the words literally. As we believe that in the socialist society of the future the entire resources of the nation must stand behind every individual, guaranteeing him against want, so today our unions must be prepared to fight with all their resources to safeguard the rights of every individual member.

The adoption of such a principle, followed by a few years of fighting on such lines to convince the world of our earnestness, would not only transform the industrial arena, but would revolutionise politics. Each side would necessarily seek to grasp the power of the state to reinforce its position, and politics would thus become what they ought to be, a reflex of the industrial battle, and lose the power to masquerade as a neutral power detached from economic passions or motives.

At present I regret to say labour politicians seem to be losing all reality as effective aids to our struggles on the industrial battlefield, are becoming more and more absorbed in questions of administration, or taxation, and only occasionally, as in the miners' national strike, really rise to a realisation of their true role of parliamentary outposts of the industrial army.

The parliamentary tail in Britain still persist in wagging the British industrial dog. Once the dog really begins to assert his true position, we will be troubled no more by carping critics of labour politics, nor yet with labour politicians' confessions of their own impotence in such great crises as that of the railway strike or the Johannesburg massacres.

Nor yet would we see that awful spectacle we have seen lately of labour politicians writing to the capitalist press to denounce the methods of a union which, with 20,000 men and women locked out in one city, is facing an attempt of 400 employers to starve its members back into slavery.

And thou, Brutus, that you should play the enemy's game at such a crisis! Every drop of ink you spilled in such an act stopped a loaf of bread on its way to some starving family.

Labour and the Proposed Partition of Ireland

Irish Worker (14 March 1914)

Britain's policy solution to various colonial or late-colonial imbroglios in which it found itself was partition – as in Ireland in 1922, and in India in 1947, and Palestine – mediated by the United Nations – in 1948. In all three cases the result was as Connolly predicted – conservative postcolonial states predicated on ethnic or religious identity.

The recent proposals of Messrs. Asquith, Devlin, Redmond and Co. for the settlement of the Home Rule question deserve the earnest attention of the working class democracy of this country. They reveal in a most striking and unmistakeable manner the depths of betrayal to which the so-called Nationalist politicians are willing to sink. For generations the conscience of the civilised world has been shocked by the historical record of the partition of Poland; publicists, poets, humanitarians, patriots, all lovers of their kind and of progress have wept over the unhappy lot of a country torn asunder by the brute force of their alien oppressors, its unity ruthlessly destroyed and its traditions trampled into the dust.[12]

But Poland was disrupted by outside forces, its enemies were the mercenaries of the tyrant kingdoms and empires of Europe; its sons and daughters died in the trenches and on the battlefields by the thousands rather than submit to their beloved country being annihilated as a nation. But Ireland, what of Ireland? It is the trusted leaders of Ireland that in secret conclave with the enemies of Ireland have agreed to see Ireland as a nation disrupted politically and her children divided under separate political governments with warring interests.

Now, what is the position of Labour towards it all? Let us remember that the Orange aristocracy now fighting for its supremacy in Ireland has at all times been based upon a denial of the common human rights of the Irish people; that the Orange Order was not founded to safeguard religious freedom, but to deny religious freedom, and that it raised this religious question, not for the sake of any religion, but in order to use religious zeal in the interests of the oppressive property rights of rack-renting landlords and sweating capitalists. That the Irish people might be kept asunder and robbed whilst so sundered and divided, the Orange aristocracy went down to the lowest depths and out of the lowest pits of hell brought up the abominations of sectarian feuds to stir the passions of the ignorant mob. No crime was too brutal or cowardly; no lie too base; no slander too ghastly, as long as they served to keep the democracy asunder.

And now that the progress of democracy elsewhere has somewhat muzzled the dogs of aristocratic power, now that in England as well as in Ireland the forces of labour are stirring and making for freedom and light, this same gang of well-fed plunderers of the people, secure in Union held upon their own dupes, seek by threats of force to arrest the

---

[12] Poland was the object of no less than three partitioning treaties, signed between the Russian Empire, Hapsburg Austria and the Kingdom of Prussia, starting in 1772, and concluding in 1795.

march of ideas and stifle the light of civilisation and liberty. And, lo and behold, the trusted guardians of the people, the vaunted saviours of the Irish race, agree in front of the enemy and in face of the world to sacrifice to the bigoted enemy the unity of the nation and along with it the lives, liberties and hopes of that portion of the nation which in the midst of the most hostile surroundings have fought to keep the faith in things national and progressive.

Such a scheme as that agreed to by Redmond and Devlin, the betrayal of the national democracy of industrial Ulster would mean a carnival of reaction both North and South, would set back the wheels of progress, would destroy the oncoming unity of the Irish Labour movement and paralyse all advanced movements whilst it endured.

To it Labour should give the bitterest opposition, against it Labour in Ulster should fight even to the death, if necessary, as our fathers fought before us.

The Real Situation in Ireland

Forward (5 September 1914)

Connolly, already by this time publicly campaigning against the War, asserts the realities of the Irish poor, as against the manoeuvres of high politics, as the First World War opens.

In these days of conflict Ireland occupies a unique position. For the first time in history an Irish leader has publicly pledged the support of the Irish nation to Great Britain in an armed struggle. But it would be a mistake to imagine that his act has indeed received the universal assent the newspapers claim. On the contrary, there is a very strong and influential body of opinion in the country which holds that the act of Mr. Redmond in proffering to the Government the armed cooperation of the Volunteers was an act sadly lacking in the first principles of statesmanship. It is felt and freely asserted by that section that Mr. Redmond gave too much and got too little in return; indeed, it is stated that he got nothing in return. His offer of cooperation with the Ulster Volunteers has been laughed at by that body, and the Government on its part had not promised to withdraw the Amending Bill, nor yet to modify it in any way favourable to the Nationalists.[13]

---

[13] Connolly here refers to the parliamentary debates and manoeuvres surrounding the passing of the third Home Rule Bill in 1914, then to be known as either the Home Rule

Great Britain was about to engage in the greatest war in her history, in a war that must inevitably strain her every resource – military and commercial – and she found herself in this position at the very moment when Ireland possessed a large force of men drilled and organised on a military basis and partially armed. When, at the close of Sir Edward Grey's speech, and pronouncements of Mr. Bonar Law and Mr. Asquith the assembled Tories and Liberals in the House of Commons began to clamour for 'Redmond, Redmond', it was a recognition of the fact that Ireland was in a strong tactical position.[14] Had Mr. Redmond at that moment sat still and let them clamour away, had he refused to be drawn into speech at that juncture, it is felt that before the night was over he would have been able to dictate his terms to the Government. Or had he been desirous to avoid seeming haste, and called in Ireland a Convention of his followers, or preferably of the Volunteers, to consider what action should be taken in view of the war, it is certain that such concessions would have been made by the Government as would have been infinitely preferable even to the Home Rule Bill in its present form.

But the malign spirit that prompted Mr. Redmond to capture the Volunteers and make himself solely responsible for its activity now impelled him to rush into speech and commit the whole people of Ireland to aggressive warfare upon Germany, solely upon Mr. Redmond's own responsibility or the responsibility of his Party, and without being able even to indicate any gain as a quid pro quo for their action.

At first the country seemed quite swept off its feet by this action. All the kept newspapers of the United Irish League immediately constituted themselves recruiting agents for the British Army, and every effort was made to stampede the Volunteers into unconditional acceptance of Mr. Redmond's blatant offer. Many thousands of recruits were obtained for the British Army during the first week or fortnight of the jingo fever promoted by the Home Rule press and wirepullers, companies of Irish Volunteers marched in parade order to see reservists off by the train and ship, their bands, to the astonishment of everyone and the horror

---

Act or as the Government of Ireland Act. The Amending Bill was a proposal of Herbert Asquith's Conservative government, in the light of massive civil and paramilitary agitation against Home Rule in Ulster, temporarily to exclude from the provisions of the Home Rule Act six of the north-eastern counties of Ulster. This achieved the support of Edward Carson and the Irish Unionist Party. With the declaration of war in August 1914, Asquith abandoned the Amending Bill, and passed instead legislation suspending the implementation of Home Rule for the war's duration.

[14] Sir Edward Grey (1862–1933), British Liberal politician, and Foreign Secretary 1905–1916. Bonar Law (1858–1923), British Conservative politician and Prime Minister.

of most, played *God Save the King*, and all sorts of erstwhile rack-renting landlords and anti-Irish aristocrats rushed in to officer these Irish Volunteers whom they had formerly despised. But gradually the nation is swinging back to sanity. The independent elements are everywhere asserting themselves, and there has already developed a fierce fight to prevent the Irish Volunteers being – as Mr. Redmond intended – handed over to the War Office.

Up to the time of writing, the Provisional Committee of the Irish Volunteers has stood firm. They have refused the offer of the War Office to supply officers to the Irish Volunteers, and insisted upon being officered by men of their own choosing under their own control, and they have stated that they prefer to buy and own their own arms rather than get them from Lord Kitchener and know that they are subject to his recall.[15]

Along with this a strong propaganda is being carried on showing that Ireland has no quarrel with the German nation; that on the contrary, Irish culture and Irish literature owe very much indeed to German friendship and to German research.

Upon the economic field a common ground has been found which is going far towards uniting all the unofficial parties and providing a common basis of action for all whose love of country is more than a political shibboleth, and for all whose conception of freedom is wider than is indicated by a mere change in administrative methods. This common ground is furnished by the question of the foodstuffs. It is realised that Ireland is able to sustain herself with her own food, but that the demand for food to feed the army and to provision Great Britain will lead to an enormous increase of prices and, perhaps to famine in the Irish towns.

The Irish farmer will sell gladly, but the prices he will obtain from the Government will send up the cost upon the poorly paid Irish workers in urban areas, and it is feared that should provisions not be available in Great Britain, should any of the trade routes be closed and grain and agricultural produce generally not be available in sufficient quantities, the British Government would commandeer the foodstuffs of Ireland as ruthlessly as it commandeered the railways during the dispatch of the Expeditionary Force of the past two weeks. It is determined on all hands that should this be done resistance will be offered, and the export of this food fought against even to the extent of armed resistance.

---

[15] Horatio Herbert Kitchener, 1st Earl Kitchener (1850–1916), English soldier and colonial administrator, later Secretary of State for War at the start of the First World War.

The Ballot or the Barricades

Irish Worker (24 October 1914)

Eighteen months before the Rising, Connolly predicts the violent struggle to come. He shows here that he was no pacifist, and also he anticipates the form of the guerrilla struggle that would come in 1919 – itself following a crisis over conscription.

Towards the close of last week the British Government flew a kite in Ireland. Flying a kite when practised by a Government means getting some person or paper to issue a statement that the Government contemplates taking certain action. If the announcement arouses no hostility of a serious nature the action is forthwith taken. If, on the contrary, the announcement is met with a storm of hostility the Government declares it did not authorise and does not contemplate any such action as was announced, and that it regrets that any such statement should have been made by unauthorised persons. Having flown its kite to learn how the wind blows, the Government then proceeds to do a little more spade work to prepare the ground better for taking the action it has just declared it does not intend to take.

The kite flown last week was the announcement that the Militia Ballot Act was to be enforced in Ireland.[16] As it evoked hostility the Government proceeded to officially repudiate it. The ground was not well prepared, the game was too shy. But nevertheless the iniquitous proposal is only temporarily abandoned. In some form or another conscription is inevitable.

The only thing that can avert conscription is the speedy collapse of the German army – a thing as remote as the conversion of England's rulers to Christian principles. Already a responsible authority, Sir Thomas Barclay, has declared that England will, before the close of the war, have two million men with the colours, an army impossible without conscription.[17] In addition to this we have the fact that the slaughter at the front is almost inconceivable. A great surgeon, Dr. Haden Guest, says, that at present the military sick and wounded in France number half a million.[18]

---

[16] The Militia Ballot Act was a law which permitted the raising of reserve soldiers without implementing full-scale conscription.

[17] Sir Thomas Barclay (1853–1941), Scottish Liberal politician and authority on international law.

[18] Leslie Haden-Guest (1877–1960), English writer, doctor and Labour Party politician.

The Lock-Out, the First World War and the Rising 239

Thus the gaps in the firing line require the presence of a continually increasing army of support to fill them. Where and how are all those soldiers to be got, if not by and through some form of conscription?

The truth about the Germany army is that its position becomes more secure every day. At the beginning of the war the Allies joyfully declared that time was on their side, that every day gained was equal to the winning of a battle, that the Allies could afford to wait and the Germans could not. It is now beginning to penetrate the heads of the military experts of Fleet Street that the boot is on the other leg. The Russians were the great hope of England. Unless the Russians can achieve victory before the closing in of the terrible Russian winter that hope is gone. It will be impossible to maintain in the field the enormous masses of Russian troops, to provision them, to keep them supplied with munitions of war, to handle all the elaborate, cumbrous but necessary machinery of transport and commissariat, whilst the snow king has his grip upon Russian railroads and rivers. Add to this the terrible cost of the maintenance of such an army as Russia requires to face the Germans – the most uneducated nation in Europe to face the most educated, and we see at once that England cannot hope to see Russia win the war for her. She must produce the men herself. Russia is bankrupt. The Czar was only able to crush the Russian Revolution because of the loans from France and England. Now these countries need all their moneys for their own salvation.

Thus on the side of Germany there are fighting the influences of time and of money, of superior equipment, and of wise provision for the future.

Therefore the Militia Ballot Act or some form of conscription will come. Are we, like our rulers, to await the evil day, and then 'muddle through' with ineffective protests? Or are we to make provision beforehand for the fight that will be necessary?

We of the Irish Transport & General Workers' Union, we of the Citizen Army, have our answer ready.[19] We will resist the Militia Ballot Act, or any form of conscription, and we begin now to prepare our resistance. Upon the Volunteers we urge similar resolves, similar preparations.

Understand what this means. It means a complete overhauling and remodelling of all the training and instruction hitherto given to those

---

[19] The Irish Citizen Army was a small force of trained trade union volunteers assembled to defend workers' and strikers' demonstrations from the police. It was formed in 1913 by James Larkin, James Connolly and Jack White. It acquired firearms in 1914, and under Connolly's leadership took part in the 1916 Rising.

corps. It means that the corps shall be taught how to act and fight when acting against an enemy equipped with superior weapons, instead of all teaching being based upon the ideas of British military text books which always presume an equality of weapons, or even a superiority upon the British side. It means that much that has been taught will be worse than useless if acted upon, as such teaching presupposed that the corps receiving instructions were to form part of a regular army in the field, an army properly supported and reinforced by complete arms of the service. The resistance to the Militia Ballot Act must of necessity take the form of insurrectionary warfare, if the resisters are determined to fight in Ireland for Ireland instead of on the Continent for England. Such insurrectionary warfare would be conducted upon lines and under conditions for which text books made no provision.

In short, it means barricades in the streets, guerrilla warfare in the country.

To all who are prepared to face that ordeal rather than shed their blood for the tyrant and exploiter we appeal to join our Citizen Army. We propose to make that force the best equipped mentally in Ireland. We want no parade ground soldiers. We want young men prepared to die for Freedom in Ireland. If the Government proposes to force us to fight against our consciences and our desire we propose to challenge it upon its own ground; and if it wants us it must take us by force.

From this date greater decision and promptitude in action will be enforced in our army though even now it is an example to follow. All those who fell away because we had not rifles enough are requested to enrol at once and take a course in the preliminary training in the new course of instruction on the lines we have indicated.

The rifles will come all right. And there are other modern weapons of warfare.

The Citizen Army Offices at Liberty Hall, Aungier Street, Inchicore, Thomas Street, and elsewhere are open every night for enrolment. We want a new muster of men prepared to face the worst and to take the best if taken it can be.

The Hope of Ireland

Irish Worker (31 October 1914)

Here the crucial role of the Irish working class to any coming radical change is reasserted – not only in Ireland but in Britain too. Class struggle in the colony is essential to the liberation of the poor of the metropolis.

The present crisis in Ireland is shattering many reputations and falsifying many predictions, but to the careful observer it is becoming daily apparent that it will leave intact at least one reputation, that of those who pinned their faith to the working class as the anchor and foundation of any real nationalism that this country can show. Here and there the working class may waver, here and there local influences may exert sufficient pressure to weaken or corrupt the manhood of the workers, but speaking broadly it remains true that in that class lay the only hope of those who held fast to the faith that this Ireland of ours is a nation distinct and apart from all others, and capable of working out its own destiny and living its own life.

The working class has ever refused to be drawn into any mere anti-English feeling; it refuses to be drawn into it now. It has always refused to consider that hatred of England was equivalent to love of Ireland, or that true patriotism required an Irishman or woman to bear enmity to the toiling masses of the English population. It still holds that position.

The working class of Ireland, when grown conscious of its true dignity, does not consider that it owes to the British Empire any debt except that of hatred. But it also realises that the best services it can render to the British people is due to them, and that service will be and will take the form of as speedy as possible a destruction of the foul governmental system that has made the British people an instrument of the enslavement of millions of the human race, of the extirpation of whole tribes and nations, of the devastation of vast territories. Enslaved socially at home the British people have been taught that what little political liberty they do enjoy can only be bought at the price of the national destruction of every people rising into social or economic rivalry with the British master class. If it requires war to free the minds of the British working class from that debasing superstition then war we shall have, for the world cannot progress industrially whilst so important a nation in Europe is perverted mentally by a belief so hostile to fraternal progress; if it requires insurrection in Ireland and through all the British dominions to teach the English working class they cannot hope to prosper permanently by arresting the industrial development of others then insurrection must come, and barricades will spring up as readily in our streets as public meetings do today.

Those who hold that the British people must learn this lesson are not necessarily enemies of the British people, of the British democracy. Rather do they hold with John Mitchel they are the truest friends of the

British people who are the greatest enemies of the British Government.[20] The Irish working class see no abandonment of the principles of the Labour Movement in this fight against this war and all it implies; see no weakening of international solidarity in their fierce resolve to do no fighting except it be in their own country to secure the right to hold that country for its own sons and daughters. Rather do they joy in giving this proof that the principles of the Labour Movement represent the highest form of patriotism, and that true patriotism will embody the broadest principles of Labour and Socialism.

The Labour Movement in Ireland stands for the ownership of all Ireland by all the Irish; it therefore fights against all things calculated to weaken the hold of the Irish upon Ireland, as it fights for all things calculated to strengthen the grasp of the Irish people upon Ireland and all things Irish. It has no war with Germany, it welcomes the German as a brother struggling towards the light. It believes that the blood guiltiness of this war lies chiefly at the door of that British Empire whose 'farflung battle line' is a far-flung shadow upon the face of civilized progress. And so believing, it counsels the Irish race to stand aloof from the battle, since it cannot intervene as a nation on the only side that honour and interest dictates.

Alone in Ireland the working class has no ties that bind it to the service of the Empire. Hunger and the fear of hunger have driven thousands of our class into the British army; but for whatever pay or pension such have drawn therefrom they have given service, and owe neither gratitude nor allegiance. For those still held to that accursed bargain as reservists, etc., we have no feelings except compassion; the British Shylock will hold them to the bond. Other classes serve England for the sake of dividends, profits, official positions and sinecures – a thousand strings drawing them to England for the one patriotic tie that binds them to Ireland. The Irish working class as a class can only hope to rise with Ireland.

Equally true is it that Ireland cannot rise to Freedom except upon the shoulders of a working class knowing its rights and daring to take them.

That class of that character we are creating in Ireland. Wherever then in Ireland flies the banner of the Irish Transport & General Workers' Union there flies also to the heavens the flag of the Irish working class, alert, disciplined, intelligent, determined to be free.

---

[20] John Mitchel (1815–1875), Irish nationalist writer and journalist at *The Nation*.

Ireland – Disaffected or Revolutionary?

Workers' Republic (13 November 1915)

This rich essay shows Connolly disputing the credentials of the country's 'revolutionaries' – they are rhetorically assertive but less actively so. Rather the country is 'disaffected' – turbulent but without proper leadership. That leadership must now emerge – note his stated admiration for Pearse, and the invocation of Mitchel.

> 'Youth of Ireland stand prepared,
> Revolution's dread abyss
> Burns beneath us all but bared . . .'

So sang Clarence Mangan in the days of '48.[21] But he sang in vain. The music of his verse charmed the cultured intellect of the leaders, but could not break through their refined distrust of the mob, nor inspire them with a confidence in its willingness to respond to the call. And the verse of Mangan never appealed to the emotions of the mob itself.

The revolutionary position was there, the people were ready, but the leaders were lacking in dash and recklessness. As another writer has it of another body of leaders similarly situated:

> 'Having all their lives sung of the glories of the Revolution, when it rose up before them they ran away appalled.'[22]

These reflections are inspired by the fact that Ireland is at present in the midst of a number of anniversaries of the great days of its patriot dead. On all hands celebrations are being or have been arranged, much oratory is on tap, many verses of more or less merit are pouring forth, and all sorts of men and women are drawing lessons and pointing morals for the edification of the Irish reading public.

It is felt that we are now in stirring times, and many people dare even to hope that we are in a revolutionary epoch. It is well then that we of the Irish working class should try and understand the position of the revolutionists of the past, that we may the better realise our position in the present.

We do not believe that this is a revolutionary epoch, no more than the days of Mitchel were revolutionary in Ireland, nor the days of Allen,

---

[21] James Clarence Mangan (1803–1849), Irish poet, admired and publicised by the Young Ireland writers, and published in *The Nation*.

[22] Prosper-Olivier Lissagaray (1838–1901), French journalist and revolutionary socialist; historian of the Paris Commune.

Larkin and O'Brien.[23] An epoch, to be truly revolutionary, must have a dominating number of men with the revolutionary spirit – ready to dare all, and take all risks for the sake of their ideals.

In 1848, as later, there were men who talked much of revolution, but when the spirit of the times called upon them to strike they all began to make excuses, to murmur about the danger of premature insurrection, of incomplete preparations, of the awful responsibility of giving the word for insurrection, etc., etc.

In 1848, as later, the real revolutionary sentiment was in the hearts of the people, but for the most part they who undertook to give it articulate expression were wanting in the essential ability to translate sentiment into action. They would have been good historians of a revolutionary movement, but were unable to take that leap in the dark which all men must take who plunge into insurrection. For, be it well understood, an insurrection is always doubtful, a thousand to one chance always exists in favour of the established order and against the insurgents.

Despite all seeming to the contrary we assert that Ireland is not a really revolutionary country. Ireland is a disaffected country which has long been accustomed to conduct constitutional agitations in revolutionary language, and what is worse, to conduct revolutionary movements with a due regard to law and order.

Our constitutionalists have been ready to defy the law; our revolutionists shine only in legal quirks to evade the letter of the law. The constitutional agitation of the Land League was one prolonged riot of illegality; the revolutionary movement of our own day shrinks from an openly illegal act as nervously as a coy maiden shrinks from a desired lover.

It is this paradoxical state of affairs that makes Irish politics so puzzling to the outsider. He listens to the politician appealing to the people to cling to constitutional methods, and at the same time exulting in the agrarian reforms gained by trampling law and order under foot. He hears the revolutionists telling that England's difficulty is Ireland's opportunity, and then, when her greatest difficulty comes, postponing action on the opportunity in order to see if the politician cannot yet succeed by legal agitation.

In his brilliant lecture on John Mitchel in the Antient Concert Rooms, on Thursday, November 4th, our friend Mr. P.H. Pearse treated his audience to a splendid review of the tendencies of opinions and

---

[23] William Allen, Michael Larkin and Michael O'Brien were the 'Manchester Martyrs', members of the Irish Republican Brotherhood executed in 1871 for their part in the death of a policeman in 1867.

movement of currents of thought, that applied so well to our own days that many of the audience forgot that it was an analysis of '48 to which they were listening or supposed to be listening.[24] It is that very similarity which enables us to so clearly understand the nature of the forces that destroyed Mitchel.

The British Government would not wait until the plans of the revolutionists were ready. It has not held Ireland down for 700 years by any such foolish waiting. It struck in its own time, and its blow paralysed the people. The leaders of the people would not follow Mitchel's lead but held the people back by talk about 'premature insurrection', and 'the desire of the Government to provoke us to act before we are ready', and such like phrases repeated glibly, with the solemnity of owls and the foolishness of idiots, until the golden moment of hot wrath was passed, and the paraders and the strutters had lost the confidence and destroyed the hopes of the nation.

In vain for Clarence Mangan to call to such a people to prepare for revolution. Revolutionists who shrink from giving blow for blow until the great day has arrived, and they have every shoe-string in its place, and every man has got his gun, and the enemy has kindly consented to postpone action in order not to needlessly hurry the revolutionists nor disarrange their plans – such revolutionists only exist in two places – the comic opera stage, and the stage of Irish national politics. We prefer the comic opera brand. It at least serves its purpose.

John Mitchel was not defeated by the British Government. He was defeated by his own associates. There are no John Mitchels left in Ireland, but of such as those who held back the hands of the people who would have rescued him there are still a goodly brood – all of them as legally seditious, as peacefully revolutionary, and as fatal to the hopes of a nation as ever were their forerunners.

O, we latter-day Irish are great orators, and great singers, and great reciters, and great at cheering heroic sentiments about revolution. But we are not revolutionists. Not by a thousand miles! Soldiers of a regular army we can be, soldiers with a well-secured base from which our provisions can come up with clock-like regularity, soldiers with our relatives and dependents securely drawing separation allowances, soldiers with an ambulance service working automatically according to railway time table, soldiers with unlimited reserves of ammunition, arms, and uniforms. For that kind of war we are ready, aye, ready.

---

[24] Patrick Henry Pearse (1879–1916), Irish teacher, barrister, poet and revolutionary; a leader, with Connolly, of the 1916 Rising.

But no revolution in history ever had any of these things. None ever will have. Hence we strictly confine ourselves to killing John Bull with our mouths.[25]

We have opened this week with a quotation from our own Irish poet – an impassioned, soul-felt appeal to the heart of a nation whose heart was greater than the spirit of its leaders. We shall close with the words of another poet, an American, a trumpet call to his people on the occasion of a crisis in his nation's history. It would be well if it were laid to heart in Ireland today:

> Once to every man and nation comes the moment to decide.

What is a Free Nation?

Workers' Republic (12 February 1916)

Here Connolly wrenches the idea of national freedom away from both Home Rulers and Unionism – the freedom of the nation he proposes will entail full recognition of the widest idea of the national and common good. In this way, he anticipates Fanon's famous critique of the 'pitfalls of national consciousness' in *The Wretched of the Earth*, forty-five years later.

We are moved to ask this question because of the extraordinary confusion of thought upon the subject which prevails in this country, due principally to the pernicious and misleading newspaper garbage upon which the Irish public has been fed for the past twenty-five years.

Our Irish daily newspapers have done all that human agencies could do to confuse the public mind upon the question of what the essentials of a free nation are, what a free nation must be, and what a nation cannot submit to lose without losing its title to be free.

It is because of this extraordinary newspaper-created ignorance that we find so many people enlisting in the British army under the belief that Ireland has at long last attained to the status of a free nation, and that therefore the relations between Ireland and England have at last been placed upon the satisfactory basis of freedom. Ireland and England, they have been told, are now sister nations, joined in the bond of Empire, but each enjoying equal liberties – the equal liberties of nations equally free. How many recruits this idea sent into the British army in

---

[25] 'John Bull' is a national personification of England, created by the Scottish writer John Arbuthnot in his 1712 pamphlet *Law is a Bottomless Pit*.

the first flush of the war it would be difficult to estimate, but they were assuredly numbered by the thousand.

The Irish Parliamentary Party, which at every stage of the Home Rule game has been outwitted and bulldozed by Carson and the Unionists, which had surrendered every point and yielded every advantage to the skilful campaign of the aristocratic Orange military clique in times of peace, behaved in equally as cowardly and treacherous a manner in the crisis of war.

There are few men in whom the blast of the bugles of war do not arouse the fighting instinct, do not excite to some chivalrous impulses if only for a moment. But the Irish Parliamentary Party must be reckoned amongst that few. In them the bugles of war only awakened the impulse to sell the bodies of their countrymen as cannon fodder in exchange for the gracious smiles of the rulers of England. In them the call of war sounded only as a call to emulate in prostitution. They heard the call of war – and set out to prove that the nationalists of Ireland were more slavish than the Orangemen of Ireland, would more readily kill and be killed at the bidding of an Empire that despised them both.

The Orangemen had at least the satisfaction that they were called upon to fight abroad in order to save an Empire they had been prepared to fight to retain unaltered at home; but the nationalists were called upon to fight abroad to save an Empire whose rulers in their most generous moments had refused to grant their country the essentials of freedom in nationhood.

Fighting abroad the Orangeman knows that he fights to preserve the power of the aristocratic rulers whom he followed at home; fighting abroad the nationalist soldier is fighting to maintain unimpaired the power of those who conspired to shoot him down at home when he asked for a small instalment of freedom.

The Orangeman says: 'We will fight for the Empire abroad if its rulers will promise not to force us to submit to Home Rule.' And the rulers say heartily: 'It is unthinkable that we should coerce Ulster for any such purpose.'

The Irish Parliamentary Party and its press said: 'We will prove ourselves fit to be in the British Empire by fighting for it, in the hopes that after the war is over we will get Home Rule.' And the rulers of the British Empire say: 'Well, you know what we have promised Carson, but send out the Irish rabble to fight for us, and we will, ahem, consider your application after the war.' Whereat, all the Parliamentary leaders and their press call the world to witness that they have won a wonderful victory!

James Fintan Lalor spoke and conceived of Ireland as a 'discrowned queen, taking back her own with an armed hand'.[26] Our Parliamentarians treat Ireland, their country, as an old prostitute selling her soul for the promise of favours to come, and in the spirit of that conception of their country they are conducting their political campaign.

That they should be able to do so with even the partial success that for a while attended their apostasy was possible only because so few in Ireland really understood the answer to the question that stands at the head of this article.

What is a free nation? A free nation is one which possesses absolute control over all its own internal resources and powers, and which has no restriction upon its intercourse with all other nations similarly circumstanced except the restrictions placed upon it by nature. Is that the case of Ireland? If the Home Rule Bill were in operation would that be the case of Ireland? To both questions the answer is: no, most emphatically, NO!

A free nation must have complete control over its own harbours, to open them or close them at will, or shut out any commodity, or allow it to enter in, just as it seemed best to suit the well-being of its own people, and in obedience to their wishes, and entirely free of the interference of any other nation, and in complete disregard of the wishes of any other nation. Short of that power no nation possesses the first essentials of freedom.

Does Ireland possess such control? No. Will the Home Rule Bill give such control over Irish harbours in Ireland? It will not. Ireland must open its harbours when it suits the interests of another nation, England, and must shut its harbours when it suits the interests of another nation, England; and the Home Rule Bill pledges Ireland to accept this loss of national control for ever.

How would you like to live in a house if the keys of all the doors of that house were in the pockets of a rival of yours who had often robbed you in the past? Would you be satisfied if he told you that he and you were going to be friends for ever more, but insisted upon you signing an agreement to leave him control of all your doors, and custody of all your keys? This is the condition of Ireland today, and will be the condition of Ireland under Redmond and Devlin's precious Home Rule Bill.

That is worth dying for in Flanders, the Balkans, Egypt or India, is it not?

A free nation must have full power to nurse industries to health,

---

[26] James Fintan Lalor (1807–1849), Irish politician and a leader of Young Ireland.

either by government encouragement or by government prohibition of the sale of goods of foreign rivals. It may be foolish to do either, but a nation is not free unless it has that power, as all free nations in the world have today. Ireland has no such power, will have no such power under Home Rule. The nourishing of industries in Ireland hurts capitalists in England, therefore this power is expressly withheld from Ireland.

A free nation must have full power to alter, amend, or abolish or modify the laws under which the property of its citizens is held in obedience to the demand of its own citizens for any such alteration, amendment, abolition, or modification. Every free nation has that power; Ireland does not have it, and is not allowed it by the Home Rule Bill.

It is recognized today that it is upon the wise treatment of economic power and resources, and upon the wise ordering of social activities that the future of nations depends. That nation will be the richest and happiest which has the foresight to marshal the most carefully its natural resources to national ends. But Ireland is denied this power, and will be denied it under Home Rule. Ireland's rich natural resources, and the kindly genius of its children, are not to be allowed to combine for the satisfaction of Irish wants, save in so far as their combination can operate on lines approved of by the rulers of England.

Her postal service, her telegraphs, her wireless, her customs and excise, her coinage, her fighting forces, her relations with other nations, her merchant commerce, her property relations, her national activities, her legislative sovereignty – all the things that are essential to a nation's freedom are denied to Ireland now, and are denied to her under the provisions of the Home Rule Bill. And Irish soldiers in the English Army are fighting in Flanders to win for Belgium, we are told, all those things which the British Empire, now as in the past, denies to Ireland.

There is not a Belgian patriot who would not prefer to see his country devastated by war a hundred times rather than accept as a settlement for Belgium what Redmond and Devlin have accepted for Ireland. Have we Irish been fashioned in meaner clay than the Belgians?

There is not a pacifist in England who would wish to end the war without Belgium being restored to full possession of all those national rights and powers which Ireland does not possess, and which the Home Rule Bill denies to her. But these same pacifists never mention Ireland when discussing or suggesting terms of settlement. Why should they? Belgium is fighting for her independence, but Irishmen are fighting for the Empire that denies Ireland every right that Belgians think worth fighting for.

And yet Belgium as a nation is, so to speak, but a creation of yesterday – an artificial product of the schemes of statesmen. Whereas, the frontiers of Ireland, the ineffaceable marks of the separate existence of Ireland, are as old as Europe itself, the handiwork of the Almighty, not of politicians. And as the marks of Ireland's separate nationality were not made by politicians so they cannot be unmade by them.

As the separate individual is to the family, so the separate nation is to humanity. The perfect family is that which best draws out the inner powers of the individual, the most perfect world is that in which the separate existence of nations is held most sacred. There can be no perfect Europe in which Ireland is denied even the least of its national rights; there can be no worthy Ireland whose children brook tamely such denial. If such denial has been accepted by soulless slaves of politicians then it must be repudiated by Irish men and women whose souls are still their own.

The peaceful progress of the future requires the possession by Ireland of all the national rights now denied to her. Only in such possession can the workers of Ireland see stability and security for the fruits of their toil and organization. A destiny not of our fashioning has chosen this generation as the one called upon for the supreme act of self-sacrifice – to die if need be that our race might live in freedom.

Are we worthy of the choice? Only by our response to the call can that question be answered.

We Will Rise Again

Workers' Republic (25 March 1916)

Connolly here reasserts the struggle for national self-determination, over and against the co-optation of forces such as the Volunteers to the British Army and imperial war-making.

The celebrations of the past week in Ireland are a welcome reminder of the indestructible nature of the spirit of freedom. Who would have thought in August, 1914, that in March, 1916, the principle of a distinct and separate existence for Irish Nationality would evoke such splendid manifestations of popular support and popular approval. In August, 1914, it seemed to many of the most hopeful of us that Ireland had at length taken its final plunge into the abyss of Imperialism, and bade a long farewell to all hopes of a separate unfettered existence as a nation.

Plans carefully laid for years before had been suddenly and relentlessly put in operation. A party of Parliamentary representatives elected to obtain Home Rule from England, and without any mandate expressing hostility to any other people, suddenly claimed the power and right to pledge the manhood of Ireland to battle with a friendly nation – a nation whose last public act towards Ireland had been an attempt to open the port of Queenstown when shut by English intrigue. The same Parliamentary Party publicly renounced all hope and desire that this country should ever attain the status of nationhood, and expressly limited the ambitions of Ireland to such freedoms as the British Government would judge to be not incompatible with the British Empire. Having so limited the claims and renounced the hopes of Ireland this Parliamentary Party consummated its treason by calling upon their fellow countrymen to go out to die, in order to win for Belgium those national rights and powers they had just renounced the right to claim for Ireland.

The public press, the vaunted guardians of public liberty, sold themselves in a body to the Government that had publicly pledged itself not to interfere with an Orange-cum-militarist conspiracy against the liberties of Ireland, and immediately became the foulest slanderers and vilifiers of all who stood by the national cause they had deserted.

The few papers that refused to be bullied, or to be bought, were ruthlessly suppressed by military force.

All over Ireland the public representatives whom a lifetime of political intrigue, vote-hunting and job hunting had debased and demoralised, yielded at the first onset of the new Irish Imperialism, and joyfully, eagerly, exultantly sold their country and their country's cause.

August, 1914, and the months immediately succeeding it, were months of darkness and of national tribulation. If the darkest hour is that before the dawn, then the dawn should not be far off, for surely no darker hour could come for Ireland than that we passed through in the beginning of this English war upon Germany.

But slowly, gradually, but persistently, the forces standing for the social and national freedom of Ireland won the people back to greater sanity and clearer visions. Despite imprisonment, despite persecution, despite suppression of newspapers, despite avalanches of carefully framed lies, the truth made headway throughout the country. The people saw clearer and clearer that nothing had been changed in Ireland, that Ireland was still denied every prerogative that makes for true nationhood, that her interests were still subject to the interests of a rival country, that the Home Rule Act expressly declared for the subjection of Ireland as a permanent condition, that the Redmond-Devlin party had sold the birthright of their country in return for the valueless promise of a Government that did not even keep faith with its own countrymen or women, that the British Empire and the freedom or prosperity of the Irish people were two things that could not exist together in Ireland, and that therefore one or the other must forever and utterly perish.

All through Ireland last week the manhood and womanhood of the nation have gladly, enthusiastically proclaimed their realisation of those truths. This 17th of March will be forever memorable for that reason. The magnificent parades of Volunteers under arms, the overflowing meetings, the joyous abandon of the Irish gatherings of all descriptions, and above all the exultant rebel note everywhere manifest, all, all were signs that the cause of freedom is again in the ascendant in Ireland.

The Cause is not lost, this 17th of March has assured us that despite all the treasons of all the traitors Ireland still remains as pure in heart as ever, and though Empires fall and tyrannies perish

We Will Rise Again.

Labour and Ireland: Dublin Working Class, amid Great Emotion, Hoist and Salute the Flag of Ireland

Workers' Republic (22 April 1916)

This report by Connolly was the editorial for the final issue of *Workers' Republic*.

On Sunday, April 16, 1916, let the date be forever remembered, Dublin witnessed a scene that moved thousands of men and women to tears of joy and thanksgiving. On that day the Irish Citizen Army, the armed forces of Labour, on the top of the headquarters of the Irish Transport Workers' Union, hoisted and unfurled the Green Flag of Ireland, emblazoned with the Harp without the Crown, and as the sacred emblem of Ireland's unconquered soul fluttered to the breeze, the bugles pealed their defiant salute, and the battalion presented arms, strong men wept for joy, and women fainted with emotion.

From early in the day the historic square was the centre of Dublin. Crowds were continually arriving to assure themselves that the ceremony was really to take place. All sorts of rumours were current all the week. Field guns were to level the Hall with the ground, all the avenues of approach were to be occupied by masses of troops with machine guns, Mr Connolly and all his officers were to be arrested at dead of night, martial law was to be declared on Saturday, and so forth; the stories were endless, and the bearers of the stories came from all quarters and ranks of society. But the preparations were quietly proceeded with, and the appointed hour found Beresford Place and all its avenues of approach blocked indeed, not by troops, but by tens of thousands of a breathless, excited, and jubilant crowd.

The duty and honour of unfurling the flag was allotted to Miss Molly Reilly, a young and beautiful member of the Irish Women Workers' Union.

In front of the Hall the Irish Citizen Army cleared a space and formed into three sides of a square. Inside their formation positions were occupied by the Women's Section, who made a splendid and beautiful show, the Citizen Army Boy Scouts, under Captain Carpenter, and the Fintan Lalor Pipers' Band. Captain Poole and a Colour Guard of sixteen men escorted the Colour Bearer who was accompanied also by the three young girl dancers known as the Liberty trio.

The flag was deposited first on a pile of drums in the centre of the square. After inspecting the troops, Commandant Connolly took up his position in front of the drums with Commandant Mallin on his left and Lieutenant Markievicz on his right.[27] Then the Colour Bearer, Miss Reilly, advanced from her escort, received the Colours from the Commandant, and turned about to face the Colour Guard. As she did so the Guard presented arms, and the buglers sounded the Salute. When the Colour Bearer had retaken her place in the centre of the Guard that body moved off around the square, whilst the Pipers' Band played appropriate music.

As the Colour Guard reached the entrance to the Hall again, and reformed to their original front the Colour Bearer carrying the Colours across her breast bore them into the hall, and up to the roof. At this point the excitement was almost painful in its intensity. So closely had the crowds been packed that many thousands had been unable to see the ceremony on the square, but the eyes of all were now riveted upon the flag pole awaiting the re-appearance of the Colour Bearer. All Beresford Square was packed, Butt Bridge and Tara Street were as a sea of upturned faces. All the North Side of the Quays up to O'Connell Street was thronged, and O'Connell Bridge itself was impassable owing to the vast multitude of eager, sympathetic onlookers.

The Fintan Lalor Pipers' Band is among the very first rank of the Pipe

---

[27] Michael Mallin (1874–1916), Irish socialist and revolutionary, second-in-command of the Irish Citizen Army. Constance Markievicz (1868–1927), Irish socialist and feminist politician, suffragist and revolutionary.

bands of Ireland, but so anxious and prayerfully eager were the people that its fine music was scarcely heeded as the hearts of all beat rapidly with longing for the appearance of the Flag upon its position.

At last the young Colour Bearer, radiant with excitement and glowing with colour in face and form, mounted beside the parapet of the roof, and with a quick graceful movement of her hand unloosed the lanyard, and

THE FLAG OF IRELAND

fluttered out upon the breeze.

Those who witnessed that scene will never forget it. Over the Square, across Butt Bridge, in all the adjoining streets, along the quays, amid the dense mass upon O'Connell Bridge, Westmoreland Street and D'Olier Street corners, everywhere the people burst out in one joyous delirious shout of welcome and triumph, hats and handkerchiefs fiercely waved, tears of emotion coursed freely down the cheeks of strong rough men, and women became hysterical with excitement.

As the first burst of cheering subsided Commandant Connolly gave the command, 'Battalion, Present Arms', the bugles sounded the General Salute, and the concourse was caught up in a delirium of joy and passion.

In a few short words at the close Commandant Connolly pledged his hearers to give their lives if necessary to keep the Irish Flag Flying, and the ever memorable scene was ended.

Last Statement

Given to his daughter Nora Connolly on the eve of his execution.

Ireland has a rich and often compelling tradition of speeches or testaments by revolutionaries at the point of imminent execution – the most famous being Robert Emmet's 'Speech from the Dock' in 1803. Connolly here aligns himself with that tradition.

To the Field General Court Martial, held at Dublin Castle, on May 9th, 1916:

I do not wish to make any defence except against charges of wanton cruelty to prisoners. These trifling allegations that have been made, if they record facts that really happened deal only with the almost unavoidable incidents of a hurried uprising against long established authority, and nowhere show evidence of set purpose to wantonly injure unarmed persons.

We went out to break the connection between this country and the British Empire, and to establish an Irish Republic. We believed that the call we then issued to the people of Ireland, was a nobler call, in a holier cause, than any call issued to them during this war, having any connection with the war. We succeeded in proving that Irishmen are ready to die endeavouring to win for Ireland those national rights which the British Government has been asking them to die to win for Belgium. As long as that remains the case, the cause of Irish freedom is safe.

Believing that the British Government has no right in Ireland, never had any right in Ireland, and never can have any right in Ireland, the presence, in any one generation of Irishmen, of even a respectable minority, ready to die to affirm that truth, makes that Government for ever a usurpation and a crime against human progress.

I personally thank God that I have lived to see the day when thousands of Irish men and boys, and hundreds of Irish women and girls, were ready to affirm that truth, and to attest it with their lives if need be.

James Connolly,
Commandant-General, Dublin Division,
Army of the Irish Republic.

Coda: Connolly's Afterlives

Just as the revolutionary period of recent Irish history – roughly speaking, the period from 1890 to 1922 – is still argued over by historians, politicians, intellectuals of many kinds, so more specifically Connolly's legacy is still argued over. Desmond Greaves, author of the first scholarly biography, saw him as a kind of Irish Lenin who latterly subscribed to the Second International's 'stage' theory of history and who made alliance with the progressive elements in the Irish middle class (Greaves 1961). Austen Morgan, on the other hand, on the right wing of the British Labour Party, saw Connolly as having betrayed his leftism by throwing in his lot with nationalists and having endorsed Germany during the First World War – a particularly common liberal view of Connolly (Morgan 1989). Kieran Allen, an Irish sociologist and Trotskyist, argues that while Connolly's militancy, and his analyses of Irish working-class politics and sentiment were acute, he misunderstood Irish republicanism in ways that damaged his project repeatedly. Connolly's essentialist views of Irish nationalism and its supposed anti-capitalism led him, finally, to concede too much ground to republicanism, right up to 1916 (Allen 1990).

More recently there has been an upsurge in interest in Connolly on the part of scholars involved in postcolonial studies. In a major study of anti-colonial and anti-imperialist movements published in 2001, Robert Young compared Connolly's position to that of Frantz Fanon, and highlighted Connolly's 'nationalist internationalism'. Echoing Marx's argument in the nineteenth century (repeated in Connolly's own time by Lenin) that Ireland was the weak point of Britain and that an insurrection there would be a potential deathblow to the Empire, Young points out that Connolly was among the first leaders to combine socialism with the demand for national self-determination in the colonial context. Connolly's willingness to think of Irish issues in the framework of British imperialism and global capitalism marks him out in the pantheon of Irish revolutionaries for his internationalism, and shows his capacity dialectically to think the local and the global. After all, he had launched the Irish Socialist Republican Party with a view to a revolutionary rearrangement of society and 'the incidental destruction of the British Empire'. In so doing, Connolly would inspire Lenin and point the way towards the Comintern, and ultimately hint at the 'tricontinental Marxism' that would underpin the great liberation movements led by Mao, Che, Fanon and Cabral (Young 2001: 303–7).

Traditional English intellectual history has poured scorn on the postcolonial vision of Irish history and of Connolly. In *Ireland and Empire*, Stephen Howe, heavily dependent on Austen Morgan's biography, suggested that references to imperialism and matters of empire in Connolly's writings amount to a mere handful (Howe 2000: 62–64). But David Lloyd, Spurgeon Thompson and Gregory Dobbins, pushing even further than Young and with a closer scholarly grasp of Connolly's texts, see in him and especially in *Labour in Irish History*, a brilliant forerunner of 'subaltern' agitation and intellectual practice. In this, they take their cue from Ranajit Guha and his colleagues in the South Asian Subaltern Studies group. Under the influence initially of Antonio Gramsci and Edward Thompson, Guha and his allies sought from the 1980s onwards to discover or account for the inner logics of Indian peasant protests, strikes, militancy and insurrections in the nineteenth and early twentieth centuries. Rather than dismiss these movements as failures or as irrational 'mob outrages', the Subaltern historians have seen in such historical ephemera actions and tendencies which were recalcitrant to British imperial understanding and to Indian nationalist historiography alike. Pushing their analysis to a wider framework, the South Asian Subaltern historians derive radically revisionist positions vis-à-vis an arguably Eurocentric Marxism on the basis of their research, questioning the metanarratives of development and modes of production that underpin orthodox thought on the left (Guha and Chakravorty Spivak 1988). Lloyd, Thompson and Dobbins argue that Connolly anticipates such thinking, suggesting that his sense of the uneven and anomalous positioning of Ireland and the Irish – geographically near the heart but functionally peripheral to the British *imperium* and Atlantic capitalism – is the true originality of his thought.

There can be no doubt, so, that Connolly's analyses of the complex relations of socialism, nationalism and enlightenment republicanism, 50 years before Fanon's scorching analyses in *The Wretched of the Earth*, make Connolly a resource for revolutionary and anti-imperialist thought everywhere. As so often with a powerful thinker, Connolly's insights are sometimes interwoven with his blindnesses – for example, his failure properly to notice the presence, agency and struggles of native African peoples even as he supported Boer resistance to the British Empire – but even in this his writings and actions are instructive to us now, alerting us to the risks of Eurocentric left analyses and the need always to historicise colonial specificities. It is hoped that this collection will contribute to the ongoing radical reassessment of his legacy.

Works Cited

Allen, Kieran (1990), *The Politics of James Connolly*, London: Pluto Press.
Fanon, Frantz (1967), *The Wretched of the Earth*, London: Penguin Books.
Greaves, C. Desmond (1961), *The Life and Times of James Connolly*, London: Lawrence and Wishart.
Guha, Ranajit and Gayatri Chakravorty Spivak (eds) (1988), *Selected Subaltern Studies*, Oxford: Oxford University Press.
Howe, Stephen (2000), *Ireland and Empire: Colonial Legacies in Irish History and Culture*, Oxford: Oxford University Press.
Lloyd, David (ed.) (2003), 'Ireland's Modernities', Special Issue of *Interventions* 5 (3).
Morgan, Austen (1989), *James Connolly: A Political Biography*, Manchester: Manchester University Press.
Morris, Catherine and Spurgeon Thompson (eds) (2008), 'Postcolonial Connolly', Special Issue of *Interventions* 10 (1).
Young, Robert J. C. (2001), *Postcolonialism: An Historical Introduction*, Oxford: Blackwell.

Index

1641 Rebellion, 115

Act of Union (1800), 4, 9, 75, 82n, 85, 112n
  and decline of Irish industry, 98–100, 182
  Repealers, 142–3, 154–5, 159, 161
AFL (American Federation of Labor), 13, 52, 55
agrarianism, Irish, 9, 12
  radical, 15, 16, 93–4, 140, 144, 152–3, 156–7; *see also* Land League; Oakboys; Ribbonism; Steelboys; Whiteboys
Allen, Kieran, 256
America
  capitalism, 43, 47; *see also* Republican Party (America)
  farmers, 43–5, 51, 52
  independence, 104
  as Ireland's economic competitor, 24, 47
  JC and, 1, 13, 45–6
  lack of true liberty, 60–2
  main political parties, 56–8
  miners, 13, 52, 60–1, 63
  native cultures misunderstood, 73
  socialism, 42–5, 54–5
  see also Irish in America; slavery
American Federation of Labor (AFL) *see* AFL (American Federation of Labor)
anarchism, 8, 14, 51, 55n, 197
Ancient Order of Hibernians, 226–7
Anglican Church *see* Church of Ireland

Anglo-Irish literature, 68–9, 70–1
Anglo-Irishness, upper- and middle-class, 72
Anglophony *see* Gaelic: language
anti-capitalism *see* capitalism
anti-colonialism *see* colonialism
anti-imperialism *see* British Empire; imperialism
Apprentice Boys of Derry, 117
aristocracy *see* upper class
Ascendancy, Protestant, 9, 140
Ashley-Cooper, Anthony, 7th Earl of Shaftesbury, 158
Asquith, Herbert, 234, 236

ballots *see* secret ballot; voting, open
Belfast, 91, 95, 227
  activism, 123–4, 125, 157, 180
  industries, 5, 172
blackleg labour, 39–40, 183
Blanc, Louis, 172, 173–4
Blatchford, Robert, 196–7
Boer War (Second), 10–11, 12, 193–4, 195, 196–7, 199–200
Bolshevism, 14, 216n
bourgeoisie *see* middle classes
Brehon legal code, 12, 67
Brennan, Joseph, 175, 179
British Empire, 17, 24, 84, 217–19
  Ireland and, 5, 10, 26, 28–9, 35, 241–2
  revolutionary movements in, 16, 90, 113; *see also* rebellions
  see also Boer War (Second); colonialism: British; First World War; imperialism; India; IPP (Irish Parliamentary Party)

British military
  in Afghanistan, 208
  in America, 95, 107
  in India, 90
  as instrument of state violence, 25, 28, 58, 59, 89–90, 173, 183, 211
  in Ireland's history, 79, 91, 92, 104, 111–12, 115n
  Irish in, 83, 84, 112, 162, 245; *see also* First World War: Irish in
  JC in and out of, 5–6
  unrest among, 170
  withdrawal from Ireland, 95, 211
  see also Boer War (Second); First World War; Napoleonic wars, aftermath; Royal Navy, Irish impressment
Bronterre's National Reformer (Irish newspaper), 179
Brotherhood, The (Irish newspaper), 150
Butt, Isaac, 3, 5, 253, 254

capitalism, 7, 8, 12, 65–6, 98–9
  in America, 43, 44, 47, 49, 60–2; *see also* Republican Party (America)
  bolstered by workers, 219
  cause of Boer War, 193–4
  exported to Ireland by England, 15, 68, 72, 73, 76
  as forerunner of socialism, 54, 197, 198
  international, 20, 191, 195
  Irish, link to Britain and Empire, 17, 74
  and Irish politics, 37, 100–1, 103, 104, 224
  and nationalism, 6, 21, 188
  newspapers, 42, 156, 201, 228, 233
  oppressive, 27–8, 33, 134–5
  responsibility for Great Irish Famine, 163, 167–8
  and revolution, 19
  see also British Empire; Grattan, Henry: Grattan's Parliament; industry; landlordism; trade, commercial; unions; working classes
Carson, Edward, 18, 227, 236n, 247
Carsonites, 211–12
Castlereagh, Lord (Robert Stewart, 2nd Marquis of Londonderry), 127, 130

Catholic Church, 30, 149, 153, 154, 161, 226; *see also* Catholic Emancipation; Catholicism
Catholic Committee, 119, 128
Catholic Confederation, 115n
Catholic Emancipation, 3, 85n, 99n, 112n, 140–1, 144
  aftermath, 152
  repercussions for the poor, 141–2, 143
Catholicism, 9
  and class, 16, 102, 103, 115, 118, 141, 142, 186
  exclusion and persecution of, 101, 103, 107, 116–17, 124, 182, 212
  and Jacobitism, 69–70, 79–80
  and land ownership, 80, 81, 82, 84–5, 88
  Wolfe Tone on, 108–9
  see also European Catholics; Irish in America
Caulfeild, James, 1st Earl of Charlemont, 103–4
Chakravorty Spivak, Gayatri, 257
Chartism, 59, 159, 160, 170, 179, 187n
Chesterfield, Lord (Philip Stanhope, 4th Earl), 88–9
chieftains *see* clan system
children
  labour of, 33, 60, 155, 158–9
  maintenance of, 22, 143, 146, 147, 148, 157
  see also education; Swift, Jonathan: *A Modest Proposal*
Church of Ireland, 17, 85n, 90, 131
  clergymen of, 86n, 87n, 102n
  disestablishment, 207
  see also tithes
clan system, 68, 69, 76, 80, 81, 115–16
Clarion, The (English newspaper), 196
class
  divisions, 9–10, 11, 105, 115–16
  in Irish history, 14–16
  and nationalism, 6, 16–17, 76–7, 92–3
  and patriotism, 26–9, 72, 74, 76, 190, 217, 241–2
  and politics, 19
  and religion, 102, 141
  in Royal Navy, 113
  war, 120

see also landlordism; middle classes; peasantry; socialism; upper class; working classes
Cluseret, Gustave Paul, 185
co-operatives, 133, 137, 138, 145–52
colonialism
  Boer, 11, 193
  British, 95, 195–6, 200, 221, 233
  European, 21
  in Ireland, 5, 9, 12, 22, 25–6, 59, 212
  socialist attitudes to, 195–9
  see also British Empire; imperialism; India
combination *see* unionisation
common ownership, 21–3, 33, 45, 60, 63, 71, 116
  of land, 12, 16, 26, 76, 191
  in practice, 149–50
communism, 12, 16, 174–5, 189; *see also* Marxism
Communist Manifesto, The (Marx and Engels), 4, 45, 82, 139
Connolly, James
  early life, 2
  military experience, 5–6, 18–19
  in Scotland, 6–7, 13
  to Ireland, 7
  to America, 13
  return to Ireland, 14, 16
  arrest, 230–1
  and revolution, 17–19, 239–40, 252–4
  final statement, 254–5
  execution, 2, 18, 19
  later assessments of, 256–8
Conservative Party (British), 3, 17, 78, 83, 205n, 224, 236
constitution of 1782, 108–10
constitutionalism *see* nationalism: constitutional
Cromwell, Oliver, 68, 80, 115n, 116, 117
culturalism *see* Gaelic: cultural revival

Davis, Thomas Osborne, 78, 89, 98, 162n, 169
Davitt, Michael, 3, 189n, 190, 224
Dawson, William James: *Lines to a Blackthorn*, 65
De Leon, Daniel, 13, 42, 51, 52
Debs, Eugene Victor, 49, 50–1
Defenders, 183
Democratic Association, 178, 179n

Democratic Party (America), 49, 56, 57, 58, 60, 174n
Despard, Edward, 130
Devlin, Joseph, 225–7, 234, 235, 248, 249, 251–2
Dobbins, Gregory, 257
Doheny, Michael, 165–6, 169, 184
Doherty, John, 180
Drennan, William, 89n
Dublin, 5, 104–5
  demonstrations, 10, 11, 108; *see also* Emmet Conspiracy
  labour movement, 3, 31, 132, 155, 157–8, 160, 188
  newspapers, 96, 123, 154, 178, 182–3
  politics, 39–40
  Rebellion *see* Easter Rising (1916)
  see also Pale, English
Dublin Lock-Out (1913), 16, 17, 19, 21n, 210, 233; *see also* Irish Transport and General Workers' Union
Dublin Parliament, 75n, 79n, 80, 82–3, 98–9, 191
  English control, 92–3, 106
  Protestant control, 120
  upper-class control, 103
  see also Act of Union (1800); Grattan, Henry: Grattan's Parliament; Penal Laws
Dublin Socialist Club, 7
Dublin Volunteers, 104–5, 124
Duffy, Charles Gavan, 161, 162n, 165

Easter Rising (1916), 1, 16, 18–19, 239n, 245n
  prelude (17 March), 250, 252
  prelude (16 April), 252–4
  aftermath, 254–5
Edinburgh, 2, 5–6, 7, 37
education, 4, 6, 36, 220–1, 239
  free, 22, 64, 135; *see also* Ralahine Agricultural and Manufacturing Co-operative Association
  in India, 201, 207
  in Ireland, 152, 224, 225, 229
  of Irish in Catholic Europe, 67–8, 69, 70
  secularisation, 9, 135
Egypt, 16, 199, 218, 248
electoral franchise expansion *see* franchise expansion

emigration, 38, 45, 143, 149–50
  driven by Great Irish Famine, 4, 163–4
  driven by unemployment, 22, 224
  see also Irish in America; Irish in Britain; Irish in France
Emmet Conspiracy, 127–31, 254
Emmet, Robert see Emmet Conspiracy
Emmet, Thomas Addis, 126
enclosures see evictions
Engels, Friedrich, 6, 8, 12, 30, 73n, 133n; see also Communist Manifesto, The; International Working Men's Association
Erin's Hope: the End and the Means, 11–12, 15, 16, 115
Established Church see Church of Ireland
European Catholics, 67–8, 69–70, 83, 102, 119
evictions, 3, 87–9, 102–3, 132, 141–2, 166
  in England, 156
  and Great Irish Famine, 167–8

famine, 45, 70, 85–7, 96, 206
  economics of, 171, 173
  in India, 201–2, 206–7, 209–10
  as likely outcome in Ireland of WWI, 213, 237
  post-evictions, 142
  see also Great Irish Famine
Fanon, Frantz, 257
farm labourers, 3, 24, 66n, 86, 118, 186
  unionisation of, 39, 132, 224
  see also agrarianism: radical; peasantry; Ralahine Agricultural and Manufacturing Co-operative Association
farming see agrarianism; America: farmers; tenants
Fenian movements, 84, 175n, 184–8
  rebellion (1867), 5, 78, 207
feudalism, 44, 82, 151, 190, 224
  imported from England, 12, 15, 73, 80–1
  see also clan system; landlordism
Fintan Lalor Pipers' Band, 253–4
First International (International Working Men's Association), 7, 188; see also Second International

First World War, 7, 16, 17, 210
  and 'civilisation', 219–21
  conscription, 238–9
  effects on working classes, 221–2
  Ireland and, 210–14, 235–7, 238–40
  Irish in, 236–7, 242, 246–7, 249, 251
  and socialism, 214–17
Fitzgerald, Lord Edward, 128
Flag of Ireland (newspaper), 184
Flood, Henry, 5, 89, 95, 105–7
Forward (Scottish newspaper), 214, 230
France, 24, 79n, 131–2, 174, 189, 218n
  Irish rebels and, 10, 110–11, 113–14, 127, 130, 184–5
  Paris Commune, 185, 188, 243n
  Republic after 1848, 171–3, 174
  see also European Catholics; First World War; French Revolution; Utopian socialism
franchise expansion, 7, 9, 100–1, 107, 120
  based on rent paid, 141
  municipal, 39, 40
  universal, 22, 125–6, 129, 134
  see also Catholic Emancipation
Free Trade, 87, 95, 103, 168, 172–3
freedom see liberty; slavery
Freeman's Journal (Irish newspaper), 207
French Revolution, 34, 125, 131, 169, 188
  Irish attitudes to, 83, 105, 119, 123
  see also Girondins; Jacobinism
Fullam, Bernard, 178

Gaelic
  cultural destruction, 67–8
  cultural revival, 4–5, 15, 23, 72
  language, 4, 69, 70, 145, 164
gentry see landlordism; private property; upper class
Germany, 7, 201n, 211, 212n
  and First World War, 215, 216, 236, 238–9, 251
  Ireland and, 213, 237, 242
  see also Utopian socialism
Girondins, 160–1, 177–8
Glorious Revolution see Jacobitism
Gonne, Maud, 10
Government of Ireland Act, 235–6n
Gramsci, Antonio, 257

Grattan, Henry, 89n, 100, 103–4
  and England, 105–7
  Grattan's Parliament, 9, 75, 82n,
    95–8, 108–10, 182
  political views, 5, 26, 107–8
Great Irish Famine, 78, 86n, 161,
    162–4, 166–8, 177–8
  aftermath, 3, 4
Greaves, C. Desmond, 256
Green, Alice Stopford, 12, 67–8, 94n
Green Flag, 170, 252–4
Gregory, Isabella Augusta, Lady, 4
Griffith, Arthur, 11, 12, 41n
Grouchy, Emmanuel de, 110–11
Guha, Ranajit, 257

Hardie, James Keir, 38–9, 40–1
Harp, The (Irish-American newspaper),
    53, 63, 66, 201
Harriman, Job, 50–1
Harrington, Timothy Charles, 39
Hearts of Oak *see* Oakboys
Hearts of Steel *see* Steelboys
Hibernian Philanthropic Society, 144
Hibernians, Ancient Order of, 226–7
historical theories
  Marxist materialist, 4, 82, 137, 198
  socialist, 67, 82, 96, 98–9
  stages theory, 8–9
history, Irish written
  control of by 'master class', 74–5,
    177, 181
  England and, 75–8, 169
  JC's view of, 12, 14–16, 67–74
  misrepresentation in, 95, 100, 126,
    160, 161, 190
  nationalist idealisation of, 23–4
  unanimity in, 102
  working classes in, 181–2, 191–2
  see also clan system; Connolly,
    James: later assessments;
    Jacobitism
Home Rule Bills, 36, 235–6n, 248, 249
Home Rule movement, 5, 16
  as anti-labour, 38–41, 190
  anti-nationalism of, 248–9
  and Boer War, 11
  capitalist nature of, 17, 37
  constitutional nationalism of, 9, 29
  and Easter Rising, 19
  and First World War, 17, 18, 235–6,
    250–1
  JC's low opinion of, 13, 95, 96

official press of, 187, 190
  and partition, 234
  and physical force movement, 35,
    36
  reactionary nature of, 31, 33
  and unionist politics, 195, 223,
    225–7, 246, 247
  see also IPP (Irish Parliamentary
    Party); Parnell, Charles Stewart
homeworkers, 32–3
Hope, James 'Jemmy', 115
Howe, Stephen, 257
Humbert, Jean Joseph Amable, 111
Hyndman, Henry, 48, 196n, 197, 198

ILP (Independent Labour Party), 6, 38,
    40, 214
imperialism, 7, 9, 195
  European, 10, 220, 234
  and revolution, 19
  see also British Empire; colonialism
independence, Irish *see* Home Rule
    movement; nationalism; socialist
    republicanism; United Irishmen
Independent Labour Party (ILP) *see* ILP
    (Independent Labour Party)
India, 16, 200–10
  Christianity in, 208
  Civil Service, 202–3
  education, 207
  famine, 201–2, 206–7, 209–10
  injustice in, 209, 210
  progress under British rule
    questioned, 203–5
  Rebellion (Mutiny) (1857), 207, 208
  wages and taxation, 202–3, 206
Industrial Revolution, 5, 96–7
industrial unionism, 14
industrialisation, 12, 16, 47, 160, 196,
    197, 241
industry, 249
  rise and decline in Ireland, 96–7,
    98–9, 100, 117, 154
  see also slavery: economic;
    unemployment; unions
insurrection *see* physical force
    movement; rebellions; violence,
    state
International Socialist Congress, 197,
    201
International Workers of the World
    (IWW) *see* IWW (International
    Workers of the World)

International Working Men's
  Association (First International), 7,
  188; see also Second International
IPP (Irish Parliamentary Party), 2–3,
  30, 211n, 247–8, 251–2; see
  also Parnell, Charles Stewart;
  Redmond, John
IRB (Irish Republican Brotherhood), 9,
  18, 78n, 152n, 179n, 184n, 244n;
  see also Griffith, Arthur; *Irish
  People* (newspaper); physical force
  movement
Irish Citizen Army, 19, 239–40, 252,
  253
Irish Confederation, 94n, 161, 164–5,
  176, 177–8
Irish Felon, The (newspaper), 173, 174,
  176n, 178
Irish in America, 13, 46, 53–4, 56–60,
  61–2, 226n
Irish in Britain, 2, 178, 179, 181, 188,
  190; see also British military: Irish
  in; First World War: Irish in; IPP
  (Irish Parliamentary Party)
Irish in France, 83, 184–5
Irish Labour and Industrial Union, 3
Irish language see Gaelic: language
Irish Monthly Magazine, 154
Irish National Guard (newspaper), 178
Irish National Land League see Land
  League
Irish National League, 3, 6, 30
Irish Parliament see Dublin Parliament
Irish Parliamentary Party (IPP) see IPP
  (Irish Parliamentary Party)
Irish People (newspaper), 41, 84, 131,
  179, 184, 187
Irish Republican Brotherhood (IRB)
  see IRB (Irish Republican
  Brotherhood)
Irish Socialist Federation (America)
  see ISF (Irish Socialist Federation,
  America)
Irish Socialist Republican Party (ISRP)
  see ISRP (Irish Socialist Republican
  Party)
Irish Transport and General Workers'
  Union, 222, 239, 242, 252
  and Dublin Lock-Out, 210, 228–9,
  230–2
  foundation, 14, 21n, 210
Irish Tribune, The (newspaper), 173,
  178, 179

Irish Unionist Party, 236n
Irish Volunteers, 94–5, 100–1, 109–10,
  252
  and First World War, 17, 235–7,
  239–40, 250
  and politics, 18, 103–5, 106, 107,
  108
  see also Dublin Volunteers
Irish Women Workers' Union, 232, 253
Irish Worker (newspaper), 210, 228
*Irish World and American Industrial
  Liberator* (newspaper), 189
Irishman, The (newspaper), 178, 179,
  184
ISF (Irish Socialist Federation,
  America), 13, 53–4, 55
ISRP (Irish Socialist Republican Party),
  7, 9, 21–3, 28–9, 40n
  and 1798 centenary, 10, 11
  and America, 12–13, 42–3, 44–5, 46,
  47–8
  and Boer War, 11, 195, 199–200
  see also *Workers' Republic, The*
  (newspaper)
IWW (International Workers of the
  World), 13–14, 49n, 53, 55

Jacobinism, 16, 122, 161n
Jacobitism, 15, 68, 69–70, 79–84, 117
Johnston, Anna, 23
Jones, Ernest Charles, 59, 170
Justice (British newspaper), 48, 51, 53,
  197

Kautsky, Karl, 8, 17
Kilkenny Confederation, 115
Kitchener, Horatio Herbert, 1st Earl
  Kitchener, 237
Know-Nothing movement (America),
  57

labour
  as concept, 28, 29, 32, 33, 144, 196
  in Irish history, 181–3
  movements, 3, 17, 20, 159, 242; see
    also Dublin: labour movement
  Party (British), 38n, 224, 225, 238n
  politics, 6, 38–9, 40–1, 55, 190, 233,
    234, 235
Labour in Irish History, 11, 12, 14–16,
  67–192
Labour Leader (British newspaper), 38,
  39, 40

Lalor, James Fintan, 11–12, 16, 161, 166, 173
  as advocate for revolution, 164–5, 170, 175–8, 248
  Fintan Lalor Pipers' Band, 253–4
land
  common ownership of, 12, 16, 21, 26, 71, 76, 191
  gifts by William III, 83–4
  reform, 4, 19, 190
  and religion, 101, 102–3
  settlement (1675), 80–1
  see also evictions; property rights
Land League, 3, 4, 188, 189–90, 191, 224n, 244
landlordism, 24, 25–6, 27, 31, 40, 87–9, 141–2
  absentee, 99–100
  anti-nationalist, 77–8
  Catholic in 17th century, 80, 115
  control of tenants' votes, 141
  impunity, 91
landowners see private property; upper class
Larkin, James, 17, 21n, 210, 232n, 239n
Lenin, Vladimir (Vladimir Ilyich Ulyanov), 8, 17, 19
Leslie, John, 6
Liberal Party (British), 3, 6, 26, 40, 190, 236
  associated individuals, 37, 41n, 167n, 187n, 209n, 238n
liberty
  lack of in America, 60–2
  of nation and class, 28, 73–4, 120, 122, 246, 248–50, 251
  religious, 147, 192; see also Catholic Emancipation
literature, 69
  Irish see Anglo-Irish literature; Gaelic: cultural revival
Lloyd, David, 257
Luby, Thomas Clarke, 178–9
Lucas, Charles, 92–3
Luxemburg, Rosa, 10, 17

MacBride, John, 11
M'Cracken, Henry Joy, 127
McNally, Leonard, 128
Madden, Richard: *Literary Remains of the United Irishmen*, 126
Magan, Francis, 128

Mahon, Charles James Patrick (O'Gorman), 143
Mallin, Michael, 253
Mangan, James Clarence, 243, 245
Markievicz, Constance, 253
marriage, 13, 64, 101, 107, 147
Martin, John, 173
Marx, Karl, 6, 12, 30, 43, 133n, 59n, 73n, 200
  Capital: Critique of Political Economy, 139, 185–6
  compared with Thompson, 131, 134, 137–9
  see also *Communist Manifesto, The*
Marxism, 1–2, 6, 7, 8, 10, 30, 43
  and colonialism, 195–6
  see also De Leon, Daniel; historical theories: Marxist materialist
Meagher, Thomas Francis, 72, 161, 165, 166
Meehan, Father Charles, 161
middle classes, 13, 15, 71, 74
  in America, 57–8
  and nationalism, 6, 9–10, 16, 76–7, 78
  and upper class, 25, 101, 104, 105
Militia Ballot Act, 238, 239, 240
Milligan, Alice, 23
miners
  American, 13, 52, 60–1, 63
  British, 37n, 38, 233
Mitchel, John, 16, 29, 59, 178, 241–2, 243, 244–5
  History of Ireland: From the Treaty of Limerick to the Present Time, The, 106, 160
  Jail Journal, 173
  quoted, 94, 171–3
  and Young Ireland, 161, 164, 165, 170–1
  see also *United Irishman*
Molyneux, William, 92–3
monarchism, 35, 38, 68, 70, 154
Morgan, Austen, 256, 257
Murphy, William Martin, 17, 228n, 231

Napoleonic wars, aftermath, 131–2, 140
Nation, The (Irish newspaper), 78n, 162n
  associated individuals, 98n, 173, 178, 181n, 187n, 188n, 242n, 243n

National Volunteers, 18
nationalisation *see* common ownership
nationalism, 12, 19, 24–5, 246–7,
   248–50
   advanced, 11, 35, 211
   and capitalism, 21, 188
   and class, 6, 9–10, 14–15, 16–17,
      76–7, 92–3, 241–2
   constitutional, 10, 30, 34–5, 37,
      244, 245; *see also* Home Rule
      movement
   cultural, 4–5, 15, 23
   socialist, 26, 188–9
   see also physical force movement;
      socialist republicanism
Native American Party, 57n
Neilson, Samuel, 121
New Yorker Volkszeitung (newspaper),
   50
newspapers, 2
   American, 44, 50–1, 52, 61, 189; *see
      also Harp, The*
   and Boer War, 196, 197
   capitalist, 42, 156, 201, 228, 233
   English, 187, 239; *see also Justice;
      Labour Leader; Times, The*
   Irish, 150, 184, 207, 210, 228,
      246–7, 251; *see also* Dublin:
      newspapers; *Irish Felon, The; Irish
      People; Irishman, The; Nation,
      The; United Irishman; Workers'
      Republic, The*
   Scottish, 48, 214, 230
   socialist, 178–81
Northern Star (Irish newspaper), 16,
   121n

Oakboys, 15, 89–90; *see also*
   Ribbonism; Steelboys; Whiteboys
O'Brien, James Bronterre, 179–80
O'Brien, Patrick 'Pat', 39–40
O'Brien, William, 41n
O'Brien, William Smith, 143, 161,
   166–7, 169, 170, 176, 184
O'Connell, Daniel, 4, 15, 128–9, 171
   and Catholic Emancipation, 3, 141
   and Repeal of the Union, 5, 99, 142,
      154, 161–2
   support for capitalists against
      workers, 155, 157–60
O'Connor, Arthur, 79
O'Connor, Fergus Edward, 159, 178,
   179

O'Connor, William Anderson: *History
   of the Irish People*, 166, 184
O'Donnell, John Francis, 181, 188
O'Grady, Standish James, 4, 15, 138
O'Leary, John, 29, 184
O'Mahony, John Francis, 184
Orange Order, 17, 225–6, 227, 234,
   247, 251
O'Reilly, John Boyle, 152, 178
outworkers, 32–3
Owen, Robert, 133, 134n, 136, 138,
   144–5

Paget, Henry, 1st Marquis of Anglesey,
   155
Paine, Thomas: *Rights of Man*, 121n
Pale, English, 75, 182, 191
parliamentary politics, 7, 8, 9, 10, 11,
   23, 30; *see also* Dublin Parliament;
   Home Rule movement; IPP (Irish
   Parliamentary Party); labour: Party
   (British)
Parnell, Charles Stewart, 3, 6, 9, 19,
   30–1, 224
partition of Ireland, 218, 233–5
Patriot Parliament, 82–3
patriot politics, 5, 15, 26, 93, 105–6;
   see also Grattan, Henry: Grattan's
   Parliament
patriotism, 17, 117–18, 188
   and class, 26–9, 72, 74, 76, 190, 217,
      241–2
   see also nationalism
pauperism *see* poverty
Pearse, Patrick Henry, 18, 244–5
peasantry, 12, 70–1, 106, 191
   Indian, 202–3, 205, 206
   see also agrarianism: radical; clan
      system; famine; farm labourers;
      tenants
Penal Laws, 84–5, 87, 88, 99n, 101–2,
   119n
People, The (American newspaper), 50
Phalanx, The (British newspaper),
   180–1
physical force movement, 11, 34–7,
   179
Pigott, Richard, 179n, 186
Pile, Thomas Devereux, 39
Pioneer (Anglo-Indian newspaper),
   207
Pitt, William the Younger, 112
Poor Law, 144, 174, 186

poverty, 1, 92, 139–40; *see also* emigration; evictions; famine; slavery: economic
Poynings' Law, 81–2, 92, 108–10
press *see* newspapers
private property, 22, 43, 58, 59, 69, 163; *see also* feudalism; property rights
property rights, 15, 25, 70–1, 82–3, 131, 168, 189, 234; *see also* common ownership; landlordism; private property
Protestant Ascendancy, 9, 140
Protestantism
  and class, 16, 85, 102, 118
  dissenters, 85n, 90–1
  and industrial ownership, 116–17
  land settlement, 80–1
  see also Catholicism; Orange Order

racism
  America, 13, 14
  South Africa, 11, 193, 200–1
Radek, Karl, 19
Ralahine Agricultural and Manufacturing Co-operative Association, 145–51
rebellions, 77
  1641 Rebellion, 115
  Boxer (China 1900–1901), 200
  Fenian (1867), 5, 78n, 184, 185n, 188n, 207
  Indian Rebellion (Mutiny) (1857), 200n, 207, 208
  Swing Riots (England, 1830s), 156n
  United Irishmen (1798), 5, 10, 16, 34, 74n, 110–12, 129n
  United Irishmen (1803), 115n; *see also* Emmet Conspiracy
  workers', 183–4, 185–6, 187
  Young Ireland (1848), 5, 72n, 78n, 94n, 143n, 168, 244
  see also Dublin Lock-Out (1913); Easter Rising (1916); Jacobitism
Redmond, John, 39, 210–11, 223, 224–5, 227, 235
  commitment to First World War, 17, 18, 235–7
  and Home Rule Bill, 248, 249, 251–2
  mistaken for socialist, 38, 40
  and partition, 234
Reilly, Thomas Devin, 161, 164, 173–5
Repeal Association, 161

Repealers *see* Act of Union (1800): Repealers
Republican Party (America), 56, 57–8
republicanism, 2, 9, 10, 12, 15, 18; *see also* socialist republicanism
revolutionary movements, 16, 162, 184
  Ireland lacking, 243–4, 245–6
  see also French Revolution; rebellions
Ribbonism, 132, 141–2, 143, 145n, 154, 184; *see also* Oakboys; Steelboys; Whiteboys
Roman Catholicism *see* Catholicism
Royal Navy, Irish impressment, 112–14, 183
Russell, John, 1st Earl Russell, 167, 170
Russia, 16, 24, 198, 209, 221, 234n
  and Britain, 197, 211, 218
  and First World War, 17, 215–16, 239
  Revolution (1905), 14, 211, 216, 239

Sarsfield, Patrick, 1st Earl of Lucan, 79, 83
Savage, John, 175
scab labour, 39–40, 183
Scotland, 1, 2, 6–7, 13, 27, 97, 157, 190; *see also* Jacobitism
SDF (Social Democratic Federation, Britain), 48–9, 196, 197
SDP (Social Democratic Party, America), 13, 43, 44, 48n, 49–53
Second International, 7, 8, 9, 13, 197n, 201n
  and colonialism, 21
  failure of, 17, 18
secret ballot, 28, 36–7, 160n; *see also* voting, open
sectarianism *see* Catholicism; Protestantism
Shan Van Vocht (Irish magazine), 23
Sheil, Richard Lalor, 159, 162
Sinn Féin, 9, 12, 41n
slavery
  in American South, 16, 57n
  colonial, 218–19
  economic, 24, 47, 54, 58–60, 155–6, 168, 189, 221–2; *see also* sweated labour
  of Irish peasantry, 70–2, 91, 109
  social, 115, 227, 241
  Thompson on, 136–7

SLP (Socialist Labor Party, America), 12–13, 14, 42, 43, 44, 51, 54
   compared favourably with SDP, 48–50, 53
   and ISRP, 46, 47–8
social democracy, 7, 22–3, 179, 192
Social Democratic Federation *see* SDF (Social Democratic Federation, Britain)
Social Democratic Herald (American newspaper), 44
Social Democratic Party (SDP, America) *see* SDP (Social Democratic Party, America)
social reformers *see* Utopian socialism
socialism
   disunity within, 8, 17–18, 43–4, 49–53, 54–6
   English, 37–8, 40
   European, 7–8, 17, 19
   in practice, 63–4, 65–6
   as science, 137
   state, 174
   see also Utopian socialism
Socialism Made Easy, 14
Socialist Labor Party (SLP, America) *see* SLP (Socialist Labor Party, America)
Socialist Party of America, 14, 43n, 48n, 49, 66
Socialist Party of Ireland, 176n, 223–4, 227
socialist republicanism, 24–6, 31, 35–7, 49; *see also* ISRP (Irish Socialist Republican Party)
Socialist, The (Scottish newspaper), 48
Society of United Irishmen *see* United Irishmen
South African War *see* Boer War (Second)
SSF (Scottish Socialist Federation), 6, 7
Stanhope, Philip, 4th Earl of Chesterfield, 88–9
starvation *see* famine
state violence *see* violence, state
Steelboys, 15, 89, 90–1; *see also* Oakboys; Ribbonism; Whiteboys
Steele, Thomas, 142
Stephens, James, 184–5
strikes, 182–3, 213, 219, 231–2, 233, 239n
   in America, 49, 60, 61
   general, 18, 215, 216

Stuart monarchy *see* Jacobitism
suffrage *see* franchise expansion
sweated labour, 31–4, 225–6, 232
Swift, Jonathan, 26, 92–3
   A Modest Proposal, 85–6, 217
syndicalism *see* unions: syndicalism

tailoring trade, 31–4, 39, 157–8, 183
Tandy, James Napper, 124
taxation, 22, 90, 101, 120, 192, 225, 233
   in America, 24, 50, 51
   in India, 202–3, 206
   see also tithes
tenants, 9, 24, 30, 69, 77–8, 189
   and franchise, 141
   Home Rule movement and, 33
   Lalor on, 176
   post-Williamite war, 84–5
   and religion, 117, 118
   rent protests, 140
   see also agrarianism: radical; clan system; evictions; landlordism
Thompson, Edward, 257
Thompson, Spurgeon, 257
Thompson, William, 133–40
   compared with Marx, 137–9
   as revolutionary, 139–40
Times, The (British newspaper), 78, 156, 186, 201
tithes, 93–4, 144, 152–3, 154, 161, 184
Tone, Theobald Wolfe, 110, 128n, 188
   An Argument on behalf of the Catholics of Ireland, 108–9
   and class, 119–20
   as revolutionary, 10, 16, 170
   and United Irishmen, 35, 121, 124
Tories *see* Conservative Party (British)
trade, commercial, 4, 101, 167, 190–1, 237
   and Act of Union, 98–100, 154, 182
   see also Free Trade; Industrial Revolution
trade unions *see* unions
Trotsky, Leon, 19

Ulster, 5, 113
   and Home Rule, 16–17, 211n, 235–6, 247
unemployment, 38, 149–50, 187
   in America, 49, 61
   in Ireland, 27, 132, 141–2, 185, 188, 224

unionisation, 3, 6, 17, 32, 228–9
unionist politics, 17, 18, 39, 211n, 234–5
  and First World War, 236n
  and Home Rule movement, 195, 223, 225–7, 246, 247
unions, 7, 8, 55
  attacked by Irish politicians, 154–5, 157–60, 224
  illegality of in Ireland, 129, 132
  syndicalism, 13, 14, 17, 210
  trade-specific, 13, 32, 33, 39, 50, 55, 180
  see also blackleg labour; Irish Transport and General Workers' Union; strikes; unionisation
United Builders Labourers' and General Workers of Dublin Trade Union, 231–2
United Irish League, 9, 39, 40, 224, 226, 227, 236
United Irishman (newspaper), 41, 160, 170, 173n, 178
United Irishmen, 16, 35, 79n, 89n, 107, 115n
  foundation and purpose, 119–23, 124–6
  rebellion (1798), 5, 9, 10, 34, 74, 110–12
  rebellion (1803), 115n; see also Emmet Conspiracy
  in Royal Navy, 113–14
United States see America
upper class, 17, 76, 83, 115n, 122, 170
  and middle classes, 25, 77, 101, 104, 105
  political power, 103, 194
  and working classes, 68, 70, 92, 119
  see also landlordism; Orange Order
uprisings see physical force movement; rebellions; violence, state
USA see America
Utopian socialism, 133–4, 136, 137, 138, 144; see also co-operatives

Vandeleur, John, 145n, 151
violence, peasant see agrarianism: radical
violence, state, 26, 28–9, 88–9, 91, 116, 153–4, 199, 231
  in America, 49
  Boer War as warning of, 194
  in England and Scotland, 156–7
  Londonderry sea disaster, 164
  in Royal Navy, 112–14
  see also British military: as instrument of state violence; rebellions
Voice of the People, The (Irish newspaper), 180
Volunteers see Irish Volunteers
voting, open, 141; see also secret ballot
voting rights see franchise expansion

wages
  in India, 202–3
  at Ralahine, 146, 148
  rates, 27, 39, 96, 159, 186
  undercut by Free Trade, 168
  undercut by outworkers, 32
Wallace, John Bruce, 150
Whately, Richard, Archbishop, 102
Whig Party (British), 26, 75n, 167n, 171–2
  O'Connell and, 155, 156–7, 158
White, Jack, 239n
Whiteboys, 3, 15, 88–9, 154, 156n;
  see also Oakboys; Ribbonism; Steelboys
Wild Geese, 69, 83
Williamite war (William III in Ireland) see Jacobitism
Williams, Richard D'Alton, 175
Workers' Republic, The (newspaper), 7, 30, 37, 42, 46
working classes, 6, 21, 23, 24, 74–5, 191–2
  bolstering capitalism, 219
  in Britain, 155–9, 187–8
  disenfranchisement of, 103
  and First World War, 213–14, 221–2
  in France after 1848, 171–3
  internationalism of, 37, 38, 169–71, 173, 176–7, 196
  and nationalism, 76–7, 241–2
  oppression of, 27–8, 118; see also slavery: economic; sweated labour
  and Parnell, 30–1
  patriotism of, 28, 217, 241–2
  revolutionary spirit, 105
  Ulster Protestant, 17
  underpayment of, 24, 27, 89–90; see also wages: rates

working classes (*cont.*)
   and upper class, 68, 70, 92, 119
   see also Emmet Conspiracy; Irish in America; Irish in Britain; labour; peasantry; rebellions: workers'; unionisation; unions
working hours restriction, 22, 185–6
World War I *see* First World War

Yeats, W. B., 4, 10, 15, 184n
Young Ireland, 72n, 94n, 161n, 162
   rebellion (1848), 5, 78, 143n, 168, 244
   weakness of leadership, 164–6, 169–70, 243
   see also Lalor, James Fintan; *Nation, The*: associated individuals
Young, Robert J. C., 256, 257